Ludwig van Beethoven

Ludwig van Beethoven

Harvey Grace

Routledge
Taylor & Francis Group
Routledge Revivals

First published in 1927 by Kegan Paul, Trench, Trubner & Co., Ltd.

This edition first published in 2018 by Routledge
2 Park Square, Milton Park, Abingdon, Oxon, OX14 4RN
and by Routledge
711 Third Avenue, New York, NY 10017

Routledge is an imprint of the Taylor & Francis Group, an informa business

A Library of Congress record exists under ISBN: 27012280

ISBN 13: 978-1-138-60199-4 (hbk)
ISBN 13: 978-1-138-60205-2 (pbk)

Crayon Drawing of Beethoven by A. v. Kloeber, 1817 or 1818

BEETHOVEN

LUDWIG VAN
BEETHOVEN

BY

HARVEY GRACE

Author of *The Complete Organist; The Organ Works of Bach;*
The Organ Works of Rheinberger; &c.

LONDON
KEGAN PAUL, TRENCH, TRUBNER & CO., LTD.
J. CURWEN & SONS, LTD.
1927

DEDICATION.

Dear Sir Henry Wood,

There are many thousands of folk who owe their intimate knowledge of Beethoven's orchestral music very largely to your work at Queen's Hall, especially at the Promenade Concerts. I am one of them, and I therefore dedicate this book to you, with sincere respect and admiration.

HARVEY GRACE.

AUTHOR'S PREFACE

The original intention was that this book should be entirely biographical. If it be true, however, that our main interest is (or ought to be) in what a composer did rather than in what he was, the truth applies especially to Beethoven, and above all at the present time. The scheme of the book has therefore been modified so as to include a survey of his work. An attempt to make such a survey cover the whole of Beethoven's output would result in little more than a catalogue, with annotations so brief as to convey hardly anything of the essential quality of the music. It seemed, therefore, that the limited space would be best used, and the needs of the general reader more fully met, by a much less rigid and comprehensive method. My aim has been to indicate some, at least, of the more important characteristics of Beethoven's works, and to show their influence on his successors. If the adoption of a somewhat discursive style needs justification, one might suggest an analogy with certain musical forms, in which material that at first seems to be irrelevant often ends by throwing unexpected light on the main theme and so increasing its significance.

In regard to the biographical section I am aware that the devout Beethovenite may regard certain passages as *lèse majesté*. But any disposition I may have felt towards toning down certain unhappy traits in Beethoven's character was checked by reading some recent books and articles which, ignoring facts now well known and beyond dispute, presented once more the traditional and totally false picture of him.

But what is a biography for, if not to tell us the truth? "Let us have one thing or the other," says Ernest Newman on this point, "either a true account of the man, or no account at all. But do not let us say that because Beethoven wrote the ninth Symphony it is right for a biographer to tell us how kind he was to his nephew, but wrong to tell how he fibbed over the state of his finances in his latter years."

In fairness, I end with a confession: For some years I had been affected by the prevalent anti-Beethoven chill, and, like my fellow-sufferers, had come to regard him as an over-rated composer. So strong was this feeling that I hesitated long before undertaking to write this book. As a result of nearly three years spent on the task, which involved a close study of his music, including much that I have never heard during a long experience of concert-going, I am once more an enthusiast.

If this were merely a personal matter it would not be mentioned. I refer to it because there are at present many thousands who are wavering in their old allegiance. I am confident that they have only to approach Beethoven's work anew, scrapping all the ready-made opinions on it, and, above all, enlarging their acquaintance with the later chamber music, in order to become converted from waverers into discriminating enthusiasts.

In the preparation of this work I have been helped in a hundred ways by one whose co-operation must be warmly acknowledged, even though she happens to be my wife. I have also to thank Mr. Robert Lorenz for kindly reading the proofs.

Wareside, Herts.
1927.

CONTENTS

PART I

BEETHOVEN

Chapter XV

Chapter XVI

Chapter XVII

Chapter XVIII

Chapter XIX

Chapter XX

PART II

PART III

LUDWIG VAN BEETHOVEN

PART I

Chapter I

Birth—Parentage—Early Studies—The Prodigy—A Sequence of Teachers—The Young Organist—A Visit to Holland.

LUDWIG VAN BEETHOVEN was born at Bonn on December 16th, 1770,[1] of a consumptive mother and a drunken father; his paternal grandmother was also a dipsomaniac, and spent the last few years of her life as a compulsory abstainer in a convent. The painful facts concerning his parentage are set out at the very beginning of this book, because a just estimate of the man and his work is possible only when his terrible handicap is borne in mind. It warped his outlook, soured his temper, adversely affected his work both in quality and quantity, and no doubt shortened his life, for he died at fifty-seven, when his creative power was at its height.

The family was of Belgian origin, the first traceable members living near Louvain, whence one of them removed to Antwerp in 1650.

The composer's grandfather, Louis, ran away to Louvain to take up an appointment as bass

[1] Only the date of baptism is recorded—December 17th. As baptism usually took place on the day following birth, the 16th is assumed.

singer, going a short time after to Bonn (1732), where he was appointed Court Musician to the Elector Clemens August.[1] Louis Beethoven had much of the forceful personality that showed itself later in his grandson. He was an excellent musician, and a man of marked integrity. Ludwig had grounds for claiming a physical likeness to him, for Wegeler tells us that the grandfather was dark-complexioned, short of stature, muscular, "with extremely animated eyes"—a description which fits the grandson in adult years. Though he died when Beethoven was little more than three years old, he left so vivid an impression on the child that his portrait was treasured and his memory honoured throughout the composer's life.

Johann, Beethoven's father, was a tenor in the Royal Choir, an appointment he no doubt owed to the paternal influence. He was tall and handsome, vain and weak in character, irregular in habit, and only moderately endowed in voice and musicianship. His wife was an estimable woman and a typical *hausfrau*, "much occupied with sewing and knitting," but with too little force of character to influence the thriftless Johann. The utmost she could do, apparently, was to refuse to pay his drinking debts. One of the few happy features of the family life was the tender feeling that always existed between

[1] It is worth noting that at least two other members of the Antwerp branch followed the arts: Gerhard, a sculptor; and Peter, a painter. There is record, too, of a priest van Beethoven in Brabant.

her and her son. A lodger in the Beethoven house gives us a pleasant picture of a domestic celebration in her honour:

> Each year the feast of St. Mary Magdalene (her birthday and name-day) was kept with due solemnity. The music stands were brought from the Tucksaal and placed in the two sitting-rooms overlooking the street, and a canopy, embellished with flowers, leaves, and laurels, was put up in the room containing Grandfather Louis's portrait. On the eve of the day, Madame van Beethoven was induced to retire betimes. By ten o'clock all was in readiness; the silence was broken by the tuning up of instruments, Madame van Beethoven was awakened, requested to dress, and was then led to a beautifully draped chair beneath the canopy. An outburst of music roused the neighbours, the most drowsy soon catching the infection of gaiety. When the music was over the table was spread, and, after food and drink, the merry company fell to dancing (but in stockinged feet to mitigate the noise) and so the festivities came to an end.[1]

So long as Grandfather Louis lived there was a measure of comfort and stability in the Beethoven *menage*; with his death began the domestic troubles that his presence had warded off. The father's drunken habits increased; the mother's health declined.

Beethoven's musical studies began early, but not phenomenally so; nor is there any evidence of infantile precocity such as was shown by Mozart

[1] Quoted in Bekker's "Beethoven," page 5.

and even by some lesser geniuses. In the dedication of his early piano Sonatinas to the Elector we read: "Music became my first youthful pursuit in my fourth year." But we know what Beethoven himself discovered only late in life, namely, that his father, anxious to exploit the child as a prodigy, falsified his age and made him out to be two years younger than he really was. Until his fortieth year Beethoven believed himself to have been born in 1772, and this date is given in most, if not all, of the early biographies. From the dedication quoted above it is evident that he was set to work when six years old. No doubt his father, remembering the triumphant and lucrative progress from court to court of the youthful Mozart—a progress that included a visit to Bonn in 1764—saw in him a means of restoring the family fortunes. That the boy was made to serve with rigour is certain, though we may discount some of the reports of the father's brutality. One so notoriously faulty as Johann Beethoven was hardly likely to be judged leniently in this or any other respect. "Give a dog a bad name." . . . When, therefore, we read that Cäcilia Fischer and Doctor Wegeler often saw from a window in the Fischer's house "the little Louis van Beethoven standing in front of the clavier and weeping," we must not hastily accept it as a proof of paternal cruelty. Many a small boy has moistened his five-finger exercises with tears, not because his father was brutal, but because his task was irksome. Beethoven never took kindly to instruction at any period of his life, and the uninteresting early stages of clavier and violin technique would hardly be attractive to him, the more so as his father was not qualified, either as musician or teacher, to make the best use of the lesson hours.

No time was lost in bringing the prodigy to market, and the following announcement appeared in the press (reproduced in the *Kölnische Zeitung* of December 18th, 1870):

> Avertissement
>
> Today, March 26, 1778, in the musical concert-room in the Sternen-gasse the Electoral Court Tenorist, Beethoven, will have the honour to produce two of his scholars, namely, Mlle. Averdonck, Court Contraltist, and his little son of six years. The former will have the honour to contribute various beautiful arias, the latter various clavier concertos and trios. He flatters himself that he will give complete enjoyment to all ladies and gentlemen, the more since both have had the honour of playing to the greatest delight of the entire court.
>
> Beginning at five o'clock in the evening. Ladies and gentlemen who have not subscribed will be charged a florin. Tickets may be had at the aforesaid Akademiesaal, also of Mr. Claren auf der Bach in Mühlenstein.

No record exists as to the programme, nor do we know how far the venture was successful.

It is evident that an eight-year-old could not be set to work thus strenuously at piano and violin without detriment to his general education. Ludwig attended an elementary school, probably in a fitful manner, and in any case his practising and lessons would leave him little zest for school work. On many a morning it must have been a very tired youngster who left his home in the Rheingasse for the day's schooling. Small wonder that he failed to distinguish himself, even in so humble an academy. Among his schoolmates was a future Electoral Councillor, Wurzer, who in his memoirs wrote :

> One of my schoolmates was Luis van Beethoven, whose father held an appointment as Court Singer. Apparently his mother was already dead at the time, for Luis v. B. was distinguished by uncleanliness, negligence, etc. Not a sign was to be discovered in him of that spark of genius which glowed so brilliantly in him afterwards. . I imagine that he was kept down to his musical studies from an early age by his father.

Wurzer was wrong in deducing from Beethoven's neglected appearance that his mother was dead. Nor need we assume that she was to blame. She must have had her hands full with her dissipated husband, three growing boys, and the job of making ends meet. For the wolf was always at the door, and for this ailing woman to have kept him outside was something of a feat. The fact seems to have been that Beethoven was constitutionally untidy—even dirty—in his habits. He inherited much of his grandfather's sterling strength of character, but there was a streak of his father's irregularity as well. No doubt it showed itself thus early in such details as a sketchy method of washing that took no account of the less accessible portions of the neck and ears.

Beethoven's school life was short as well as unsatisfactory: it ended when he was eleven years old, and he was never able to make good the deficiencies later. He had a smattering of French and Latin but he was always a poor hand at two of the "three R's." His actual writing was fair —at the start, that is—but his spelling and punctuation were always speculative. Even weaker was his arithmetic. All his life, when faced by calculations other than the simplest, he was forced to help himself by the use of the fingers; and there is no more tragi-comic picture in the history of music than that of the composer of the Ninth Symphony whiling away some of the hours on his death-bed by wrestling with the mysteries of the multiplication table.[1]

Inevitably his musical attainments soon got beyond the limited range of his father, and there ensued a succession of teachers, mostly unsatisfactory. The old Court organist, van den Eeden, tried his hand when the boy was eight years old, but apparently he was a failure. A

[1] Thayer, iii. 194.

tenor singer in a theatrical company, and a good pianist, Friedrich Pfeiffer succeeded him. Pfeiffer was a man of parts, but a scapegrace; he appears to have lodged with the family, and to have become a boon companion of the father. Painters have often idealized the childhood of famous musicians, showing them picturesquely at the clavier, practising secretly by moonlight, or holding admiring groups spellbound. Nobody seems to have depicted a scene that frequently occurred during the boyhood of Ludwig: Johann Beethoven and Pfeiffer reeling in at midnight, and dragging the nine-year-old from his bed, to the key-board, where they would sometimes keep him till it was time to consider breakfast and school. No wonder he struck his schoolmate Wurzer as neglected, dirty, and dull!

Pfeiffer taught him for a year, and then left Bonn—as he had left other cities—in a significant hurry. There followed some lessons on the violin and viola from a court musician named Rovantini.

Ludwig had always been attracted by the organ and (apparently at his own request) he became a pupil of a Franciscan friar named Koch, who was expert both in playing and in organ construction. The boy made such progress that he soon became Koch's assistant. He also struck up an acquaintance with the organist in the Minorites cloister, and undertook to play at the six o'clock Mass. His practical interest in the organ is shown by the fact that one of his memorandum books contained the measurements of the pedalboard of the Minorite instrument. He is said to have studied also at this time with Jensen, the organist of the Münsterkirche at Bonn. (An interesting reminder of this side of his youthful activities is seen in a conversation, towards the end of his life, with a young organist named Freudenberg: "I, too, played the organ a great deal in my youth, but my nerves could not stand the power of the gigantic instrument. I place an organist who is master of his instrument first among virtuosos.")

Mention should be made at this point of a journey to Holland with his mother, apparently a combination of concert tour and visit to a friend of the family. A glimpse of this undertaking is given us by the Widow Karth, who as a child lived in the upper storey of the Beethoven house. She remembered sitting on her mother's knee, and hearing Beethoven's mother, "a quiet suffering woman," tell how, during the journey, the cold was so intense that she had to wrap up the boy's feet and keep them in her lap to prevent frostbite. Ludwig played a great deal during the visit, created a sensation, and received valuable presents. But the actual pecuniary results must have been poor, for he is reported to have said on his return, "The Dutch are skinflints (Pfennigfuchser); I'll never go to Holland again."

Although tradition says that he already composed (we hear of a Funeral Cantata being written and performed in January, 1781, when he was eleven) he appears to have had no instruction in composition until Neefe took him in hand.

CHAPTER II

Neefe, Friend and Teacher—An Early Reference to Beethoven in the Press—Beethoven as Deputy-Kappellmeister—First Publications—Appointment as Assistant Court Organist—Word Portrait of Beethoven as a boy—Operatic Experiences.

THE name of Christian Gottlob Neefe would probably have been long since forgotten but for his connection with Beethoven. If he has received a kind of shadowy immortality it is no more than he deserves for his fostering care of young Ludwig. He came to Bonn in 1779 as musical director of the Grossmann theatrical company, on the invitation of the Elector, who wished to do his part in the attempt then being made to form a national theatre. Neefe succeeded van den Eeden as Court organist in 1781, to the disappointment of the Beethovens, who had hoped that Ludwig, already assistant, would step into the post. However, so busy a man as Neefe would need a responsible deputy, and the next best thing to the appointment itself was the post of assistant, with payment in the shape of all-round instruction. Neefe rose well to the responsibility of training such a boy. He was severe, but apparently not more so than was desirable in the case of a pupil who, as a result of frequently changing and generally indifferent tuition, must have developed much that was unsatisfactory in technique and taste. Moreover, we may be sure that the "prodigy" atmosphere had not been without ill-effects. Neefe seems to have recognized both the boy's genius and the need of corrective discipline. He has been accused of undue severity, but he is acquitted by the results; and Beethoven's own gratitude, handsomely expressed in after years, shows that, although the boy probably resented drastic criticism at the time, he ultimately realized its value. Ten years later, on his departure from Bonn for Vienna, we find him writing to Neefe: "I thank you for the counsel which you gave me so often in my progress in my divine art. If I ever become a great man, yours shall be a share of the credit."

From Neefe himself came the first printed notice of Beethoven. Writing to "Cramer's Magazine," on March 2nd, 1783, concerning the musical life of Bonn, he said.

> Louis van Beethoven, son of the tenor singer mentioned, a boy of eleven years[1] and most promising talent. He plays the clavier very skilfully and with power, reads at sight very well, and—to put it in a nutshell—he plays chiefly "The Well-Tempered Clavichord" of Sebastian Bach, which Herr Neefe put into his hands. Whoever knows this collection of preludes and fugues in all the keys—which might almost be called the *non plus ultra* of our art—will know what this means. So far as his duties permitted,

[1] The reader must not forget to add two years to Beethoven's age in early references of this kind.

> Herr Neefe has also given him instruction in thorough-bass. He is now training him in composition, and for his encouragement has had nine variations for the pianoforte, written by him on a march (by Ernst Christoph Dressler) engraved at Mannheim. This youthful genius is deserving of help to enable him to travel. He would surely become a second Wolfgang Amadeus Mozart were he to continue as he has begun.

Thayer points out, justly, that Neefe's reference to Mozart shows his perception, for Mozart had at this date produced few of his finest compositions.

Deputizing for Neefe in the Court Chapel was no sinecure, musical services being frequent and elaborate. Further responsibilities were placed on Ludwig's shoulders in 1783, when, Neefe being called on to deputize for Kappellmeister Lucchesi during the latter's absence on leave for several months, the boy filled his place as "cembalist in the orchestra" at the stage rehearsals of the Grossmann company. In this capacity he had to conduct the musical part of the performance, seated at the pianoforte, and playing, when necessary, from the score—no small responsibility for a youngster of thirteen. It would be difficult to over-estimate the value of the experience in Beethoven's development.

Two works were published at this period—a song, and a pianoforte Rondo in Bossler's "Blumenlese fur Liebhaber," the former signed, the latter anonymous. A few months later the same publisher brought out the three Sonatas for pianoforte dedicated to Maximilian Friedrich, "composed by Ludwig van Beethoven, aged 11 years." (At the time of publication—1783—Beethoven was thirteen, but the actual composition may have taken place a good deal earlier.)

Meanwhile the work of the young assistant increased in both chapel and theatre. Nevertheless he received no salary and had no official standing. At the beginning of 1784, his year of probation being more than fulfilled, he petitioned for a salaried appointment. The petition has been lost, but the High Lord Steward's report on it survives, wherein that official, "referring to the petition of Ludwig van Beethoven for the post of Assistant Court Organist, is of the humble opinion that the grace ought to be bestowed upon him, together with a small compensation." The "small compensation" was urgently needed just now, for things at home were going from bad to worse. The report, in fact, states that Ludwig's father was "no longer able to provide for his care and subsistence." The petition was granted, but before the salary was fixed the Elector died, and the musical arrangements at the Court underwent sweeping changes. The theatrical company was dismissed, and Neefe found himself no longer in need of an assistant. The new Elector, Maximilian Franz, was faced with urgent need of economy, and at once began to scrutinize the pay-sheets. It was lucky for Ludwig that his name appeared as a regular member of the staff, though so far unpaid. The reports made out for the new Elector's information call for quotation so far as they concern the Beethovens and Neefe. Ludwig's father appears in the list of tenors :

> J. van Beethoven, age 44 . . . has three sons living in the Electorate, aged 13, 10, and 8 years, who are studying music; has served 28 years, salary 315 florins. His voice has long been stale . . . very poor, of fair deportment . . .

The " fair deportment " was no doubt a charitable view inspired by the writer's kindly feeling towards Ludwig, of whom we read :

> Ludwig van Beethoven, aged 13, born at Bonn, has served two years, no salary . . . during the absence of the Chapelmaster Luchessi he played the organ ; is of good capability . . . of good and quiet deportment, and poor.

The writer was evidently no friend to Neefe, and twice suggests his dismissal, in one case indicating the extent of the saving in cash. (Neefe's salary was 300 florins—about £30) :

> Item. If Neefe were to be dismissed another organist would have to be appointed, who, if he were to be used only in the Chapel could be had for 150 florins . . . the same is small, young, and the son of a Court *musici*, and in case of need has filled the place for nearly a year very well.

In the upshot Neefe's salary was reduced by a third (restored to the original sum a year later) and we learn from the pay-roll that " tenorist

Beethoven" and "Beethoven jun." received sums equivalent to £30 and £15 per annum respectively.

A note as to Ludwig's personal appearance at this period is of interest. Ries and Simrock both describe him as "a boy powerfully, almost clumsily built," and Fischer says: "Short of stature, broad shoulders, short neck, large head, round nose, dark brown complexion; he always bent forward slightly when he walked. In the house he was called 'der Spagnol' (the Spaniard)."

The three years that followed the accession of Max Franz call for few words. Save for occasional visits by touring companies, the Bonn theatre was closed, and Beethoven had ample time for study. Infrequent as they were, however, the theatrical performances were of a kind that must have profoundly influenced Ludwig, for the operatic works included Gluck's "Alceste" and "Orpheus," Salieri's "Armida" and works by Grétry (eight), Paisiello (five), Gossec, Pergolesi, Philidor, Monsigny, etc. We may figure the youth, then, making the most of these opportunities of hearing dramatic music (mostly of a light kind), composing, pursuing his studies under the faithful Neefe, and playing the Chapel organ. He seems also to have studied the violin under Franz Ries.

The compositions of this period include three pianoforte quartets (published after his death) the thematic material of which was used in later works.

Chapter III

Visit to Vienna—Lessons from Mozart—Recalled to Mother's Death-bed—A Terrible Family Bill of Health—The von Breunings—Count von Waldstein—Beethoven's Father loses his Post.

"This genius deserves support to enable him to travel." So wrote Neefe in 1783, and four years later the means were found, though from what source is not known.

Early in 1787, Ludwig, now sixteen years old, (though held to be fourteen, the reader will remember) went to Vienna for a short stay, and during his visit received a few lessons from Mozart. Concerning his introduction to the latter, Jahn says:

> Beethoven, who as a youth of great promise came to Vienna in 1787, but was obliged to return to Bonn after a brief sojourn, was taken to Mozart and at that musician's request played something for him which he, taking it for granted that it was a show piece prepared for the occasion, praised in rather a cool manner. Beethoven, observing this, begged Mozart to give him a theme for improvisation. He always played admirably when excited, and now he was inspired too, by the presence of the master whom he reverenced greatly; he played in such a style that Mozart, whose attention and interest grew more and more, finally went silently to some friends who were sitting in an adjoining room, and said, vivaciously, "Keep

your eyes on him; some day he will give the world something to talk about."

The lessons seem to have been in composition, though it has been conjectured that the chief aim of the visit was to study the piano under Mozart. Perhaps the piano lessons would have followed, had not Ludwig been recalled to Bonn by news of his mother's illness. Certainly the boy appears to have attracted little attention by his pianoforte playing, for although the Vienna press of that time made mention of the infant prodigies Hummel and Scheidl, there is silence concerning Beethoven. Yet he must have become a topic of conversation in musical circles, for Haydn, writing to Artaria, the Vienna music publisher, in May, 1787 (a few weeks after Ludwig's arrival) says, "I should like to know who this Ludwig is"—presumably a reference to Beethoven, though of course there may have been a musician surnamed Ludwig.

The stay at Vienna had lasted only three months when the lad was summoned home. He returned via Augsburg, making friends there with the family of Schaden, a pianoforte maker, and borrowing £3 to help him on his way. A letter written to Schaden a few weeks after his arrival at Bonn shows him to be in poor health and even poorer spirits:

I must tell you that from the time I left Augsburg my cheerfulness as well as my health began to decline;

the nearer I came to my native city, the more frequent were the letters from my father urging me to travel with all possible speed, as my mother was not in a favourable state of health. I therefore hurried forward as fast as I could, although myself far from well. My longing once more to see my dying mother overcame every obstacle, and assisted me in surmounting the greatest difficulties. I found my mother still alive but in the most deplorable state; her disease was consumption, and about seven weeks ago, after much pain and suffering, she died. She was such a kind, loving mother to me, and my best friend. Ah, who was happier than I when I could still utter the sweet name, mother, and it was heard? And to whom can I now speak it? Only to the silent image resembling her evoked by the power of the imagination. I have passed very few pleasant hours since my arrival here, having during the whole time been suffering from asthma, which may, I fear, eventually develop into consumption; to this is added melancholy, almost as great an evil as my malady itself. Imagine yourself in my place, and then I shall hope to receive your forgiveness for my long silence. You showed me extreme kindness and friendship by lending me three Carolins in Augsburg, but I must entreat your indulgence for a time. My journey cost me a great deal, and I have not the smallest hopes of earning anything here. Fate is not propitious to me in Bonn.

Ludwig's mother died on July 17th, 1787, aged 40. The family at this time was in sore straits. Franz Ries apparently put his hand in his pocket on their behalf, but there seems to have been no response to the following petition to the Elector :

> Court Musician [Johann Beethoven] makes obedient representation that he has got into a very unfortunate state because of the long-continued sickness of his wife, and has already been compelled to sell a portion of his effects and pawn others, and that he no longer knows what to do for his sick wife and many children. He prays for the benefaction of an advance of 100 rthlr. on his salary.

The "many children" consisted at this time of Ludwig, Caspar, Anton, Carl (aged 13), Nickolaus Johann (aged 11), and Maria Margaretha Joseph, now about a year old, and fated to die five months later; August Franz George, born in 1781, had died at two and a half; the first-born—Ludwig Maria, had lived only six days; and another child—a girl—had succumbed after four days.

This aspect of the family history is summarized here, because it throws a vivid light on the whole of Beethoven's early life. What a bill of health! Small wonder that Ludwig began at this time to worry concerning the probability of his having inherited consumption—a source of anxiety that never left him.

The year 1787, wretched though it was, closed with a happy circumstance in his appointment as pianoforte teacher to the son and daughter of Madame von Breuning. Concerning the date of his acquaintance with the members of this family there is a conflict of evidence, but the probability is that during his violin studies with Ries a year or two before, Stephan von Breuning, then a boy four years younger than Ludwig, had been a fellow pupil. His entry into this family circle was an event of the first importance. The von Breunings were cultured, and occupied a good social position; and the children were sufficiently near Beethoven in age to admit of genuine companionship. The fact that he soon became on such terms of intimacy as to spend whole days and nights at the von Breuning's house points to his having thus early exercised the power of personal attraction that subsequently bridged even wider social gaps. Without this attractive power his already manifest genius would, socially, have availed little, for at that time a musician, even when he happened to be a Haydn, could exist only by attaching himself to the establishment of a wealthy amateur, where his status was that of a superior type of domestic servant.

The von Breuning circle gave him just what was needed at this time. It enabled him to make good some of the deficiencies in his education, especially on the literary side. He improved in health and spirits, and also, no doubt, in manners and personal habits, though throughout his life the latter were always irregular.

Another fruitful acquaintance dates from this period—that with Count von Waldstein, an enthusiastic and generous-hearted amateur. Wegeler calls him " the first, and in every respect the most important, of the Mæcenases of Beethoven " :

> He was not only a connoisseur but also a practitioner of music. He it was who gave all manner of support to our Beethoven, whose gifts he was the first to recognize worthily. Through him the young genius developed the talent to improvize variations on a given theme. From him he received much pecuniary assistance bestowed in such a way as to spare his sensibilities, it being generally looked on as a small gratuity from the Elector.

The Count has been well rewarded. How many would know his name to-day but for the dedication of the great C major Sonata ? Without belittling his generosity, we may say that, like others of Beethoven's benefactors who were rewarded with dedications, their reflected immortality was cheap at the price.

The " pecuniary assistance " must have been badly wanted when the Count came on the scene, for matters at home were still on the down grade. The end of this chapter of home troubles was reached in 1789, when Ludwig was forced to take the drastic step of petitioning the Elector to discharge his father from the Court service, paying him only half his salary (on condition that he retired " to a village in the Electorate " and conducted himself with reasonable sobriety), the remainder going to his son, "besides the salary which he now draws, and the three measures of grain for the support of his brothers."

(The edict of banishment was not enforced. It probably served its purpose by being held over Johann's head *in terrorem.*)

A glimpse of the stage to which Johann had sunk is given us by Stephan von Breuning, who speaks of seeing Ludwig rescuing his drunken father from a police officer.

Chapter IV

Beethoven as Head of the Household—Congenial Work in the Theatre Orchestra—Meets Haydn in Bonn—An Estimate of Beethoven as Pianist—Haydn again visits Bonn and Encourages Beethoven—Beethoven a Busy but Reluctant Teacher—An Extempore Duet—The First of the Love Affairs—Ardent . . . but Transient—Departure for Vienna.

The eighteen-year-old Ludwig was thus placed at the head of the family. His brother Carl was no doubt preparing for the musical career planned for him; and Nickolaus Johann was apprenticed to the Court Apothecary.

Despite his responsibilities as head of a household consisting of a besotted father and two unsatisfactory—or at least uncongenial—brothers, Ludwig now entered on a period of about four years of happiness. His position, both social and professional, improved steadily. The Elector's revival of his predecessor's project of a national theatre increased his opportunities of musical development. Bonn found itself with a busy circle of excellent musicians, and Ludwig's official duties made him one of them. He composed a romantic ballet, which was performed (anonymously), but he appears to have been chiefly esteemed as a pianist. More important for his future as an orchestral composer was the fact of his playing the viola in the theatre band for four years. Nothing could have been better for him, both as man and musician, than a long spell of work calculated above all to give him an insight into the practical side of orchestration, and at the same time so undistinguished as to offer no temptation to display—a wholesome contrast to his earlier piano-playing activities. Thayer, with reason, ascribes to the influence of this period, with its almost daily contact with music of an essentially melodic and dramatic quality, much of Beethoven's powers as a writer of tunes. To it may also be attributed some at least of that sense of form that showed itself even in the earliest of his compositions.

During this spell of congenial and fruitful work he saw Haydn, who passed through Bonn *en route* for London. During a journey up the Rhine with the Court, he met the Abbé Sterkel, a famous pianist, to whom he played his recently published set of Twenty-four Variations on a theme of Righini. Beethoven's playing at this period seems to have been somewhat rough technically, but full of character. Carl Ludwig Junker, chaplain to Prince Hohenlohe, writing in a journal of this date, gives us a glimpse of his playing, and incidentally adds one more proof of the attractiveness of Beethoven's personality:

> I heard also one of the greatest of pianists, the dear, good Bethofen, (*sic*) some compositions by whom appeared in the Spires "Blumenlese" in 1783, written in his eleventh [thirteenth] year. True, he

did not perform in public; probably the instrument here was not to his mind. It is one of Spath's make, and at Bonn he plays upon one by Steiner. But, what was infinitely preferable to me, I heard him extemporize in private; yes, I was even invited to propose a theme for him to vary. The greatness of this amiable, light-hearted man, as a virtuoso, may in my opinion be safely estimated from his almost inexhaustible wealth of ideas, the altogether characteristic style of expression in his playing, and the great execution which he displays. I know, therefore, no one thing which he lacks, that conduces to the greatness of an artist. I have heard Vogler upon the pianoforte—of his organ playing I say nothing, not having heard him upon that instrument—have often heard him, heard him by the hour together, and never failed to wonder at his astonishing execution; but Bethofen, in addition to the execution, has greater clearness and weight of idea, and more expression—in short, he is more for the heart—equally great, therefore, as an *Adagio* or *Allegro* player. Even the members of this remarkable orchestra are, without exception, his admirers, and all ears when he plays. Yet he is exceedingly modest and free from all pretension. He, however, acknowledged to me, that, upon the journeys[1] which the Elector had enabled him to make, he had seldom found in the playing of the most distinguished virtuosos that excellence which he supposed he had a right to expect. His style of treating his instrument is so different from that usually adopted, that it impresses one with the idea that by a path of his own

[1] This reference is obscure, as Thayer points out. It may be conjectured however, that Junker had in mind such expeditions of the Court Orchestra as the one on which this meeting occurred.

discovery he has attained that height of excellence whereon he now stands.

This quotation is worth noting on several grounds. It shows that though now past his twentieth year (an age at which most great composers have made their mark as creative musicians) Beethoven's success was chiefly as a pianist; indeed, it appears that even Haydn fell in with the general view. Far more important, however, is the fact that thus early Beethoven began to reveal the emotional appeal and originality of method that was destined to change the whole current of music. This point can only be touched on here; its development belongs to a later chapter.

One other circumstance of this period calls for mention—a second visit of Haydn on his return from London to Vienna. Again there was complimentary feasting (a breakfast given by the orchestra) and Beethoven took advantage of the occasion to bring a Cantata to the notice of Haydn, "who encouraged its author to continue study." Probably the question of lessons with Haydn was now broached.

Beethoven seems now to have been in considerable request as a teacher, though we may well understand his dislike of the work. Wegeler tells us that Madame von Breuning frequently found it necessary to keep him up to the mark—no easy task, for sometimes when she had coaxed him as far as the door he would slip back: it was impossible to teach to-day; he would do a double turn to-morrow. Whereat Madame would with a shrug own herself beaten: "It's no use to-day; he has his *raptus* again." However, Beethoven never ceased to be grateful to this excellent tactful woman: he described the von Breunings as "his guardian angels of that time"; and, speaking of Madame's "many reprimands" said:

> "She knew how to keep insects off the flowers." By insects he meant certain friendships which had already begun to threaten danger to the natural development of his talent and a proper measure of artistic consciousness by awakening vanity in him by their flatteries. He was already near to considering himself a famous artist, and therefore more inclined to give heed to those who encouraged him in his illusions than such as set before him the fact that he has still to learn everything that makes a master out of a disciple.[1]

So far as good friends could make up for the unhappiness of his early home life, Beethoven was richly compensated. To picture him as a lonely, friendless, and neglected genius, as has often been done, is shabby treatment of Neefe, the von Breunings, Waldstein, and the rest of the loyal (and long-suffering) friends who were never lacking to the end of his life.

A curiosity in the way of improvisation may

[1] Schindler, quoted in Thayer, i. 119.

be mentioned here, as it took place at the von Breuning's. Wegeler says:

> Once when Beethoven was improvising at the house of the Breunings (on which occasions he used frequently to be asked to characterize in the music some well-known person) Father Ries was urged to accompany him upon the violin. After some hesitation he consented, and this may have been the first time that two artists improvised a duo.

Improvisation is necessarily a solo affair, and doubt is often expressed as to this "duo." It may have been somewhat in the nature of a joke or "stunt". On the other hand, it should be remembered that pianoforte improvisations at this period consisted very largely of more or less superficial passage-work over a simple harmonic basis. Despite their frequent touches of originality, all the evidence goes to show that those of Beethoven (certainly in his early years) conformed to custom. This being so, there is no reason to doubt Ries's ability to add a violin melody to a harmonic scheme that must have run on familiar lines. For example, Beethoven's Fantasia in G Minor, despite its late opus number (77), is clearly an early work, and was probably based on an improvisation. Much of it is of the type of music in which a good musician can see a bar or two ahead, and it would be no startling feat for a violinist with no previous knowledge of the work to add a countertheme, and even join in some of the decorative passages. The point is not important, perhaps; but it is one of many interesting by-paths in music that are worth a moment's thought.

At the von Breuning's occurred the first of Beethoven's many love-affairs. Among the visitors were Jeanette d'Honrath and Maria Anna Westerhold, and for both damsels Beethoven (says Wegeler) "at various times indulged transient, but not the less ardent, passions." Both adjectives may be applied to the many similar affairs that occurred throughout Beethoven's life. The facility with which he fell in love was happily equalled by the ease with which he fell out. He once admitted to Ries that a certain woman "had held him in the strongest bonds for the longest time, viz., fully seven months."[1] Nobody was a penny the worse, and as the experiences inevitably served to stimulate composition, posterity owes something to the long line of Beethoven's flames. No doubt the emotional intensity which was one of the distinguishing features of his output (compared with the music of his predecessors) was due in part to the series of such crises.

One is tempted to speculate as to the probable effect on his music had one of these youthful affairs led to a happy marriage. The fact that in practically all his love affairs the attraction was mutual is a further reminder of his strange

[1] Thayer, i, 325.

power of personal appeal, especially where women were concerned. "So long at any rate as I knew him," says Wegeler, "Beethoven was never without a love, and he achieved conquest where many an Adonis had failed before him." And other friends, such as von Breuning, Ries, and Romberg, corroborate.

His invariable disappointments are perhaps explained by his unpractical habit of falling in love with women of high social position. ("Alas! she is not of my station," he writes to Wegeler in 1801 concerning the Countess Guicciardi.) It was the tale of the moth and the star, *da capo, ad libitum*.

In November, 1792, Beethoven left Bonn for Vienna, there to take up with Haydn the course of study that had no doubt been discussed when the two met a few months earlier. Neefe says that Beethoven went "at the expense of the Elector," and there is evidence that Maximilian had intended to defray the cost. But political and other troubles caused the flight of the Elector, and, beyond a small sum to help him on the journey, Beethoven received nothing.

Chapter V

Early Struggles in Vienna—Death of Johann Beethoven—Dawning Prosperity—Pupil of Haydn—A Pianistic Duel—Lessons from Schenk and Albrechtsberger—A Difficult Pupil.

Beethoven, now twenty-two years old, arrived in Vienna in the early days of November, 1792. Such details as are available concerning his early days there are of the most prosaic type, yet not without interest. Lodgings had to be found and a complete equipment purchased. For the former, a garret over a printer's shop was secured, but it was soon exchanged for a room on the ground floor—probably from motives of economy, for the notebook, in some details of expenses, says: "It is not necessary to give the housekeeper more than 7 florins per month, the rooms are so close to the ground." The book gives a list of immediate needs, "wood, wigmaker, coffee, overcoat, boots, shoes, pianoforte-desk, deal writing-desk, pianoforte-money." A note as to the address of a dancing-master is significant, especially when read in conjunction with such entries as "Black silk stockings: 1 ducat; 1 pair of winter silk stockings: 1 florin, 40 kreutzers;" etc. Here is a young man who means to cut a figure in other than musical circles! Unfortunately he seems to have been lavish on the strength of his expectations from the Elector. A few pages later we read, " In Bonn I counted on receiving 100 ducats here ; but in vain. I have got to equip myself completely anew." Instead of the looked-for 100 ducats, only 25 had been received, and Beethoven at once had to dip into the small savings he had brought with him.

His difficulties were increased a few weeks later by the sudden death of his father (December 18th, 1792). This meant the lapse of the pension of 200 thalers, half of which had been coming regularly to Ludwig. What was now to be done in regard to the maintenance of brothers Carl and Nickolaus ? He at once petitioned the Elector, and the payments were continued until the following year, when they ceased with the further decline in Maximilian's fortunes. Happily, good friends were soon forthcoming in Vienna. He had gone thither with the status of a Court appointment and with the warmest wishes of Waldstein and other important amateurs ; and he was already favourably known, either personally or by repute, to many prominent Viennese folk who had visited Bonn. Thayer gives a lengthy list of aristocratic families in Vienna who within a short time welcomed Beethoven on a footing partly social, partly professional ; and within a year we find him lodged in Prince Lichnowsky's house, and, later, in receipt of a substantial annuity from the Prince. So much for the long-popular conception of Beethoven as a friendless, starving genius !

The fact is that after the few straitened months that followed his arrival in Vienna, Beethoven found in private engagements, gifts, and pupils, an ample income.[1]

Meanwhile, he had started his lessons with Haydn, only to become dissatisfied in a short time. It may be imagined that he was not the most tractable of pupils, and it is evident that Haydn was too much occupied to give him proper attention. At all events, the relations between the two, never very cordial, became less and less so. Still, there was no open breach, and that the association of master and pupil was not limited to lesson hours is shown by such entries in Beethoven's notebook as "22x chocolate for Haidn and me;" "Coffee, 6x for Haidn and me." (The dates are October 24th and 29th, 1793, nearly a year after Beethoven began the lessons.) The story of the pupil's disillusionment is worth telling: Among the most famous of virtuosi in Vienna at that time was the Abbé Joseph Gelinek, "a brilliant pianist and so prolific a composer of variations that he was nick-named 'the variation-smith.'" Beethoven soon got to know him; indeed, shortly after Beethoven's arrival in the city there was a pianistic contest between them—an event which demands a word in passing. Gelinek was seen one day by Carl Czerny's father going off decked in his best. Czerny asked him where he was going. Gelinek

[1] Thayer, i, 168.

replied that he had been invited to measure himself with a young pianist who had just arrived. "I'll use him up," he added. A few days later Czerny met him again, "Well, how did the contest go?" "Ah," replied Gelinek, "he is no man; he's a devil. He will play me and all of us to death. And how he improvises!"

In Gelinek's lodging Beethoven met Johann Schenk, an excellent all-round musician and composer. Here is Schenk's own account of the meeting:

> In July [1793] Abbé Gelinek informed me that he had made the acquaintance of a young man who displayed extraordinary virtuosity on the pianoforte, such, indeed, as he had not observed since Mozart. In passing, he said that Beethoven had been studying counterpoint with Haydn for more than six months and was still at work on the first exercise. . . . Beethoven, eager to learn, became discontented and often gave expression to his dissatisfaction to his friend. . . . Gelinek came to me with the question whether I felt disposed to assist his friend in the study of counterpoint. . . . A day was fixed to meet him in Gelinek's lodgings and hear him play.

The meeting duly took place, and Schenk was astounded by Beethoven's improvising. On the following day he called on Beethoven, and found "on his writing desk a few passages from his first lesson in counterpoint." A mere glance showed that, brief as the examples were, they bristled with errors. Schenk, "feeling sure that

Beethoven was unfamiliar with the preliminary rules of counterpoint," gave him the "Gradus" of Fux, and undertook to help him in his studies, a condition being that the instruction was to be gratuitous and kept secret. The lessons began in August, 1793, and lasted about a year. Beethoven's trip to Eisenstadt with Haydn in May, 1794, broke off the lessons, and they were never resumed.

No doubt Beethoven had good grounds for dissatisfaction with Haydn as a teacher. Yet some excuse may fairly be made for the older man. Temperamentally, there was a wide gulf between Haydn, the product of the patronage system, and the young Beethoven who, though indebted to the system throughout his life, was destined to do more than any other in making the musician independent of it. To the amiable Haydn the youth must have seemed a truculent boor. Moreover, Beethoven's development as a composer was slow, owing no doubt to the intermittent and unsatisfactory nature of his early instruction. It is not surprising that Haydn, to whom composition had always been almost as easy and natural a function as breathing, should share in the general estimate of Beethoven as an exceptionally gifted pianist and improviser rather than as a composer. Yet though Beethoven learned little from Haydn in such matters as strict counterpoint and fugue, he could hardly have failed to gain much from so polished a master of style and form; and no one knew better than Beethoven himself the social and professional advantages of being known as the pupil and familiar of the most famous musician of the time. The latter point no doubt explains the care with which he avoided anything in the nature of a breach with Haydn.

Haydn continued to teach Beethoven until the former's departure for England at the end of 1793, and in the following January Beethoven began a course of study with Albrechtsberger. Here was a contrapuntist who was all for the rigour of the game, and no better testimony as to Beethoven's consciousness of his deficiencies in theory, and his determination to overcome them, can be found than his subjecting himself to the strictest teacher of the day, and continuing with him for about fifteen months, with three lessons a week.

Entries in Beethoven's notebooks show that during this period he took also three lessons a week in violin-playing from Schuppanzigh. Nor does this exhaust the list of teachers. More or less casually, he received at this time instruction on the horn from Stich (better known as Punto); from Kraft and Linke on the violoncello; and from Friedlowsky on the clarinet. To Salieri he went for lessons in vocal writing.

No doubt he found much of the Albrechtsberger regimen irksome; but those who figure him always as an inveterate despiser and breaker of rules are mistaken. The 160 pages of exercises that have survived show otherwise. " Every line," says Thayer, " bears witness that he entered into his studies with complete interest and undivided zeal." Yet the somewhat crabbed Albrechtsberger and his pupil must often have crossed each other, and we feel no surprise on reading that Beethoven in after years described him as " a musical pedant," while the theorist said of Beethoven, " Have nothing to do with him! He has learnt nothing, and will never do anything in decent style." Thayer probably takes too rosy a view of Beethoven's teachableness, and quotes in support the marginal query Beethoven wrote concerning an unprepared suspension: " Is it allowed?" But it is far more likely that the apparently docile query was satirical. Ries confirms Beethoven's unpopularity with his teachers: " I know them all well. All three [Haydn, Albrechtsberger, and Salieri] had a high regard for Beethoven, but only one opinion concerning his studies. They agreed that Beethoven was so obstinate and self-willed that he had to learn afterwards, through hard experience, many a truth he refused to accept from his teachers. This was especially the opinion of Albrechtsberger and Salieri". And Haydn's nickname for his pupil, " the Great Mogul," partly referred less to his swarthy appearance than to his arrogance.

CHAPTER VI

Progress in Composition—Guest of the Lichnowskys—Oppressive Hospitality—First Viennese Appearance as Pianist—An Aristocratic Musicmaker—van Swieten and the "48"—The B flat Concerto—The Trios, Op. I—Profitable Publication—First Pianoforte Sonatas.

THIS is a suitable point at which to report on Beethoven's progress as a composer. A glance at the list of works at the end of the book will show that his output so far was small, compared with that of Mozart, Haydn, and other great com posers at the same age. The cause is no doubt to be found in the lack of regular study of harmony and counterpoint in his early years, and to the small part such study played compared with his work at the pianoforte. We must remember, too, that the method of composition practised in his maturity—often a painful kind of evolution rather than invention—seems to have been more or less habitual from the first. However, some important works of a later date were undoubtedly conceived at this time. Even the Ninth Symphony is linked with his boyhood, for before going to Vienna he had already expressed his intention of setting the "Ode to Joy" that was eventually to form the chorale finale.

Mention has been made of Beethoven's taking up his abode with Prince Lichnowsky, and the fact is significant of the curious social position of Beethoven. All doors seem to have been open to him, and no more striking proof of the genuine enthusiasm for music on the part of the aristocracy of Vienna could be brought forward than the readiness with which they condoned the *gaucherie* and even downright bad manners of Beethoven. The Lichnowskys must have swallowed much. For example, Beethoven soon slighted their hospitality by treating their establishment as a mere house of call, rather than as the permanent haven his generous patrons had in view. The restrictions of a well-run household were too much for him. He rebelled especially at the obligation to appear at dinner at a fixed hour, and probably even less to his liking was the necessity for appearing at his host's table in proper attire. Hence his frequent meals at neighbouring inns, at such hours as suited him best. His dislike of restraint even led him to take lodgings of his own, while still retaining his rooms at the Lichnowskys' as a kind of headquarters. (The lodgings were changed so frequently that historians have long since given up the attempt to trace them. He is known to have occupied at least thirty—an average of one a year!) Perhaps the Prince—and even more the Princess—showed too openly their intention of taking care of him; and their hospitality may not have been free from a suspicion of "lion-hunting." At all events, Beethoven found it irksome, and escaped from it with growing frequency. "They wanted to train me there with grandmotherly love," he explained, "and the Princess would have liked to put me in a glass case."

We may sympathize with Beethoven in his dislike of a hospitality that no doubt tended to become oppressive at times; but there is little excuse for his breaches of manners and taste. These were generally caused by his suspicious nature seeing in an act of kindness a reflection on his independence—a curious contradiction in one who all his life owed so much to patrons. He was ready enough to accept a handsome annuity from the Prince, yet at the same time he could misread as insults the ordinary courtesies of a host to his guest.

Thus, the Prince gave order that if he and Beethoven happened to ring their bells at the same time, the latter should receive attention first. Beethoven got to hear of this, flew into a passion, and engaged a servant for himself. Again, on his expressing a desire to learn to ride, the Prince quite naturally offered him the run of his stables. This was a further offence, at which Beethoven showed his resentment by promptly buying a horse. Instances might be multiplied. The subject will be touched on later in discussing Beethoven's personal character. Here it must suffice to quote from one of Beethoven's letters (written in 1801), a sentence or two which throws an unfavourable light on his attitude to his benefactors :

> How sad is my lot ! I must avoid all things that are dear to me, and live amongst such miserable and egotistical men as —— and —— and others. I must say that amongst them all Lichnowsky is the most satisfactory, since last year he has settled an income of 600 florins on me, and the good sale of my works enables me to live without care. . . . I use —— and —— only as instruments on which I play when I please. . . . I estimate them only at what they are worth to me ——

a cynical utterance to come from a young man so accustomed to parade his love of liberty and independence.

Beethoven's first public appearance in Vienna as a solo performer took place in 1793—three years after his arrival. Bearing in mind the high reputation he had at once achieved as a pianist, this concert appearance seems belated. It must be remembered, however, that the concert as we know it to-day had not yet come into existence. Enterprising virtuosi sometimes gave subscription concerts, but such events were few, as is shown by the fact that after the death of Mozart no such event appears to have taken place in Vienna for many years. The nearest approach to our present-day public concert was the series of four given annually in aid of a fund for musicians' widows and orphans.

Even to-day the public concert is an unreliable guide as to the actual musical life of the community: in the Vienna of Beethoven's day it signified far less. Thus, there was an abundance of music-making, but practically all of it was private, and apparently there were almost as many folk ready to take a hand in its performance as there were listeners. Note this as an example of musical culture in high places, and at unusual hours: In 1782 Mozart took a regular part in a series of concerts organized by Martin, the performances being held at an hour when most musicians of to-day are still abed, and the orchestra consisting of amateur strings and professional wind. These concerts generally numbered twelve in each season, and continued regularly for several years. Hence, at the time of Beethoven's arrival in Vienna

> the extraordinary spectacle was still to be seen of princes and nobles joining in the performance of orchestral music to an audience of their own class at the strange hours of from 6 *to* 8 *in the morning.*[1]

And Thayer quotes Risbeck as to the status of music in Vienna at this period:

> Musicians are the only artists concerning whom the nobility exhibit taste. Many houses maintain private bands for their own delectation, and all the public concerts prove that this field of art stands in

[1] Thayer i, 166.

> high respect. It is possible to enlist four or five large orchestras here, all of them incomparable. The number of real virtuosos is small, but as regards the orchestral musicians scarcely anything more beautiful is to be heard in the world.

(Vienna at this time had a population of 200,000).

Here is a note giving a pleasant glimpse of a different and perhaps even better type of connoisseur, Gottfried van Swieten, an admirer of Beethoven, to whom the First Symphony was dedicated:

> To M. Beethoven in Alstergasse, No. 45, with the Prince Lichnowsky: If there is nothing to hinder next Wednesday I shall be glad to see you at my home at half past 8 with your nightcap in your bag. Give me an immediate answer.
>
> Swieten.

Some commentators see in the reference to the "nightcap" an invitation to stay the night. More probably it was a waggish allusion to the "Forty-eight" of Bach; for Schindler says that at the frequent musical evenings at van Swieten's, the old man often persuaded Beethoven to remain after the departure of the company, and "add a few fugues of Sebastian Bach as an evening blessing."

On March 29th and 30th, then, Beethoven made his first appearance before the Viennese public, at a couple of concerts given for the benefit of widows of musicians. At the first he played a Concerto of his own (probably that in B flat, Op. 19); at the second he gave an improvisation. The Concerto was not completed until two days before the concert, the Rondo being written in the afternoon, and handed out, sheet by sheet, to four copyists in an adjoining room—an eleventh hour method to which Beethoven was addicted throughout life, often with disastrous results in performance.

These two concert appearances were followed by the playing of a Mozart Concerto on the following night, between the acts of Mozart's "La Clemenza di Tito" given at the Burgtheatre by Mozart's widow.

A notable fact in regard to Beethoven's progress as a composer calls for record here. The three trios for pianoforte, violin and violoncello may have been written, or at least sketched out, at Bonn. (We know they were played in 1793 at the Lichnowskys' in the presence of Haydn, who gave offence to Beethoven by expressing doubts as to the advisability of publishing the third, in C minor.) The three works had attracted so much attention that the time seemed ripe for their publication, and a subscription was opened for the purpose in May, 1795. Two hundred and forty-one copies were subscribed for, the subscription price being one ducat, and Beethoven paying Artaria the publisher one florin per copy—representing a profit of nearly £200. How many modern composers make half that sum from a chamber work? How many even succeed in getting their Opus 1 printed at all?

The following year saw the publication of the first group of pianoforte sonatas, the three dedicated to Haydn, Op. 2. The dedication, and the fact that Beethoven appeared as pianist at a concert given by Haydn at about this time, shows that the two maintained at least an appearance of cordial relations. But Beethoven could not forget Haydn's deficiencies as a teacher. He was willing to dedicate the Sonatas to him (especially as a dedication to the outstanding musician of his day would confer prestige on a young composer); and he was ready enough to appear at a concert given by Haydn[1]—again for not entirely unselfish reasons. But when Haydn asked him to add to the dedication "Pupil of Haydn," (a natural request, seeing that he was ignorant of the fact that Schenk had been supplementing his lessons) Beethoven declined. "Though I have taken some lessons from Haydn," he told a friend, "I have never learned anything from him"—which was only partially true. He may not have learned exactly what he paid for, but he almost certainly received good value in other ways. (The fee, by the way, was two groschen—about 9½d. per lesson.)

[1] At this concert were played for the first time at Vienna three new symphonies of Haydn, the fruits of his recent visit to London. Beethoven's contribution appears to have been his own Concerto in B flat.

Meanwhile, Beethoven's former intention of returning to his birth-place had been abandoned. Father, mother, and four children, lay in the churchyard at Bonn, and Ludwig's two brothers had no desire to remain in the old home. They came to Vienna therefore in 1795, and Beethoven never saw Bonn again.

CHAPTER VII

Successful Tours—A Himmel Episode—Warnings of Deafness—The "Eroica" suggested—Production of First Symphony—Contests with Steibelt.

THE record of Beethoven's life from this point provides little material for ordinary biographical purposes. The fourth year of his life in Vienna saw him well-established and prosperous. His position as the first of pianists was acknowledged; his compositions were attracting increased attention; his financial prosperity is shown by his being able to maintain a servant and a horse. Even a genius could not complain of having gone no farther at the age of twenty-six.

Nor does he seem to have been called on to give more than very slight aid to his brothers, and that only for a short time after their arrival. Carl soon obtained a position in the musical world—undistinguished, it is true, but apparently lucrative enough to keep him; and Johann, established as an apothecary's assistant, prospered sufficiently to save money, and in a few years set up in business on his own account.

During 1796 and 1797 Beethoven made numerous journeys, some of them probably as a member of Lichnowsky's suite—Prague (twice), Berlin, Nuremberg, and apparently also Dresden, Pressburg, Buda-Pesth and Leipzig. These excursions were highly profitable, if we may take those to Prague as evidence. He wrote to his brother Nickolaus during his second visit to that city:

> I am getting on well—very well. My art wins for me friends and respect; what more do I want? This time, too, I shall earn considerable money. I shall remain here a few weeks more and then go on to Dresden, Leipzig, and Berlin.

At Berlin he played at the Singakademie, and also at the Court, being rewarded at the latter by a gold snuff-box, "not an ordinary snuff-box," exclaimed Beethoven, proudly, "but the kind generally given to Ambassadors." He had even more solid grounds for satisfaction in that it was out of the ordinary in another respect, being filled with Louis d'ors instead of snuff.

In Berlin he made the acquaintance of, among other musical notabilities, Friedrich Himmel, concerning which meeting a story is told showing Beethoven's curious simplicity and lack of humour —humour, that is, outside his own peculiar and primitive type. He had held an improvising contest with Himmel, and had offended his rival by saying, after the latter had been playing for some minutes, "When are you going to begin?" The two made it up, but Himmel neither forgave nor forgot. However, they corresponded after Beethoven's return to Vienna, and Himmel, knowing Beethoven's avidity for news, wrote one day that the latest sensation was the invention of a lamp for the blind. Beethoven swallowed the tale, and passed it on to his friends, who naturally asked for particulars. The still unsuspecting Beethoven wrote to Himmel for further information, receiving instead a letter ("not fit for publication," says Ries) which ended the correspondence abruptly. Even then Beethoven must needs make matters worse, and involve himself in further ridicule by showing the letter round among his friends.

The Singakademie performance may be noted, because of a comment of Beethoven. Describing the occasion to Madame von Arnim some years after, he told her that the audience, instead of applauding, gathered round him, weeping: "That is not what we artists wish for," he added; "we want applause!"

Only two matters call for notice in connection with the year 1798. The first is of tragic significance. Beethoven began to be aware of the defect in his hearing that was eventually to shut him off from the world of sound, and, in an almost equal degree, to isolate him socially. The other point is that the genesis of the "Eroica" Symphony may be traced to the Spring of this year. The suggestion that Beethoven should write a symphony in honour of Napoleon Bonaparte is credited to General Bernadotte, who at this time came to Vienna as French Ambassador. Some years, however, were to elapse before Beethoven began the work. He was still busy on the first Symphony, which was produced at a concert in the Burg Theatre on April 12th, 1800, the occasion being a concert given by Beethoven (his first) for his own benefit. The programme is worth reproducing :

> To-day, Wednesday, April 2nd, 1800, Herr van Beethoven will have the honour to give a grand concert for his benefit in the Royal Imperial Court Theatre beside the Burg. The pieces which will be performed are the following :
>
> 1. A grand symphony by the late Kapellmeister Mozart.
> 2. An aria from "The Creation" by the Princely Kapellmeister Herr Haydn, sung by Mlle. Saal.
> 3. A grand Concerto for the pianoforte, played by Herr Ludwig van Beethoven.
> 4. A Septet, most humbly and obediently dedicated to Her Majesty the Empress, and composed by Herr Ludwig van Beethoven for four stringed and three wind-instruments, played by Messrs. Schuppanzigh, Schreiber, Schindlecker, Bär, Nickel, Matauschek and Dietzel.
> 5. A Duet from Haydn's "Creation," sung by Mr. and Mlle. Saal.
> 6. Herr Ludwig van Beethoven will improvise on the pianoforte.
> 7. A new grand symphony with complete orchestra, composed by Herr Ludwig van Beethoven.

Not much has survived in the way of critical comment. The *Allgemeine Musikalische Zeitung* praised the concert as being of exceptional interest; the new concerto "had many beauties, especially in the first two movements"; the Septet showed "taste and feeling"; the Symphony contained "much art, novelty and wealth of ideas." There was, however, "too much use of wind-instruments, so that the music sounded more as if written for a military band than an orchestra." The performance could hardly have been first-rate, for the critic roundly scolds the players for disregarding the conductor. (They acted thus, not because they were incompetent, but because Beethoven had managed to make himself disliked by them.)

Later in the same month Beethoven made another platform appearance, at a concert given by his friend Punto, the horn-player. The two played a new Sonata for horn and piano composed for the occasion, and finished only the day before the concert. It was so great a success that it had to be repeated in full.

Reference has been made to various pianistic duels between Beethoven and his rivals. One such contest that took place at about this time is perhaps worth recounting in detail. The opponent was Steibelt, a showy player, and, incidentally, composer of a "Storm Rondo" that for a time agitated the drawing-rooms of England hardly less than the "Battle of Prague."

He came to Vienna at the height of his reputation, and first met Beethoven at the house of Count Fries. Among the music played was Beethoven's B flat Trio. Op. 11, in which the pianist's part gives little opportunity for display. Steibelt listened complacently, and delivered himself of a few compliments. Evidently there was not much to fear from this uncouth composer! After a performance of a quintet of his own, Steibelt improvised in his usual showy manner, "making a great effect with his tremolos, which were then something entirely new," says Ries. Beethoven made no kind of response, and victory appeared to rest with Steibelt.

A week later there was again a musical evening at the same house, and again the rivals were present. Steibelt scored his usual success with another quintet, and then gave an improvisation which (says the partial Ries) "had, obviously, been carefully prepared." It was evidently intended to be provocative, for the theme was that which Beethoven had used for the variations in the Trio played the week before. (But Steibelt may justly have claimed that the theme was at least as much his as Beethoven's, seeing that its source was an opera by Weigl.) The choice of subject angered Beethoven and his friends, and nothing short of an improvisation would relieve his feelings. He blundered his way to the piano, picking up as he went the violoncello part of Steibelt's quintet, placed it on the piano-desk upside-down ("intentionally?" Ries asks, but need he?); and with one finger hammered out a tune of sorts from the inverted page. He then fairly let himself go, and such a hail of notes ensued that Steibelt hastily left the room before Beethoven had finished. The pair never met again; in fact, Steibelt thereafter accepted no invitations without first stipulating that Beethoven should not be among the guests.

Chapter VIII

The Op. 18 Quartets—Influence of Förster—Deafness increases—Despair and Resolution—Countess Guicciardi and the "Moonlight" Sonata fiction—Beethoven's playing of Bach—A subscription for Bach's Daughter—Sixteen subscribers!—Prometheus Ballet Music.

Beethoven had by this time essayed all the branches of composition on which his fame rests. For pianoforte solo he had written numerous sets of variations and ten of the sonatas, and this year (1800) was to see the appearance of the eleventh, in B flat, Op. 22; his first symphony had been well received, and was on the point of publication; he had to his credit three concertos, (B flat, C, and C minor); two 'cello and three violin sonatas; many works for wind ensemble—a medium for which he had a strong partiality at first, but for which he wrote nothing during the last twenty-six years of his life, save the Equali for four trombones; some choral works and songs, among the latter being "Adelaide" and the scena "Ah! perfido"; and he had tried his hand at stage work with some ballet music. He was now to develop the form in which his genius was to reveal itself more completely, perhaps, than in any other—the string quartet.

Concerning the date of the composition of the

first six quartets (Op. 18) nothing certain is known. Probably a good deal of the material had existed for some years, and had undergone repeated revision. After exhaustive—even exhausting—discussion of the subject, Thayer concludes that their composition was begun in 1798, the Quartet in D (published as No. 3) being the first to be undertaken. Beethoven worked on them till 1800-1, and they were published in the latter year. They probably owed their inception (and certainly much of their quality) to the influence of Emanuel Aloys Förster, an excellent writer of chamber music from whom Beethoven learned so much in an informal way that he afterwards spoke of him as his "old master." Förster's house was a rendezvous of musicians, and string quartet parties took place regularly on Sunday mornings and Thursday evenings. Beethoven was often present, and also had many other meetings with Förster, discussing composition. We may reasonably conjecture that but for this admirable musician and worthy man the chamber music of Beethoven would have been less important, both in quantity and quality. Some credit should go to Prince Lichnowsky as well. At his house the Schuppanzigh Quartet met constantly, and Beethoven was able to experiment and test effects to his heart's content; and about the time of the composition of the first six quartets the Prince (at the suggestion of Schuppanzigh) gave

Beethoven a valuable quartet of Italian instruments—violins by Guarnerius and Amati, viola by Vincenzo Ruger, and violoncello by Guarnerius.

Apropos of the Schuppanzigh Quartet, it may be mentioned here that Prince Lobkowitz, another patron of Beethoven (and one so lavish in his expenditure on music that he became bankrupt) afterwards made these four players the nucleus of an orchestra designed for Beethoven's use for rehearsal purposes. Probably no composer was ever so fortunate as Beethoven in patrons at once munificent and practical.

Some of the letters written in 1801 show that Beethoven's deafness was steadily increasing. He writes to his friend Carl Amenda :

> How often do I wish you were with me, for your Beethoven is living an unhappy life. . . . My noblest faculty, my hearing, has greatly deteriorated. When you were still with me I felt the symptoms but kept silent; now it is continually growing worse, and whether or not a cure is possible has become a question. . . . Oh, how happy would I be if my hearing were completely restored . . . but as it is I must refrain from everything, and the most beautiful years of my life must pass without accomplishing the promise of my talent and powers. . . . My affliction causes me the least trouble in playing and composing, the most in association with others. . . . I beg of you to keep the matter of my deafness a profound secret *to be confided to nobody, no matter who it is.*

Again in a letter to Wegeler, after describing his prosperous circumstances, he goes on :

> The only pity is that my evil demon, my bad health, is continually putting a spoke in my wheel, by which I mean that my hearing has grown steadily worse for three years.

There follow some details of medical treatment of the dysentery which was supposed to be responsible for the ear trouble ; after which he proceeds :

> Since then I can say I am stronger and better, only my ears whistle and buzz continually, day and night. I can say I am living a wretched life ; for two years I have avoided almost all social gatherings because it is impossible for me to say to people : " I am deaf." If I belonged to any other profession it would be easier, but in my profession it is an awful state, the more since my enemies, who are not few, what would they say ? In order to give you an idea of this singular deafness of mine I must tell you that in the theatre I must get very close to the orchestra in order to understand the actor. If I am a little distant I do not hear the high tones of the instruments and singers, and if I be but a little further away I do not hear at all. Frequently I can hear the low tones of a conversation, but not the words, and as soon as anybody shouts it is intolerable. It seems singular that in conversation there are people who do not notice my condition at all, attributing it to my absent-mindedness.

Later in the year he writes again to Wegeler at great length. Here are a few extracts showing the mixture of despair and resolution that marked his attitude at this time, and, indeed, for the remainder of his life. The letter contains also a reference to a love affair on which a good deal of ink has been shed, and which has still some interest because of its long and mistaken association with one of the most popular of the piano Sonatas—the so-called " Moonlight " :

> . . . The ringing and sounding in my ears has become less than usual, especially in the left ear, where my deafness began ; but my hearing has not been improved and I dare not say it has not grown worse rather than better . . . Miracles are told of *galvanism* ; what have you to say about it ? A doctor told me that he had seen a deaf and dumb child recover his hearing again, and a man who had been deaf seven years got well. I am living more pleasantly since I lived amongst men. You will scarcely believe how lonely and sad my life was for two years ; my bad hearing haunted me everywhere like a ghost, and I fled from mankind and seemed like a misanthrope, though far from being one. This change has been wrought by a *dear*, *fascinating* girl, who loves me and whom I love. There have been a few blessed moments within the last few years, and it is the first time I feel that marriage might bring me happiness. Alas ! she is not of my station, and now it would be impossible for me to marry. I must still hustle about most actively. . . . Oh, if I were rid of this affliction I could embrace the world ! I feel

that my youth is just beginning, and have I not always been ill? . . . No! I cannot endure it. I will take my fate by the throat; it shall not wholly overcome me.

The "dear, fascinating girl" was the Countess Guicciardi, a pupil of Beethoven, and at the date of the letter (November 16th, 1801) seventeen years old. Thayer says that, despite the wealth of comment inspired by this attachment, there is no reason to suppose that it lasted longer than other affairs of the kind.[1] The main interest in the affair now lies in the fact that much of the romantic glamour surrounding the "Moonlight" Sonata has been due to the dedication. Its inscription to the Countess, the reference to the "dear, fascinating girl," and the title "Moonlight" conferred by the poet Rellstab, have led to its being made the subject of more windy nonsense, perhaps, than any other piece of music ever written. Yet all the sentimental stories and "programmes" have the bottom knocked out of them by the most prosaic of statements made by the fascinator herself, fifty years later, in a conversation with Otto Jahn: Beethoven had given her the Rondo in G, but wishing after all to dedicate that work to the Countess Lichnowsky, he had asked her (Julia) to return it.

[1] We have seen that, on the word of Beethoven himself, he was once so hard hit that his devotion lasted "fully seven months"!

He then dedicated the C sharp minor Sonata to her instead.[1]

Thayer says, " What a blow to all the supposed romantic significance ! " and he adds that the C sharp minor Sonata was not very highly esteemed by the composer himself. Beethoven said to Czerny, " Everybody is always talking about the C sharp minor Sonata ! Surely I have written better things. There is the Sonata in F sharp major—that is something very different."

Composers are notoriously bad judges of the relative value of their achievements, and the mere fact of a work being neglected or adversely criticised is often enough to give them a strong bias in its favour. The " Moonlight " is still over-rated, and the F sharp major comparatively neglected, and the fact is not entirely due to the romantic fable or the moonshine label. The C sharp minor Sonata would always be widely popular, for of all the thirty-two it is the only mature specimen that contains two movements free from considerable difficulty. The popularity of a concert-room battle-horse is as nothing compared with that won by a work of which a recognizable version may be extracted from the domestic piano.

Bach played but a small part in the musical life

[1] That the Sonata had a poetic basis seems, however, to be established. Its origin is held to be a poem by Seume, called " Beterin " (" Prayer ") descriptive of a maiden kneeling at the altar praying for her sick father (*Adagio*) ; angels come to her aid (*Allegretto*) ; and the face of the suppliant is transfigured with a glow of hope (*Presto*).

of Beethoven's day; save for the "Forty-eight" few of the clavier works were known, and the choral masterpieces had yet to be discovered. The few points at which Beethoven came in touch with Bach are therefore of great interest. The reader will remember that amongst the material for study given him in early boyhood by Neefe was the "Forty-eight"; and we have recently seen that these works were in constant request with his patron, van Swieten. Among the reports of his playing are frequent references to the excellence of his playing of Bach's fugues; indeed, he seems to have left his rivals far behind in this respect. The correspondence of the period we have now reached—1800-1—contains some interesting Bach references. Writing to Hoffmeister (a composer who had recently started in business with a partner Kuhnel as a music publisher)[1] he says:

> Your enterprise delights me also, and I wish that if works of art ever bring profit it may go to real artists instead of mere shopkeepers.
>
> The fact that you purpose to publish the works of Sebastian Bach does good to my heart, which beats only for the lofty and magnificent art of this patriarch of harmony, and I hope soon to see them in vigorous sale. I hope to be helpful in many ways, especially if you offer the works for subscription.

A letter, dated April 22nd, 1801, to Breitkopf and Härtel, contains a reference to a scheme on

[1] Since 1814 the firm has become famous under the name of Peters.

behalf of Bach's youngest and last surviving daughter, Regina Johanna, who was described in the appeal as "starving." Evidently the fund was being poorly supported:

> Coming recently to a friend who showed me the amount which had been collected *for the daughter of the immortal god of harmony*, I marvel at the smallness of the sum which Germany, especially your Germany, had contributed in recognition of the individual who seems to me worthy of respect for her father's sake, which brings me to the thought how would it do if I were to publish a work for the benefit of this person by subscription, acquaint the public each year with the amount and its proceeds in order to assure her against possible misfortune. Write me quickly how this might best be accomplished so that something may be done before this *Bach* dies, before this brook [*bach*] dries up and we be no longer able to supply it with water. That you would publish the work is self-evident.

(Beethoven could never resist an opening for a pun. This "bach-brook" specimen, obvious as it is, shows his verbal humour in a comparatively favourable light.)

It is satisfactory to read that thanks to this subscription, the old lady was enabled to spend her last days in comfort. In the *Allgemeine Musikalische Zeitung* for December, she returned thanks for 96 thalers and 5 silbergroschen contributed by sixteen persons (!) The fact that the greater part of this amount came from *four* subscribers in Vienna, is a reminder of the almost total eclipse of Bach's fame in his native country.

In 1801 the ballet "Prometheus" was produced, with such success that sixteen performances were given in this year, and thirteen in the following. The chief interest of "Prometheus" lies in its connection with the "Eroica," a theme in its Finale forming the basis of the closing movement of the Symphony. (It was used also as a Contredanz, and as a theme for the Variations and Fugue for piano, Op. 35.)

Chapter IX

Letter to "The Immortal Beloved"—The Heiligenstadt "Will"—A long Concert—"A Terrible Rehearsal"—Thomson of Edinburgh—First performance of the "Eroica"—"Can't the damned hornist count?"—French occupation of Vienna—"Fidelio" produced—The four Overtures.

Quite an extensive literature has grown up around a letter that was probably written at this period. Beethoven's susceptibility to female charm has been mentioned, and there will be no need to spend space in discussing the various objects of his attachment. But that he was really hard hit at least once seems to be proved by the famous letter to the "Immortal Beloved." As the letter gives neither the year in which it was written, the place of origin, nor the name of the recipient, there is ample room for conjecture as to the Beloved's identity. Thayer is only one of the writers who have devoted many pages to a discussion of the matter; but after all the marshalling of evidence, nothing conclusive has emerged. The reader who is curious is referred to Thayer, i, chap. xxi, and to other authorities there cited. The rest of us will gladly let the affair join the long list of mysteries whose solution is really of little importance. The letter itself, however, is given, if only as an example of

Beethoven's epistolary style at its most fervid and incoherent:

July 6, in the morning.

My angel, my all, my very self—only a few words to-day and at that with pencil (with yours) not till to-morrow will my lodgings be definitely determined upon—what a useless waste of time. Why this deep sorrow where necessity speaks—can our love endure except through sacrifices—except through not demanding everything—can you change it that you are not wholly, I not wholly thine. Oh, God! look out into the beauties of nature and comfort yourself with that which must be—love demands everything and that very justly—*thus it is with me as far as you are concerned, and you with me.* If we were wholly united you would feel the pain of it as little as I. My journey was a fearful one; I did not reach here until 4 o'clock yesterday morning; lacking horses the post-coach chose another route—but what an awful one. At the stage before the last I was warned not to travel at night, made fearful of a forest, but that only made me the more eager and I was wrong; the coach must needs break down on the wretched road, a bottomless mud road—without such postillions as I had with me I should have stuck in the road. Esterhazy, travelling the usual road hitherward, had the same fate with eight horses as I had with four—yet I got some pleasure out of it, as I always do when I successfully overcome difficulties. Now a quick change to things internal from tidings external. We shall soon surely see each other; moreover I cannot communicate to you the observations I have made during the last few days touching my own life—if our hearts were always close together I would make none of the kind. My heart is full of many things to say to you—Ah! there are moments when I feel that speech is nothing after all—cheer up—remain my true, my only treasure, my all as I am yours; the gods must send us the rest that shall be best for us.

Your faithful Ludwig.

Evening, Monday, July 6.

You are suffering, my dearest creature—only now have I learned that letters must be posted very early in the morning. Mondays, Thursdays,—the only days on which the mail coach goes from here to K. You are suffering—Ah! wherever I am there you are also. I shall arrange affairs between us so that I shall live and live with you, what a life!!!! thus!!!! thus without you—pursued by the goodness of mankind hither and thither—which I as little try to deserve as I deserve it. Humility of man towards man—it pains me—and when I consider myself in connection with the universe, what am I and what is he whom we call the greatest—and yet—herein lies the divine in man. I weep when I reflect that you will probably not receive the first intelligence from me until Saturday—much as you love me I love you more—but do not ever conceal your thoughts from me—goodnight—as I am taking the baths I must go to bed. Oh, God! so near so far! Is our love not truly a celestial edifice—firm as Heaven's vault.

Good-morning, on July 7.

Though still in bed my thoughts go out to you, my Immortal Beloved, now and then joyfully, then sadly, waiting to learn whether or not fate will hear us. I can live only wholly with you or not at all—

yes, I am resolved to wander so long away from you until I can fly to your arms and say that I am really at home, send my soul enwrapped in you into the land of spirits.—Yes, unhappily it must be so—you will be the more resolved since you know my fidelity—to you, no one can ever again possess my heart—none—never—Oh, God, why is it necessary to part from one whom one so loves and yet my life in W [Wien = Vienna] is now a wretched life—your love makes me at once the happiest and the unhappiest of men—at my age I need a steady, quiet life—can that be under our conditions? My angel, I have just been told that the mail-coach goes every day—and I must close at once so that you may receive the L. at once. Be calm, only by a calm consideration of our existence can we achieve our purpose to live together—be calm—love me—to-day—yesterday—what tearful longings for you—you—you—my life—my all—farewell. Oh continue to love me—never misjudge the most faithful heart of your beloved L.

ever thine
ever mine
ever for each other.

The years just recorded are so typical of those that followed that the remainder of Beethoven's life, so far as actual incidents are concerned, might be summarized in a half dozen pages. A detailed record would consist of little more than a recital of quarrels and reconciliations, alternations of dejection and resolution, of comparatively blank periods followed by feverish productivity. More and more he lived apart from the world, and as the newspapers of the period, unlike those of to-day, dealt little with the private life of persons, however distinguished, the records of Beethoven's later years tend to resolve themselves into a collection of his letters, and such documents as programmes, business correspondence with publishers, etc. As his own letters are often undated, and the reminiscences of his friends usually disagree in matters of fact (as is natural, owing to their having been written many years afterwards, with consequent distortions and haziness of memory) it will be seen that the biographer of Beethoven's maturity must either be content with a summary, or must reconstruct the records, year by year, from a mass of documentary evidence that is often obscure and frequently biassed. The latter plan has been carried out, once and for all, by Thayer, whose three large volumes appear to contain everything that can be ascertained concerning Beethoven.

Such a detailed biography is essential, yet a study of it leaves one convinced that the man is infinitely less important than the musician. This may, of course, be said in a greater or less degree of all creative artists, but it is peculiarly the case with Beethoven, partly because of the uneventful character of his life, and even more because his music expresses his personality with a fulness probably without parallel in any branch of art. In fact, his natural means of expression was music, not words.

His clumsiness in the use of language as a medium has been shown in the letter to the Immortal Beloved. Another document, the famous "Will," must be given here, if only because of its date. It has, moreover, a deep human interest, and, despite its occasional incoherence, is not without a kind of primitive eloquence. It rings more true than the letter, as well it might. This was no expression of a lifelong devotion that might last (in his own words) "fully seven months"; it was a cry wrung from the heart of one suffering under the heaviest of physical infirmities. If its frequent high-flown verbosity suggests a pose, we must remember that the literary style of the period was on the florid and emotional side; that Beethoven had little self-control either in words or actions; and that the document was to be read only after his death:

For my brothers Carl and —— Beethoven.

O ye men who think or say that I am malevolent, stubborn or misanthropic, how greatly do ye wrong me, you do not know the secret causes of my seeming, from childhood my heart and mind were disposed to the gentle feeling of good will, I was even ever eager to accomplish great deeds, but reflect now that for 6 years I have been in a hopeless case, aggravated by senseless physicians, cheated year after year in the hope of improvement, finally compelled to face the prospect of a *lasting malady* (whose cure will take years or, perhaps, be impossible), born with an ardent and lively temperament, even susceptible to the diversions of society, I was compelled early to isolate myself, to live in loneliness, when I at times tried to forget all this, O how harshly was I repulsed by the doubly sad experience of my bad hearing, and yet it was impossible for me to say to men speak louder, shout, for I am deaf. Ah, how could I possibly admit an infirmity in the *one sense* which should have been more perfect in me than in others, a sense which I once possessed in highest perfection, a perfection such as few surely in my profession enjoy or ever have enjoyed—Oh I cannot do it, therefore forgive me when you see me draw back when I would gladly mingle with you, my misfortune is doubly painful because it must lead to my being misunderstood, for me there can be no recreation in society of my fellows, refined intercourse, musical exchange of thought, only just as little as the greatest needs command may I mix with society, I must live like an exile, if I approach near to people a hot terror seizes upon me, a fear that I may be subjected to the danger of letting my condition be observed—thus it has been during the last half-year which I spent in the country, commanded by an intelligent physician to spare my hearing as much as possible, in this almost meeting my present natural disposition, although I sometimes ran counter to it yielding to my inclination for society, but what a humiliation when one stood beside me and heard a flute in the distance and *I heard nothing*, or someone heard *the shepherd singing* and again I heard nothing, such incidents brought me to the verge of despair, but little more and I would have put an end to my life—only art it was that withheld me, ah it seemed impossible to leave the world until I have produced all that I felt called upon to produce, and so I endured this wretched existence—truly wretched, an excitable body which a sudden change can throw from the best into the worst state—Patience—it is said I must now choose for my guide, I have done so, I hope my determination will remain firm to endure until it pleases the inexorable parcæ to break the thread, perhaps I shall get better, perhaps not, I am prepared. Forced already in my 28th year to become a philosopher, O it is not easy, less easy for the artist than for any one else—Divine One thou lookest into my inmost soul, thou knowest it, thou knowest that love of man and desire to do good live therein. O men, when some day you read these words reflect that ye did me wrong and let the unfortunate one comfort himself and find one of his kind who despite all the obstacles of nature yet did all that was in his power to be accepted among worthy artists and men. You my brothers Carl and —— as soon as I am dead if Dr. Schmid is still alive ask him in my name to describe my malady and attach this document to the history of my illness so that as far as is possible at least the world may become reconciled with me after my death. At the same time I declare you two to be the heirs to my small fortune (if so it can be called), divide it fairly, bear with and help each other, what injury you have done me you know was long ago forgiven. To you brother Carl I give special thanks for the attachment you have displayed towards me of late. It is my wish that your lives may be better and freer from care than I have had, recommend *virtue* to your children, it alone can give happiness, not money, I speak from experience, it was virtue that upheld me in misery, to it next to my art I owe the fact that I did not end my life by suicide—Farewell and love each other—I thank all my friends, particularly *Prince Lichnowsky* and *Professor Schmid*—I desire that the instruments from Prince L. be preserved bv one of you but let no quarrel result from this, so soon as they can serve you a better purpose sell them, how glad will I be if I can still be helpful to you in my grave—with joy I hasten towards death—if it comes before I shall have had an opportunity to show all my artistic capacities it will still come too early for me despite my hard fate and I shall probably wish that it had come later—but even then I am satisfied, will it not free me from a state of endless suffering? Come when thou wilt I shall meet thee bravely—Farewell and do not wholly forget me when I am dead, I deserve this of you in having often in life thought of you how to make you happy, be so—

LUDWIG VAN BEETHOVEN.
(seal)

Heiligenstadt,
October 6,
1802.

For my brothers Carl and —— to be read after my death.

Heiligenstadt, October 10th, 1802, thus do I take my farewell of thee—and indeed sadly—yes that beloved hope—which I brought with me when I came here to be cured at least in a degree—I must wholly abandon, as the leaves of autumn fall and are withered so hope has been blighted, almost as I came—I go away—even the high courage—which often inspired me in the beautiful days of summer—has disappeared—O Providence—grant me at last but one day of pure *joy*—it is so long since real joy echoed in my heart—O when—O when, O Divine One—shall I feel it again in the temple of nature and of men—Never ? no—O that would be too hard.

So far from " joyfully hastening to meet death," however, Beethoven at once proceeded to show his tenacious hold on life by entering on an unusually productive period. The country holiday that produced the " Will " must have been busily spent in composition. The oratorio " Christus am Olberg " (known in England as " The Mount of Olives "), several sonatas, and the second Symphony are among the works known to have been completed this summer, the sequel being a concert in the following Spring (April 5th, 1803) at which the Oratorio, the Symphony, and the C minor Pianoforte Concerto had their first performance.

The programme included also the first Symphony. Other works were down for performance (probably some vocal items for relief purposes) but were omitted owing to lack of time—which is not surprising ! This concert is notable also because some of its circumstances show how powerful had become Beethoven's position as a composer. The whole of the music was by him, and the charges for admission were largely increased. He " doubled the prices of the first chairs, tripled those of the reserved, and charged 12 ducats (about six pounds) instead of 4 florins for each box." The result was a profit of 1,800 florins (about £180), a handsome return, seeing the value of money at that period.

Apropos of the excessive length of this concert, here are some particulars concerning the rehearsal. It began at 8 in the morning, "and," says Ries, "was a terrible rehearsal; at half-past 2[!] everybody was exhausted and more or less dissatisfied." The long-suffering Lichnowsky was present throughout, and did the practical thing, as usual, by sending for food—"bread and butter, cold meat and wine in large baskets,"—inviting all and sundry to help themselves. Having thus restored something like comfort and amity,

> the Prince requested that the oratorio be rehearsed once more from the beginning, so that it might go well in the evening, and Beethoven's first work in this genre be worthily presented. And so the rehearsal began again.

An interesting connection with this country calls for note here. Beethoven received a letter from a Scottish folksong enthusiast, George Thomson, of Edinburgh, inviting him to contribute to a series of sonatas on Scottish airs. Beethoven replied, offering to write six for a fee of £150—too much for Thomson, who answered that he would pay no more than £75. Nothing came of the project at the moment, but some years later Beethoven wrote accompaniments for about a hundred Scottish, Welsh and Irish airs, chiefly the latter. (The fact that England also had a few national songs had yet to be discovered.) He seems to have enjoyed the work ; certainly it was lucrative, for he received in all nearly £600, a large increase on the fee paid to Haydn—£291 18s. for 230 arrangements. (Thomson, by the way, made no profit on the collections.)

The year 1804 saw the first performance of the "Eroica." Concerning its dedication and title Ries says :

> In this symphony Beethoven had Buonaparte in his mind, but as he was when he was First Consul. Beethoven esteemed him greatly at the time and likened him to the greatest Roman consuls. I as well as several more of his intimate friends saw a copy of the score lying upon his table, with the word "Buonaparte" at the extreme top of the title page and at the extreme bottom "Luigi van Beethoven", but not another word. Whether, and with what the space between was to be filled out, I do not know. I was the first to bring him the intelligence that Buonaparte had proclaimed himself Emperor, whereupon he flew into a rage and cried out : "Is then he, too, nothing more than an ordinary human being? Now he, too, will trample on all the rights of man and indulge only his ambition. He will exalt himself above all others, and become a tyrant!" Beethoven went to the table, took hold of the title-page by the top, tore it in two and threw it on the floor. The first page was rewritten and only then did the Symphony receive the title : "Sinfonia Eroica".

It is amusing to read that Czerny and others held that the opening Allegro was descriptive of a naval battle, and that the Funeral March commemorated Nelson or Abercrombie. Czerny wrote:

> According to Beethoven's long-time friend, Dr. Bertolini, the first idea of the "Sinfonia Eroica" was suggested by the death of the English general Abercrombie; hence the naval (not land-military) character of the theme and the entire first movement.

Evidently Czerny thought General Abercrombie was a naval officer! Yet it must be admitted that the character of the first movement is no more "land-military" than naval; nor, indeed, is it easy to see in the music anything of a specially "heroic" character. Beethoven's real "heroic" first movement is surely that of the ninth Symphony. It is reasonable to suppose, however, that Beethoven, if he intended his music to be descriptive at all, had in view neither a battle nor a hero in the ordinary conquering sense of the word. His own political views were revolutionary (though of a far milder brand than is generally supposed), and he probably saw in Buonaparte (as did others at that time) not so much a great soldier as a champion of his country's freedom. As Ries shows, in the passage quoted above, his homage was for the Consul, not the soldier. The only apparent way in which the Symphony lives up to its dedication is in its scope and freedom. It was one of the first works written in what Beethoven called his "new style," and marks a great advance on the second Symphony. What was more natural than that the composer should pay tribute to his hero in a work large in scale, bold and free in style, and combining perfect construction with unconventionality in form?

The "Eroica," after private performances by Prince Lobkowitz's orchestra, was first heard publicly on April 7th, 1805. It had a rather poor reception, being too long and generally too tough a morsel for ready acceptance. Czerny told Jahn that during its progress "somebody in the gallery cried out 'I'll give another kreutzer if the thing will but stop!'" Yet it was not too long for Prince Ferdinand Louis of Prussia, who happened to visit Prince Lobkowitz at that time. By way of surprise to the visitor, the work was played by Lobkowitz's orchestra. Prince Ferdinand listened attentively, and at the end asked for a repetition. This was given, whereupon he expressed a desire for still another performance, and after an hour's interval for the resting and refreshing of the band, it was played a third time, when, says one who was present, "the impression made by the music was general, and its lofty contents were now recognized."

By the way, the much-discussed entry of the horns in the tonic against the dominant harmony of the violins is a small thing in dissonance to the ear of to-day. As to whether it is due to a copyist's error seems to be settled by the following note by Ries :

> At the first rehearsal of the symphony, which was horrible, but at which the horn player made his entry correctly, I stood by Beethoven and, thinking that a blunder had been made, I said, "Can't the damned hornist count ? It sounds infamously false ! " I think I came pretty close to receiving a box on the ear. Beethoven did not forgive the slip for a long time.

In 1803 Beethoven had been commissioned by Schikaneder, director of the Vienna Theatre, to write an opera, and rooms in the Theatre had been given him. Both commission and accommodation lapsed a year later, when Schikaneder sold his interest in the concern ; but Beethoven was already at work on his task, and "Fidelio" was produced a few months after the first performance of the "Eroica." A more unfavourable moment could hardly be imagined. The French army, under Beethoven's former "hero," had a few days before occupied Salzburg and Ulm, and Vienna itself was entered on November 13th, the aristocratic patrons of music promptly going out as the French came in. (The faithful Lichnowskys were exceptions ; both were at rehearsals, as well as performance, score in hand.) In these distracting conditions, and inadequately rehearsed, "Fidelio" was performed on November 20th, 21st, and 22nd (to an audience largely consisting of French soldiers) and then withdrawn. With improved libretto, a new overture, and judiciously "cut," it had another performance in March of the following year, and one in April, and then disappeared from the stage for some years.

As is well known, Beethoven wrote four Overtures for "Fidelio": that now known as No. 2 was played for the opening performances; No. 3 was written for the two 1806 productions; No. 1 was designed for a proposed revival of the opera at Prague in 1807, which, however, did not take place; and No. 4 made its appearance in May, 1814, at Vienna. Only No. 4 is called "Fidelio," the others being known as "Leonora." Incidentally, the confusion that long existed as to the order in which the overtures were written led to an amusing example of the way critical judgment is apt to be influenced by chronology. Thayer says that there was

> much eloquent dissertation on the astonishing development of Beethoven's powers as exhibited in his progress from No. 1 to No. 3.

"Astonishing" indeed, seeing that the so-called No. 1 was written at least a year after No. 3, and was deliberately conceived in a simpler style in order to suit the needs of the Prague theatre!

Chapter X

Operatic projects—Fourth Symphony, etc. produced—The Op. 59 Quartets unfavourably received—First performance of Fifth and Sixth Symphonies—Choral Fantasia—Beethoven offered post of Kappellmeister at Cassel—Subsidy induces him to to remain in Vienna—the " Adieu " Sonata—Bombardment of Vienna.

Had Beethoven's one operatic venture been a success, the subsequent history of music-drama might have been profoundly affected. True, he never showed much aptitude in setting words to music—rather the reverse ; but the strong sense of drama that is at the back of almost all his finest music would have more than made amends. Nor is it conceivable that his early experiences of operatic rehearsal at Bonn could have been fruitless. That he was drawn to the operatic form is clear from his subsequent petition to the Directors of the Royal Imperial Court Theatre for an appointment as composer, undertaking to compose " every year at least one grand opera " and to " deliver gratis a small operetta, divertissement, choruses or occasional pieces according to the wishes or needs of the Worshipful Direction." The salary he suggested was 2,400 florins per annum (about £250) and the use of the theatre for a yearly benefit concert. The petition was not granted, despite the fact of the directorate including Prince Lobkowitz and others well-disposed towards the composer. Various reasons have been suggested, but we need look no farther than Beethoven's deafness, his procrastinating habits, and his cantankerousness in dealing with the performers and theatre staff. However, his friends eased the blow of the disappointment, Prince Esterhazy commissioning him to write a Mass, and preparations being at once put in hand for two benefit concerts that brought him a handsome sum. Three new works were produced at these concerts—the fourth Symphony, the G major Pianoforte Concerto, and the "Coriolan" overture.

Meanwhile the F minor Pianoforte Sonata (named by the publisher "Appassionata") and the Quartets, Op. 59, had been completed. The last named, now among the most prized of Beethoven's works, had a very unfavourable reception. (Even Schuppanzigh and his colleagues laughed when trying the Quartet in F, under the impression that the composer was playing a joke on them.)

The fifth Symphony had long since been on the stocks, its commencement dating from 1805. This, the most famous of orchestral works, would have been labelled No. 4 had not Beethoven become engaged to Countess Theresa Brunswick in 1806, and laid it aside in order to give vent to his happiness by writing the light-hearted B flat Symphony. The C minor and the

"Pastoral" Symphonies had their first performances on December 22nd, 1808, the programme including also the Choral Fantasia (another first performance) the Gloria and Sanctus from the Mass in C (the work commissioned by Prince Esterhazy as a solatium for Beethoven's operatic disappointment), the G major Pianoforte Concerto, an improvisation, and the Scena "Ah perfido"—truly an orgy, even for those days when folk sat long at their music. Unfortunately a lack of rehearsal and an unwarmed hall combined to make the audience more than usually conscious of the inordinate length of the programme, and the new works had an inauspicious start. The Choral Fantasia is now generally regarded as one of Beethoven's failures, but it is of importance as forerunner of the Choral Symphony, and also because the long opening section for pianoforte solo is said by Czerny to be a good example of Beethoven's methods in improvising free variations. (The description of this work in the announcement of the concert is worth quoting: "No. 4. Fantasia for the pianoforte which ends with the gradual entrance of the entire orchestra and the introduction of choruses as a finale." Nottebohm points out on the evidence of the sketchbooks that Beethoven's original intention was to begin not with the pianoforte but with the string quartet of the orchestra; also, the work was begun before the text had been found. A very interesting anticipation of the Choral Symphony is shown in Beethoven's first intention of introducing the voices by a kind of rhetorical flourish: "Hört ihr wohl?"

A few months before this concert Beethoven received an offer of the post of First Kapellmeister to King Jerome of Westphalia at Cassel, with a salary of 600 ducats (about £300). Beethoven was strongly disposed to accept, judging from a letter to Breitkopf and Härtel:

> At last I am forced by the intrigues and cabals and contemptible actions of all kinds to leave the only surviving German fatherland on the invitation of his Royal Majesty of Westphalia, I am going thither as Chapelmaster with an annual salary of 600 ducats in gold. I have only to-day sent my assurance that I will come by post and am only waiting my decree before making preparations for my journey.

The reference to his treatment at Vienna calls for a word. To the end of his life Beethoven indulged in such splenetic attacks, and they have been too readily accepted by writers who appeared to hold the view that a genius must, *ipso facto*, be despised by the public of his day. This was certainly not true of Beethoven, as has been shown elsewhere in these pages. The specific charge in the letter quoted above is best answered by Czerny, who, more than most musicians of his time, was able to speak with certainty. In his notes to Jahn he says:

> It has repeatedly been said in foreign lands that Beethoven was not respected in Vienna, and was suppressed. The truth is that already as a youth he received all manner of support from our high aristocracy, and enjoyed as much care and respect as ever fell to the lot of a young artist. . . . Later, too, when he estranged many by his hypochondria, nothing was charged against his often very striking peculiarities; hence his predilection for Vienna, and it is doubtful if he would have been left so undisturbed in any other country. It is true that as an artist he had to fight cabals, but the public was innocent in this. He was always marvelled at and respected as an extraordinary being, and his greatness was suspected even by those who did not understand him. Whether or not to be rich rested with him, but he was not made for domestic order.

The genuineness of Beethoven's expressed desire to accept the Westphalian offer is open to doubt. Despite his unmethodical habits and improvidence, he had a keen eye to the main chance, and we may be sure that he saw his way to using the offer for bargaining purposes. His patrons, hearing of the project, at once laid their heads together, as Beethoven no doubt expected of them. They had a double reason for inducing him to remain in Vienna, and the genuine esteem and admiration so constantly shown ever since his arrival in their midst was probably the chief. They could hardly conceive that his eccentric character would receive elsewhere the consideration that had been forthcoming in Vienna.

Moreover, there was little guarantee of permanency in a post under the twenty-four-year-old Jerome—as indeed events proved a few years later.[1] Added to these disinterested considerations was no doubt a feeling that Vienna would be disgraced if she allowed Beethoven to depart ostensibly because the Vienna public would not provide him with a living. Hence a series of negotiations after Beethoven's own heart,[2] resulting in an agreement (dated March 1st, 1809) which deserves quotation :

AGREEMENT

The daily proofs which Herr Ludwig van Beethoven is giving of his extraordinary talents and genius as musician and composer, awaken the desire that he surpass the great expectations which are justified by his past achievements.

But as it has been demonstrated that only one who is as free from care as possible can devote himself to a single department of activity and create works of magnitude which are exalted and which ennoble art, the undersigned have decided to place Herr Ludwig van Beethoven in a position where the necessaries of life shall not cause him embarrassment or clog his powerful genius.

To this end they bind themselves to pay him the fixed sum of 4,000 (four thousand) florins a year, as follows :—

[1] A little link with London may be noted. During his stay in the United States, Jerome married, while still in his 'teens, Elizabeth Patterson. His father annulled the marriage, and she settled in Camberwell.

[2] Thayer, ii, 135.

His Imperial Highness, Archduke Rudolph	Fl. 1,500
The Highborn Prince Lobkowitz	„ 700
The Highborn Prince Ferdinand Kinsky	„ 1,800
Total	Fl. 4,000

which Herr van Beethoven is to collect in semi-annual instalments, *pro rata*, against voucher, from each of these contributors.

The three signatories pledged themselves to pay the subsidy until Beethoven should obtain an appointment of equal value; should such an appointment not be obtained (as was practically certain) or Beethoven be prevented from following his calling through accident or old age, the salary would be granted for life.

On his part, Beethoven was to remain in Vienna, save for reasonable absences on leave for business and artistic journeys.

Beethoven's elation at this handsome provision is shown in his letters of this period. Unfortunately, as a result of the Austrian Finanzpatent the depreciation of the florin was such as to reduce the endowment considerably. Schindler, writing in 1840, calculated that the 4,000 florins were reduced to a fifth. But the researches of Thayer[1] show that the loss was not nearly so great, especially as the Archduke Rudolph at once made up the difference so far as his part of the annuity was concerned. Nevertheless, the rosy prospect held out by the agreement faded soon after with

[1] For a detailed discussion of a somewhat complex financial question see Thayer, ii, 211-213.

the bankruptcy of Lobkowitz and the death of Kinsky, although by means of a long and worrying legal process Beethoven obtained a settlement that satisfied him; Lobkowitz nobly did his best to see that his bankruptcy affected Beethoven as little as possible.

The discussion of this affair of the subsidy has taken us ahead somewhat, but it happens that there is little of musical importance to record in connection with the intervening years. A few months after the signing of the salary agreement Vienna was besieged by the French, and the Archduke Rudolph left Vienna with the Imperial family. One of the finest of the pianoforte sonatas, Op. 81a, "Les Adieux, l'Absence et le Retour" was evoked by the incident. This is one of the few examples of Beethoven's use of descriptive titles. Even so, had not the manuscript contained in Beethoven's own handwriting a statement that the absence, etc., was that of the Archduke, a very different interpretation would have become general; a description by the critic Adolf Marx (1795-1866) reads:

> A soul picture, which brings before the mind the Parting—let us say of two lovers; the deserted—let us assume again sweetheart or wife; and Reunion of the Parted Ones.

This was a distressful summer for Beethoven. On May 12th the city capitulated, after a bombardment during which he was forced to take refuge in a cellar, with his head surrounded by pillows—not so much from cowardice, we may believe, as from anxiety as to the effect of the gunfire on his poor enfeebled ears. As he crouched there, did he reflect on the irony of the fact that the man behind the guns was the "Hero" of his third Symphony?

CHAPTER XI

Death of Haydn—A barren period—More love affairs—"Help me to hunt a wife"—Domestic worries—"Comical" episode in a restaurant—Personal habits.

A FEW weeks later the death of Haydn must have added to his depression. Yet he seems to have been hard at work composing—or at least making sketches—till the end of the year, the seventh Symphony, among other important works, being well on the way.

With 1810, however, began a series of comparatively barren years. A variety of explanations suggest themselves, among them the likelihood that the partial blank was merely a pause before entering on his third period. It must be remembered, too, that the political disturbance and the high cost of living that followed the capitulation to the French, hindered the publication and performance of new music. Beethoven was not the man to hasten works to completion when there was no prospect of making, either in public or in private, any present use of them.[1] But may we not, at least to some extent, ascribe the decreased output to his sudden acquisition of an annual income which at that time represented a competence? When all has been said in derision of "potboilers," the plain fact remains

[1] Thayer, ii, 209.

that a very large proportion of the great things in art would almost certainly never have been undertaken but for the need of earning money. That this was so with Beethoven is clear. For example, writing to Wegeler in 1801, he says, apropos of his being able to ask good terms from no fewer than six or seven publishers ("and more if I chose"):

> You see it is very convenient. I see a friend in need and my purse does not permit me to help him at once. I have only to sit down and in a short time help is at hand.

The fact that in such cases the pot to be boiled is that of a friend does not invalidate the theory put forward above. Support for it might be found in many of his bargaining letters, and above all in certain negotiations that (to be frank) were dishonest. Of these, more later. Whatever the cause, the three generous patrons were (says Thayer) "bitterly disappointed" at the sudden drying up of the fount they had thought to stimulate to even greater and more regular activity.

A couple of love affairs call for mention at this point. No doubt the subsidy (plus a substantial sum received from Clementi for the English rights of some works) led Beethoven to turn his thoughts once more towards marriage. Writing to his friend, Count Gleichenstein, shortly after the signing of the agreement, he speaks of his improved circumstances, and says, "Now you can help me to hunt a wife"; in 1810 we find him suddenly taking unwonted thought as to his wardrobe and personal appearance (the Count is to buy him among other articles of wear "at least half a dozen neck-ties"); and a little later he writes to Wegeler urgently asking him to obtain his (Beethoven's) baptismal certificate, a request which Wegeler construed as a hint of approaching marriage. His choice seems to have fallen on Therese Malfatti. Nothing came of it, however, and shortly afterwards the inveterate lover succumbed to Elizabeth (Bettina) Brentano, a prominent figure in the literary branch of the Romantic movement, and a friend of Goethe—for whom, indeed, she experienced an unrequited passion. (She afterwards married Baron von Arnim.)

Like his other adventures of the kind, Beethoven's attachment to Bettina has led to a great deal of disputation. Never, surely, did love affairs so barren in themselves produce such a mountain of commentary! The curious in such matters will find all they want (and probably a good deal more) in Thayer and in the books cited by him. The rest of us are not greatly interested in the long list of women before whom Beethoven fell with monotonous persistence.

Our interest lies rather in the manner and degree in which the fruitless quest affected his work as a composer. On the positive side must be set the emotional stimulus that has always been associated with such one-sided attachments. It would, however, be a mistake to attempt a particular and detailed relation between cause and effect. As a result of Beethoven's habit of working at several compositions at the same period and of allowing very long intervals to elapse between their start and finish, the association of a given work with a particular incident or crisis in his career is too hazardous to be of value. (The so-called "Moonlight" Sonata and its dedication will recur to the reader.) We must be satisfied with seeing in Beethoven's chequered love affairs the origin of much of the vivid (even violent) emotional contrast that was a new thing in music. There were other factors, it is true, and some of them will be discussed later. But we may assume that this—the most human and intimate of all—was not the least vital.

But the failure of his quest had other results, as was suggested above. If the axiom, "it is not good for man to be alone," be true in a general sense, it applies above all to so erratic, and in many ways so helpless, an individual as Beethoven. His domestic troubles have their ludicrous aspect, but they were desperately serious in their effect on his health and output. The traditional conception of a creative artist (especially a composer) dies hard, and the weight of opinion still favours the view that his achievements are the result of some abnormality in conduct, or eccentricity in habit. Yet it is impossible to read of Beethoven's constant change of lodgings, endless troubles with servants, irregular and unsuitable meals, and innumerable vagaries, without being convinced that but for them his tale of masterpieces might have been largely increased.

He was no more than middle-aged when he died, and the ninth Symphony and last Quartets show that his natural force, so far from being abated, was capable of flights into an atmosphere so rarified that he is almost alone in it. One is tempted to say that the epitaph on Schubert's grave (only a few paces from his own, by the way):

"Music has here entombed a rich treasure, but much fairer hopes,"

might almost be shared between them.[1] For, despite his immensely great volume and wider scope, Beethoven's work was hardly less incomplete than that of the younger man; although the powers of invention, thought, and development shown in his last works were such that "fairer hopes" is an inadequate term.

No biography of Beethoven would be complete without some details of his domestic vicissitudes, so the subject, having been broached, may be conveniently developed here.

[1] Some months after this page was written, the author discovered that the same parallel had been drawn by Dr. Ernest Walker in his excellent monograph on Beethoven.

The fact of his having occupied about thirty lodgings during his thirty-five years in Vienna has been mentioned; and he changed his servants with no less frequency—though probably "notice" was as often as not given by the servant. In either case it is safe to lay the blame at his door, if we may judge from recorded instances of his ungovernable temper and irregular habits.

Even the publicity of a restaurant could not curb his passion. Ries tells us of a noonday meal at an inn they were accustomed to frequent; the waiter made a mistake in carrying out an order. Beethoven's bullying complaint being answered with some resentment, he threw a dish of stewed lights "with plenty of gravy" at the waiter's head. The man was carrying an armful of plates and could not protect himself; "the gravy ran down his face," and he and Beethoven stormed at one another while all the other guests roared with laughter, Beethoven himself being finally "overcome with the comicalness of the situation." (What a sense of humour these German Romantics had!) A man who could thus conduct himself in public must have been a terror in his own rooms; it is easy to picture his servants coming and going—especially going.

Even if his temper had been that of an angel, his personal habits would have soon sickened any domestic worth employing:

> He seldom took anything into his hands without dropping and breaking it. Thus he frequently knocked his inkwell into the pianoforte. . . . No piece of furniture was safe from him, least of all a costly piece. Everything was overturned, soiled and destroyed.

This was not the worst, however, for Marie von Breuning, in a memorandum written for Thayer, tells us of "his habit of expectorating in the room"; and Frau Streicher, a good soul who at one time took pity on him and tried to improve matters, told Schindler that "she found Beethoven in the Summer of 1813, in the most desolate state as regards his physical and domestic needs—not only did he not have a single good coat, but not a whole shirt." Schindler considerately leaves us to imagine the rest, adding: "I must hesitate to describe his condition exactly as it was."

An attempt at reform was made when he was arranging for his nephew Carl to come and live with him. Kind-hearted Streicher had got things fairly ship-shape, and Beethoven evidently meant to turn over a new leaf. In the State Library at Berlin is preserved a large sheet of paper on which he wrote a list of questions submitted to some friend (perhaps Madame Streicher). The questions, duly answered, are:

> What ought one to give two servants to eat at dinner and supper, both as to quantity and quality?
>
> How often ought one to give them roast meat?

Ought they to have it at dinner and supper too ?

That which is intended for the servants, do they have in common with the victuals of the master, or do they prepare their own separately, i.e., do they have different food from the master ?

How many pounds of meat are to be reckoned for three persons ?

What allowance per day do the housekeeper and maid receive ?

How about the washing ?

Do the housekeeper and maid get more ?

How much wine and beer ?

Does one give it to them and when ?

Breakfast ?

It is hardly possible to overestimate the benefit in health (and therefore in longevity and productiveness) that Beethoven would have derived from a happy marriage. Think of such scenes as those described above, multiply them a hundred fold, and imagine the difference a wife would have made—the right sort of wife, that is: no Countess Theresas or blue-stocking Bettinas, but a good manager and cook with no nonsense about her (and perhaps even no music).

Chapter XII

Folksong arrangements for Thomson—The "Emperor" Concerto produced—Two good hagglers—Goethe on Beethoven—Beethoven on Goethe.

Beethoven's habit of saddling himself with far more commissions than he could carry out in a reasonable time is shown in a typical letter to Thomson of Edinburgh, written in 1811. After announcing the completion of the arrangements of forty-three Welsh and Irish songs he had undertaken for 100 ducats, he says:

> Your offer of 100 ducats in gold for the three Sonatas [for violin and piano] is accepted for your sake [!] and I am also willing to compose three quintets for 100 gold ducats; but for the dozen English songs my price is 60 ducats in gold (for four songs the price is 25 ducats). For the cantata on the naval battle in the Baltic Sea, I ask 50 ducats, but on condition that the text contains no invectives against the Danes, otherwise I cannot undertake it.[1] . . . I will not fail to send you the arrangements of my symphonies in a very short time, and will gladly undertake the composition of an oratorio if the words be noble and distinguished and the honorarium of 600 ducats in gold be agreeable to you.

Apart from the production of the "Pastoral" Symphony and the "Egmont" Overture in

[1] This work was to have been a setting of Campbell's *Battle of the Baltic.*

May and of the "Coriolan" Overture in July, there appears to have been no other public performance of Beethoven's music during this year—chiefly owing to the disturbed state of public affairs. The B flat Pianoforte Trio, Op. 97—known as "The Archduke," from its dedication to the Archduke Rudolph—was finished, as was also the unimportant incidental music to the "Ruins of Athens" and "King Stephen"; and among the publications for the year were the "Adieu" Sonata and the Choral Fantasia.

The following year was almost devoid of musical interest. Beethoven's career as a pianist was practically over; his infirmity alone was sufficient to make him incapable of playing in public with credit, especially now that some powerful rival exponents (among them Czerny) were on the scene.

A note by Körner, dated February 15th, records one of the few musical events of the year:

> On Wednesday, for the benefit of the Society of Noble Ladies for Charity, a concert and tableaux, representing three pictures by Raphael, Poussin and Troyes as described by Goethe in his "Elective Affinities," were given. The picture offered a glorious treat; a new pianoforte concerto by Beethoven failed.

The failure of the "Emperor" at this, its first Vienna performance, was no doubt due to its being out of place in a programme that must have attracted a large proportion of folk with no ears for so long and exhausting a work.

More correspondence with Thomson occurs at this time, and shows the Scot pitted against a good haggler. Evidently Thomson would not rise to Beethoven's demands; hence these comparisons:

> Haydn himself assured me, that he also got four ducats in gold for each song, yet he wrote only for violin and pianoforte without ritornellos or violoncello. As regards Herr Koželuch, who delivers each song to you for two ducats, I congratulate you and the English and Scotch publishers on a taste that approves him. In this field I esteem myself a little higher than Herr Koželuch (*Miserabilis*), and I hope and believe that you have sufficient discrimination to do me justice.

And the letter ends with a repetition of a demand for nine ducats in gold, and a hint about a tour:

> We need the gold here, for our country is at present only a paper fountain, and I in particular need the gold, for I shall probably leave this country and go to England and then to Edinburgh in Scotland, and rejoice in the prospect of there making your personal acquaintance.

Goethe and Beethoven met for the first time during this year. Here is the poet's impression of the composer:

> I made Beethoven's acquaintance in Teplitz. His talent amazed me; unfortunately he is an utterly

untamed personality (not altogether in the wrong in holding the world to be detestable) but who does not make it any the more enjoyable either for himself or others by his attitude. He is to be excused, on the other hand, and much to be pitied, as his hearing is leaving him, which, perhaps, mars the musical part of his nature less than the social. He is of a laconic nature, and will become doubly so because of his lack.

For the sake of completeness, the composer's recollections of the meeting may be given here, though they belong to a later date. They occur in the record of a conversation with Friedrich Rochlitz, a Leipsic musical litterateur who visited Beethoven in 1822. Rochlitz was asked if he knew Goethe. He nodded his "yes." "I do, too," said Beethoven, "I got acquainted with him in Carlsbad—God knows how long ago." [It was in Teplitz ten years before.] He went on, "I was not so deaf then as I am now, but hard of hearing. How patient the great man was with me! How happy he made me then! I would have gone to my death for him; yes, ten times! It was while I was in the ardour of this enthusiasm that I thought out my music to his 'Egmont.'[1] Since that summer I read Goethe every day, when I read at all. He has killed Klopstock for me. You are surprised? Now you smile? Aha! You smile

[1] The enthusiasm was well in advance, for the "Egmont" music was written two years *before* the meeting—another proof of the necessity for caution in reading autobiography into Beethoven's works.

that I should have read Klopstock! I gave myself up to him many years—when I took my walks and at other times. Ah, well! I didn't understand him always. He is so restless; and he always begins too far away, from on high down; always Maestoso, D-flat major! Isn't it so? But he's great, nevertheless, and uplifts the soul. When I did not understand I divined pretty nearly. But why should he always want to die? That will come soon enough. Well; at least he always sounds well, etc. But Goethe—he lives and wants us all to live with him. That's the reason he can be composed. Nobody else can be so easily composed as he."

A good many anecdotes survive concerning the association of Goethe and Beethoven. Probably some of them are apocryphal, but here is one that at all events deserves to be true: The pair were walking one day in a public place when Goethe assumed an air of annoyance at the constant salutations of the passers by. "Don't let that trouble you," said Beethoven, "The greetings are most likely intended for me!"—not the only little touch in Beethoven that reminds English folk of their own Samuel Johnson.

CHAPTER XIII

Dispute with brother Johann—The eighth Symphony—Maelzel and the Allegretto—Maelzel's "Panharmonicon"—First performance of the seventh and "Wellington" Symphonies—Dispute with Maelzel—Spohr on Beethoven's playing—End of career as pianist.

THESE pages purposely concern themselves with Beethoven's brothers only so far as they materially affect the tenor of his life. One unhappy episode in which Beethoven came into conflict with his brother Johann occurred at this time, and has to be recorded, if only for the light it throws on the composer's blundering way of carrying out good intentions. Johann had contracted an irregular union with one Therese Obermeyer, and Beethoven, instead of being content with putting his objections as one brother might to another, must needs descend on their home at Linz, and try to bully them into separating. Of course he stormed in vain, Johann naturally telling him in effect to mind his own business. Whereupon Beethoven may be said literally to have moved heaven and earth to gain his ends, for he applied both to the Bishop and the civil authorities for support. He got it, too, in the shape of an order to the police to remove Therese to Vienna if she did not leave Linz by a specified date. The result was a scene between the brothers on which biographers have agreed to draw a veil. All that need be said is that Johann won by promptly doing what anybody less obtuse than Beethoven in such matters would have foreseen: he married the girl, and so gave Beethoven a sister-in-law whom he cordially detested.

During this wretched visit to Linz, Beethoven put the finishing touches to the happy eighth Symphony—"the little one," as he called it. The mention of this work serves as a reminder of Maelzel, a character who had a good deal to do with Beethoven at this time, and who was concerned with him in a little bit of musical history curious in itself, and also illustrative of the composer's occasional strange lapses in standard.

Maelzel was a well-trained and capable musician who succumbed to a passion for mechanical invention. More of this side of him later; first let us see his alleged connection with the Allegretto of the eighth Symphony. The popular story is that he had recently invented the ticking instrument which has so frequently failed to keep time with many of us, and that at a supper given to him by Beethoven and others just before a projected visit to England, the composer improvised a canon in which the theme consisted of rapidly reiterated semiquavers to the syllable "ta," in burlesque of the metronome's ticking. Thayer elaborately disposes of this story by a series of dates that seem unassailable. Moreover the metronome was not yet invented. So far, the nearest approach was Maelzel's "Chronometer," an instrument constructed on another principle. The farewell supper no doubt took place, and probably the truth is that the Allegretto had already been composed, and that Beethoven and his companions, in convivial mood, lifted up their voices canon-wise, fitting to it some such text as that given in Grove's "Beethoven and his nine Symphonies" . . . "Ta, ta . . . lieber Maelzel, lieben Sie wohl, sehr wohl."

Our chief interest in Maelzel, however, is with the "Panharmonicon," a mechanical instrument he constructed at about this time, and with which he proposed to visit England. The Panharmonicon seems to have been the forerunner of the powerful steam organs heard to-day in connection with "roundabouts." Its repertoire included such works as Cherubini's "Lodoiska" Overture, Haydn's "Military" Symphony, overtures and choruses by Handel, etc. Maelzel proposed that Beethoven should compose a work for the machine, and accompany the inventor on an English tour. Maelzel was not only a genius in his way; he had also more than a touch of the showman. He shrewdly reckoned that the genuine musical public would be attracted by the Haydn and Handel works, and by the name and fame of Beethoven; "battle" and "storm" pieces would bring in the many-headed. Why not rope in both publics by inducing Beethoven to concoct a "battle" piece for the Panharmonican, and to become himself a part of the show? The victory of Wellington at Vittoria in the summer of this year (1813) provided just the subject for an English tour.

Beethoven rose to the bait and set to work promptly. Moscheles, in a note to his English translation of Schindler's biography gives some details of this "freak" piece:

> I witnessed the origin and progress of this work, and remember that not only did Maelzel decidedly induce Beethoven to write it, but even laid before him the whole design of it; himself wrote all the drum marches and the trumpet-flourishes of the French and English armies; gave the composer some hints, how he should herald the English army by the tune of "Rule Britannia"; how he should introduce "Malbrook" in a dismal strain; how he should depict the horrors of the battle and arrange "God save the King" with effects representing the hurrahs of a multitude. Even the unhappy idea of converting the melody of "God save the King" into a subject of a fugue in quick movement, emanates from Maelzel. All this I saw in sketches and score, brought by Beethoven to Maelzel's workshop, then the only suitable place of reception he was provided with.

Beethoven clearly enjoyed himself. "It is certain," he said naïvely, "that one writes most beautifully when one writes for the public, also that one writes rapidly." The only certainty, however, is the rapidity, as is proved by "Wellington's Victory, or the Battle of Vittoria," which, despite the illustrious name on the title page, turned out to be merely our old friend "The Battle of Prague" blown up to bursting point.

It had an immense popular success, however—or (shall we say ?) therefore—though the success was not on the lines originally contemplated. It came about thus: Both Beethoven and Maelzel badly needed funds to meet the heavy travelling expenses of the journey. The inventor therefore proposed that a concert should be given at which Beethoven's new Symphony (the seventh) should be given its first performance: this would ensure the attendance of musicians. The rest of the public were to be drawn by an orchestral version of the "Battle" Symphony, and (an astute touch) by the announcement that the profits would be given to the fund in aid of the wounded at the battle of Hanau.

Maelzel (with good reason, as the sequel showed) counted on such a success that repetitions of the performance would be called for; from these would come the profits for himself and collaborator.

Here is the programme of the concert, which took place on December 8th, 1813:

1. "An entirely new Symphony" by Beethoven. [The A major.]

2. Two Marches by Dussek and Pleyel, played by Maelzel's Mechanical Trumpeter, with full orchestral accompaniment.
3. " Wellington's Victory."

The orchestra included practically all the most distinguished musicians in Vienna at the moment —Dragonetti, Meyerbeer, Hummel, Salieri, Romberg, Spohr, etc. To these, no doubt, the occasion was mainly a " rag," and there is good ground for the report that Beethoven himself " declared the work to be folly, and that he liked it only because with it he had thoroughly thrashed the Viennese."[1]

The success was such that the programme was repeated on the following Sunday. The profits of both concerts—about £400— were handed over to the fund for the wounded. Further performances followed, and Beethoven suddenly found himself a popular composer in the widest sense of the term. Schindler says that " this was one of the most important moments in the life of the master, at which all the hitherto divergent voices, save those of the professional musicians, united in proclaiming him worthy of the laurel. . . . A work like the battle-piece had to come, in order that divergent opinions might be united, and the mouths of all opponents, of whatever kind, be silenced."

Before showing the solid advantage that

[1] Tomaschek, in Thayer, ii, 256.

Beethoven derived from this sudden access of popularity, it has to be recorded that the overwhelming success of the battle-piece led to a breach with Maelzel. The inventor certainly had cause for complaint. As we have seen, the idea of the Symphony—even a good deal of its actual working out—was his.[1] When, therefore, Beethoven, as a result of the financial and other success of the concert, gave up the idea of joining Maelzel in the English tour, the inventor felt that he had been shabbily treated. Moreover, the success of the Battle Symphony was such that crowds flocked to repeated performances without the aid of his "Mechanical Trumpeter," its place being taken by various works of Beethoven. Maelzel, therefore, quietly collected the band parts of the Symphony, with a view to giving performances on his own account. When Beethoven accused him of stealing the work Maelzel very reasonably claimed that it belonged to the mechanical instrument for which he and Beethoven had designed it. The result was a lawsuit which, after dragging on for some years, was settled amicably.

Among the more important results of the success of the Battle Symphony was a revival of "Fidelio," for which a revised version was prepared. Owing to hindrances (among them the dispute with Maelzel) the new version was some months in the making, and the revival did

[1] Thayer, ii, 253.

not take place until the end of May, 1814. Even so, however, the public's admiration for the composer of the Battle Symphony was equal to the strain caused by the delay, and the opera was received with acclamation.

Meanwhile, the eighth Symphony had been brought to a hearing (February 27th, 1814). Its success was not great, partly, no doubt, for the reason suggested in the *Allgemeine Musikalische Zeitung*—" the faulty judgment which permitted the Symphony to follow that in A major, " a work which had already established itself as a firm favourite. The Symphony in F having been made to sound smaller than it was by the A major, received further damage by being followed by the " Wellington," the Battle section of which had to be repeated.

The production at this time of the B flat Pianoforte Trio, Op. 97, has an interest to-day because Spohr happened to be at one of the rehearsals, and heard Beethoven play. It was Spohr's only experience of the kind, and he says:

> It was not a treat, for, in the first place, the pianoforte was badly out of tune, which Beethoven minded little, since he did not hear it; and secondly, there was scarcely anything left of the virtuosity of the artist which had formerly been so greatly admired. In *forte* passages the poor deaf man pounded on the keys till the strings jangled, and in *piano* he played so softly that whole groups of tones were omitted, so that the music was unintelligible unless one could look

> into the pianoforte part. I was deeply depressed at so sad a fate. If it is a great misfortune for anyone to be deaf, how shall a musician endure it without giving way to despair? Beethoven's melancholy was no longer a riddle to me.

And Moscheles, writing of the first performance of the Trio, says in his Diary:

> In the case of how many compositions is the word "new" misapplied! But never in Beethoven's, and least of all in this, which again is full of originality. His playing, save for its intellectual element, satisfied me less, being wanting in clarity and precision; but I observed many traces of the grand style of playing which I had long recognized in his compositions.

Evidently Beethoven was well aware of his deficiencies as a pianist, for, after playing in the Trio again a few weeks later, he appeared no more as a soloist in public.

Chapter XIV

"The Mount of Olives" produced in England—A letter to Thomson—Death of Brother Carl—Disputed Guardianship of Nephew Carl—Shabby treatment of Royal Philharmonic Society—Beethoven's "poverty"—The "Hammerklavier" Sonata finished—The Mass in D started, and ninth Symphony sketched—A present from Broadwood—An offer from the Philharmonic Society.

The first performance in England of the oratorio "The Mount of Olives" took place during this year, and some of the attendant circumstances are sufficiently curious to deserve mention. In 1813 Sir George Smart gave a Lenten Oratorio Season at Covent Garden. Casting round for a novelty for 1814, and hearing the Beethoven work mentioned he offered £50 to anyone who would procure him a copy. The work had been published by Breitkopf and Härtel, but owing to Napoleon's embargo against England, copies could not be obtained in the ordinary way. In the winter of 1813-14, an eating-house keeper named Jack Morris brought Smart a copy of the Oratorio. "Well," said the astonished and delighted conductor, "I'll give you the £50."

"No," was the reply, "I'll take only two guineas, for that's what I paid for it."

"How did you get it?" asked Smart.

"A friend of mine who is a King's Messenger bought it for me in Leipsic."

The only acknowledgment that Morris would take, beside the two guineas, was that Smart should accept an invitation from him to be present at a pugilistic exhibition and at the supper afterwards. The score bears the date of reception, January 7, 1814.[1]

The work was given ten times during the Spring of 1814, and was highly successful, though Smart's friends, on hearing it at rehearsal, had told him he was mad to produce it. If this view was based on the quality of the music there was good ground for it. The work is now almost as neglected as it deserves to be. However, its benefits for Smart did not cease with its tenth performance. Encouraged by his success with the oratorio, Smart followed it up with the Battle Symphony, to such good purpose that its performance became an annual event for several years, and put £1,000 into his pocket.

Apart from the eighth Symphony the outstanding composition for the year 1814 was the fine Pianoforte Sonata in E Minor, Op. 90. The Autumn saw the completion of the "Name-Day" Overture in C, which had been on the stocks for some years. Altogether this period, with its capture of the two main sections of the musical public by means of the "Wellington" and A Major Symphonies, may be said to mark the culminating point in Beethoven's life. Honours and recognitions of various kinds were showered on

[1] Thayer, ii, 309.

him, including the freedom of the City of Vienna, with relief from all taxation. Commissions came thick and fast—more than he could carry out. He was in a state of affluence, despite the habitual pleas of poverty in his correspondence with English clients.[1] His productivity began to decline, however, partly no doubt as a result of his greatly improved financial condition.

A letter, dated February, 1815, written in English, to Thomson of Edinburgh, is of interest at this juncture :—

Mr. George Thomson, merchant in the musical line.
Edingbourgh, Scottland.

Sir,

Many concerns have prevented my answers to your favours, to which I reply only in part. All your songs with the exception of a few are ready to be forwarded. I mean those to which I was to write the accompaniments, for with respect to the 6 Canzonettes which I am to compose, I own that the honorary you offered is totally inadequate. Circumstances here are much altered and taxes have been so much raised after the English fashion that my share for 1814 was near 60£, besides, an original good air,—and what you also wish—an Overture, are perhaps the most difficult undertakings in musical compositions. I therefore beg to state that my honorary for 6 songs or airs must be 35£ or seventy impl. Ducats—and for an Overture 20£ or 50 impl. Ducats. You will please to assign the payment here as usual, and you may

[1] For a full discussion of this point, with details of Beethoven's income at the end of 1815, see Thayer, ii, 323.

depend that I shall do you justice. No artist of talent and merit will find my pretensions extravagant.

Concerning the Overture you will please to indicate in your reply whether you wish to have it composed for an easy or more difficult execution. I expect your immediate answer having several orders to attend, and I shall in a little time write more copiously in reply to your favours already received. I beg you to thank the author for the very ingenious and flattering verses obtained by your means. Allow me to subscribe myself

Sir,

your very obedt. & humble servant

LUDWIG VAN BEETHOVEN.

Vienna, Feb. 7(?), 1815.

On November 16th of this year occurred an event that was destined to affect profoundly the remainder of Beethoven's life: his brother Carl died of consumption, leaving instructions in his will that the guardianship of the nine-year-old son Carl was to be shared by his widow and Ludwig. This dual responsibility was an afterthought on Carl's part, expressed in a codicil. Knowing that no love was lost between his wife and brother, and that the latter was desirous of adopting young Carl, he wrote:

> . . . I have found it necessary to add to my will that I by no means desire that my son be taken away from his mother, but that he shall always, and so long as his future career permits, remain with his mother, to which end the guardianship of him is to be exercised

> by her as well as my brother. Only by unity can the object which I had in view in appointing my brother guardian of my son, be attained, wherefore, for the welfare of my child, I command *compliance* to my wife, and more *moderation* to my brother.
>
> God permit them to be harmonious for the sake of my child's welfare. This is the last wish of the dying husband and brother.

—a wish that was uttered in vain. Neither compliance nor moderation was forthcoming, and there followed a series of lawsuits, bickerings, and domestic and financial worries that clouded the rest of the composer's life. Faults there were on the parts of both guardian and ward. The wretched affair need not be gone into fully here. It will suffice to state that Beethoven succeeded in obtaining the full custody of the boy, and that the result was in every way disastrous, mainly, no doubt, through his temperamental unfitness for such a responsibility. The legal proceedings were spun out till 1820, at a heavy cost to Beethoven's health and output.

The years 1816 and 1817 were almost a blank so far as composition was concerned, the only works of note being the Pianoforte Sonata in A and the song cycle, "An die ferne Geliebte."

At about this time occurred an episode which, unfavourably as it reflects on Beethoven's rectitude, cannot be passed over. Beethoven attempted, through Neate, to dispose in London of a batch of works—the Violin Concerto, and a pianoforte transcription thereof; two Sonatas for Violoncello and Pianoforte, Op. 102; the seventh Symphony; "Fidelio"; and the F Minor String Quartet. Unfortunately, he had spoilt his chances with London publishers by his treatment of the Royal Philharmonic Society a few months earlier. Asked by this body to compose something specially for them, Beethoven replied by sending three works that had been written some years before, and that were, moreover, among his poorest efforts—the "King Stephen," "Ruins of Athens," and "Name-Day" Overtures. The first-named had in fact already been published by Haslinger, of Vienna, in 1815. The Society's disappointment with the music, and resentment at such dishonest treatment, was reflected in the attitude of the London publishers. To make matters worse, at this same period, Beethoven treated the publisher Birchall very shabbily by withholding the assignment of some works of which Birchall had purchased the English copyright, sending, instead of the important document, a claim for an additional five pounds for copying and postage. No wonder Neate, armed though he was with some of the master's choicest works, met with a chilly response in London publishing circles! He was, in fact, prepared for it by a remark in a letter written to him by a publisher after the trial of the Overtures sent to the Philharmonic Society: "For God's sake, don't buy anything of Beethoven!" And Birchall answered Neate's request to purchase the Overtures by saying flatly that he wouldn't take them, even as a gift. There followed a good deal of correspondence between Birchall and Beethoven concerning the assignment and the £5—correspondence in which the publisher cuts the more honourable figure. In fact, so bad was the impression made by Beethoven, that on Birchall's death a little later his successor, Lonsdale, did not consider it worth while to continue the connection with the composer.

This is perhaps a suitable moment in which to dispose finally of the popular conception of Beethoven as a neglected and poverty-stricken genius. On this subject Thayer quotes the following from William Henry Fry, a prominent American musical writer in the mid-nineteenth century, and describes it as "a common opinion":

> Beethoven worked hard for thirty years. At hi death, after the cup of glory had overflowed, his name resounding through Christendom, he left in all a beggarly sum of two or three thousand dollars, having lived as anyone acquainted with his career knows, a penurious life, fitted to his poverty and servile position in Vienna.

Fry added that the public indifference to his music "doomed Beethoven to a garret which no Irish Emigrant would live in."

Thayer easily disproves the popular fallacy as to Beethoven's poverty, and in regard to the alleged neglect of his music by press and public says:

> Taking 1821-1822 as a medium date, the leading political and literary journals in Vienna in those years were the *Weiner Zeitung*, Joseph Carl Bernard, editor; the *Beobachter*, Joseph Pilat, editor; the *Sammler*, Portenschlag and Ledermeyer, editors; the *Weiner Zeitschrift*" (fashion journal), Kohann Schickh, editor; and the *Theater-Zeitung*, Adolph Bauerle, editor. Most of these editors were personal friends of Beethoven; and whoever performs the weary task of looking through their myriads of pages sees that all were his admirers and let no opportunity pass unimproved of adding a leaf to his laurels. Still, disappointment at the comparative paucity of matter relating to him follows such an examination. The cause, however, lay in himself; in the small number of new compositions of high importance; and in the rarity of his appearance before the public. True, there were newspapers, and in divers languages, that took no note of Beethoven and his works because music and musicians were not within their scope; but not one of them was hostile. In short, whether the periodical press be considered as the exponent or the guide of public opinion, in either case its tone at Vienna during the ten years which remained of Beethoven's life · is ample refutation of the so oft-asserted disregard for and contemptuous neglect of their great composer on the part of the Viennese.

And Thayer goes on to quote a passage from Schindler which helps us to understand the smallness of Beethoven's output at this period of his life—a period which under normal conditions should have yielded the finest fruits of his genius.

> During these years our composer, instead of writing many notes, as had been his wont, wrote many letters, referring in part to his domestic affairs, in part to the litigation, and in part to the education of his nephew. These letters are, in general, among the least encouraging and most deplorable testimonials to the excitement which attended his passionate prosecution of these objects. Those of his friends and nearer acquaintances who permitted themselves to be drawn into these three matters were so overwhelmed with documents and communications that they blessed the hour in which the lawsuit was brought to a conclusion.

The fact is, Beethoven's nature was becoming more and more suspicious, and even his best friends did not escape from oral and written outbursts of ill-temper. It was perhaps inevitable that during the period of hero-worship that followed his death, these outbursts should have been regarded as a great composer's protest against a neglectful public, rather than as the splenetic utterances of a harassed and afflicted man.

The years 1817-19 saw the composition of no more than a few unimportant vocal works, the Quintet Fugue in D (written for a manuscript collection of Haslinger, and published ten years later as Op. 137), and the great Sonata in B flat for Pianoforte, Op. 106. The Mass in D, however, was taking shape in the composer's mind, and parts of the ninth Symphony were sketched.

In the midst of his worries Beethoven was cheered, at least temporarily, by the arrival in 1818 of the gift of a grand pianoforte from John Broadwood and Sons. The instrument bore the inscription "Hoc Instrumentum est Thomas Broadwood (Londini) donum, propter Ingenium illustrissimi Beethoven."

At Beethoven's death the pianoforte was bought for 181 florins, by music publisher Spina, who gave it to Liszt. It is now in the Buda Pesth National Museum. On the right of the keyboard are scratched the autographs of Kalkbrenner, Ries, Ferrari, Cramer, and Knyvett.

Meanwhile (1817) the Philharmonic Society had invited Beethoven to visit London and to write for them two symphonies for a fee of 300 guineas, with the prospect of handsome pickings from concerts and other engagements. Beethoven accepted with alacrity, but failed to appear at the period agreed on, explaining in a letter to Ries that ill-health was the obstacle, and expressing a hope that he might be able to come later in the year—a hope that was not to be fulfilled.

Chapter XV

More litigation with Carl's widow—A Glimpse of Beethoven composing—An English admirer, Gardiner of Nottingham—Transactions concerning the Mass in D—Krehbiel on Beethoven's character—Some excuses.

The year 1819 opened with one of the regularly recurring squabbles, followed by litigation, between Beethoven and his sister-in-law (the "Queen of Night" as he called her) concerning young Carl, who had run away from his uncle to his mother. The Spring found Beethoven starting his annual spell in the country at Mödling, and hard at work on the Mass in D—how hard may be seen from this note of Schindler:

> Towards the end of August, accompanied by the musician Johann Horsalka still living in Vienna, I arrived at the master's home in Mödling. It was 4 o'clock in the afternoon. As soon as we entered we learned that in the morning both servants had gone away, and that there had been a quarrel after midnight which had disturbed all the neighbours, because as a consequence of a long vigil both had gone to sleep and the food which had been prepared had become unpalatable. In the living-room, behind a locked door, we heard the master singing parts of the fugue in the *Credo*—singing, howling, stamping. After we had been listening a long time to this most awful scene, and were about to go away, the door opened and Beethoven stood before us with distorted features, calculated to excite fear. He looked as if he had been

in mortal combat with the whole host of contrapuntists, his everlasting enemies. His first utterances were confused, as if he had been disagreeably surprised at our having overheard him. Then he reached the day's happenings, and with obvious restraint he remarked: "Pretty doings, these! (*Saubere Wirthschaft.*) Everybody has run away and I haven't had anything to eat since yesternoon!" I tried to calm him and helped him to make his toilet. My companion hurried on in advance to the restaurant of the bathing establishment to have something made ready for the famished master. Then he complained about the wretched state of his domestic affairs, but here, for reasons already stated, there was nothing to be done. Never, it may be said, did so great an artwork as is the Missa Solemnis see its creation under more adverse circumstances."

He was now once more pressed to visit England. A passage in the Conversation Book (apparently written by Schindler) giving particulars of some commissions from Donaldson of Edinburgh, ends:

> These Englishmen speak of nothing else than their wish for you to come to England—they give assurance that if you come for a single winter to England, Scotland, or Ireland, you will earn so much that you can live the rest of your life on the interest.

This was no wild estimate, as was proved by the experience of Haydn twenty-five years before. His two English visits yielded him a sum sufficient to ensure peace and comfort for his old age.[1]

[1] *Haydn*, by Michel Brenet, English translation by C. Leonard Leese. p. 53.

Meanwhile, the Mass grew, every movement taking on larger dimensions than had been originally planned. The work had been promised for the installation of the Archduke Rudolph as Archbishop of Olmütz, but was not nearly ready in time.

This year's publications included the two Sonatas for Violoncello and Pianoforte, Op. 102; an arrangement for Quintet of the C minor Trio, Op. 1, No. 3; and the "Hammerklavier" Sonata.

Beethoven was very much alone just now, partly because of his deafness and even more because most of his oldest and closest friends had died, or had become estranged through his repellent manner. That his later works should tend to become more and more remote in feeling is natural. His fierce absorption in the Mass, for example, was such as could have been possible only in one who was more or less cut off from the society of his fellows. We may even ascribe to his loneliness and almost constant exasperation the impracticable nature of a good deal of the vocal writing—though it is true that he was always disposed to scorn the convenience of the performer.[1]

[1] Thus, on Kraft, the 'cellist, complaining that a certain passage did not "lie within his hand," Beethoven's curt answer was, "It *must* lie;" and again, on hearing of a similar complaint from the violinist, Schuppanzigh, he said "Does he imagine that I think of his wretched fiddle when the spirit is on me?" Curiously, these incidents are sometimes quoted as a kind of proof of Beethoven's greatness, whereas of course they are nothing of the kind. An important part of a composer's job *is* to think of the limitations, as well as the possibilities, of the "wretched" instrument for which he happens to be writing.

An episode of interest to English readers occurred in 1820. Among the very earliest of Beethoven enthusiasts in England was William Gardiner, a Nottingham stocking manufacturer, over whose activities as musical amateur and writer on art, natural history and other subjects one would like to dwell did space permit.[1] Among his musical dabblings at this period was a curious compilation entitled "Judah," an oratorio made up of extracts adapted from various composers, eked out by passages from his own pen. In a letter to Beethoven, undated, but evidently belonging to 1820, he wrote:

Dear Sir:

At the house of Lady Bowater in Leicestershire in 1796, I met with your Trio in E-flat (for Violin, Viola and Bass). Its originality and beauty gave me inexpressible delight; indeed it was a new sense to me. Ever since, I have anxiously endeavoured to procure your compositions as much so as the war could permit. Allow me to present to you the first volume of my "Sacred Melodies" which contain your divine Adagios appropriated to the British church. I am now engaged upon a work entitled "The Oratorio of Judah," giving a history of that peculiar people from the Jewish scriptures. The object of this letter is to express a hope that I may induce you to compose an Overture for this work, upon which you can bring all the force of your sublime imagination (if it please you) in the key of D minor. For this service my friend

[1] See an article by Orlando A. Mansfield, in the *Musical Times* of October, 1926.

Mr. Clementi will accept your draft upon him for one hundred guineas.

I have the honour to be, dear Sir,

Your faithful servant,

William Gardiner.

Apparently the domestic and legal distractions that afflicted Beethoven at this time accounted for the letter remaining unanswered—despite the handsome bait. Probably, too, Beethoven was less flattered than Gardiner expected him to be by the news that his "divine Adagios" had suffered a sea-change into hymn-tunes for the "British church." We may smile at Gardiner and his "Judah," but let it go to his credit that he perceived the greatness of Beethoven as composer as early as 1796—a period when so many of Ludwig's contemporaries and familiars thought of him mainly as a brilliant pianist. In Gardiner's "Italy, her Music, Arts and People," he writes:

> Recently we arrived at Bonn, the birthplace of Beethoven. About the year 1786, my friend the Abbé Dobler, chaplain to the Elector of Cologne, first noticed this curly, blackheaded boy, the son of a tenor singer in the cathedral. Through the Abbé I became acquainted with the first production of this wonderful composer. How great was my surprise in playing the viola part to his Trio in E flat [from Op.1], so unlike anything I have ever heard. It was a new sense to me, an intellectual pleasure which I had never received from sounds.

It is pleasant to know that Gardiner, who began his Beethoven-worship so early, lived to round it off by being present—an octogenarian—at the unveiling of the monument to the composer at Bonn in 1848. More: he was given the honour of writing his name (with what swelling heart may be imagined!) under the signatures of Queen Victoria and the Prince Consort on the roll which was placed in the base of the memorial.

The Archduke Rudolph was duly installed as Archbishop on March 30th, 1820, but the Mass which Beethoven had undertaken to provide for the ceremony was, as we have seen, not ready. It was, however, sufficiently advanced for Beethoven to begin an elaborate series of negotiations concerning its publication. Unfortunately, it is difficult to negotiate both elaborately and honestly, and it has to be recorded that the transaction concerning this masterpiece was the most discreditable of all Beethoven's business activities. The whole of the complicated affair is too lengthy to be set out in detail, because of the amount of correspondence that would call for quotation. Here is an attempt at a compressed record of involved machinations that covered a period of some years (the confusing financial details, varying currencies, etc., are omitted, as are also the particulars of the sums advanced by the publishers, and the hawking of other manuscripts in company with the Mass—that work being used not only for the purpose of raising the wind, but also as a decoy) :

March 18th, 1820: Beethoven writes to Simrock offering the Mass " for the honorarium of 100 Louis d'ors " ; May 13th, 1822 : Simrock reminds Beethoven that the Mass has not yet been delivered ; May 19th : Beethoven tells his friend Brentano that he will keep faith with Simrock, " even at a sacrifice " ; ten weeks before this, however, he had written to Schlesinger of Berlin concerning the Mass, urging a speedy reply, " chiefly because two other publishers " are pressing for the work ; July 2nd : Schlesinger writes accepting Beethoven's terms for the Mass ; July 26th : Beethoven writes to Peters of Leipsic (to whom he had already offered the Mass), " In no event will Schlesinger ever get anything more from me . . . he is not among those who might have received the Mass " ; May 18th, 1822 : Peters writes expressing a desire to publish anything of Beethoven ; June 5th : Beethoven replies, offering a collection of manuscripts, among them the Mass ; June 15th : Peters expresses an urgent desire for the Mass, above all the works proposed ; June 26th : Beethoven writes to Peters, " I give you the Mass for the sum of a 1,000 florins . . . you will in all likelihood receive the score by the end of July " ; August 23rd, 1822 : Beethoven writes to Artaria, publishers of his early works, " As regards the Mass, I have been offered a 1,000 florins.

The state of my finances do not permit me to take a smaller honorarium from you. All that I can do is to *give you the preference* . . . I beg of you to keep everything secret about the Mass" [an injunction given to the other publishers !]; March 23rd: Beethoven puts off the importunate Peters, and begins to hedge—"As regards the Mass . . . the time is approaching when you will receive *one or the other*.[1] Besides yourself there are two other men who also desire each a Mass. I am resolved to write at least three"; March 10th, 1824: Beethoven offers to Schott "a new Grand Mass . . . my greatest work"; *on the same day* he writes to Probst of Leipsic offering the Mass at the same sum quoted to Schott; Diabelli (who was a publisher as well as a composer) was also involved in tortuous negotiations—dates not clear; in the upshot the favoured one of the seven publishers was Schott, who issued the work in 1827.

The reader who desires the depressing experience of seeing how far a great man may decline in the pursuit of money may find all he wants, and to spare, in Vol. iii. of Thayer.

The unhappy business is there summed up in an indictment that is severe, but not unjust. It throws so much light on the Jekyll-and-Hyde aspect of Beethoven's personality, that it deserves quotation:

[1] The author's italics: the sentence shows Beethoven neatly shifting the discussion from *the* Mass to *a* Mass.

Careful readers of this biography can easily recall a number of lapses from high ideals of candour and justice in his treatment of his friends and of a nice sense of honour and honesty in his dealings with his publishers; but at no time have these blemishes been so numerous or so patent as they are in the negotiations for the publication of the *Missa Solemnis*—a circumstance which is thrown into a particularly strong light by the frequency and vehemence of his protestations of moral rectitude in the letters which have risen like ghosts to accuse him, and by the strange paradox that the period is one in which his artistic thoughts and imagination dwelt in the highest regions to which they ever soared. He was never louder in his protestations of business morality than when he was promising the Mass to four or more publishers practically at the same time, and giving it to none of them; never more apparently frank than when he was making ignoble use of a gentleman, whom he himself described as one of the best friends on earth, as an intermediary between himself and another friend to whom he was bound by business ties and childhood associations which challenged confidence; never more obsequious (for even this word must now be used in describing his attitude towards Franz Brentano) than after he had secured a loan from that friend in the nature of an advance on a contract which he never carried out; never more apparently sincere than when he told one publisher (after he had promised the Mass to another) that he should be particularly sorry if he were unable to give the Mass into his hands; never more forcefully and indignantly honest in appearance than when he informed still another publisher that the second had importuned him for the Mass (" bombarded " was the word), but that he had never deigned to answer his letters. But even this is far from compassing the indictment; the counts are not even complete when it is added that in a letter he states that the publisher whom he had told it would have been a source of sorrow not to favour, had never even been contemplated amongst those who might receive the Mass; that he permitted the friend to whom he first promised the score to tie up some of his capital for a year and more so that "good Beethoven" should not have to wait a day for his money; that after promising the Mass to the third publisher he sought to create the impression that it was not the *Missa Solemnis* that had been bargained for, but one of the two masses which he had in hand.[1]

In a footnote, the American editor of the 1921 edition of Thayer, Henry Edward Krehbiel, takes responsibility for this passage, adding, by way of justification, that Thayer's notes fail at this point, and that "the indictment . . . is not only demanded by historical truth, but also wholly within the spirit of Thayer as manifested in the earlier volumes." Mr. Krehbiel adds:

> Dr. Deiters makes no effort to conceal the facts, though he does not marshal them so as to present the moral delinquency in the strong light in which it appears when Beethoven's words and deeds are brought sharply into juxtaposition; nevertheless, after presenting a plea in extenuation fully and fairly, he says: "We pay the tribute of our profoundest sympathy for Beethoven under these circumstances;

[1] Thayer, iii, 51 *et seq.*

we know sufficiently well the noble impulses of his soul in all other fields; we are aware of the reasons which compelled him to try anything which promised to better his condition; but the conscientious reporter cannot ignore facts which lie notoriously before him, and, hard as it may be, cannot acquit Beethoven of the reproach that his conduct was not in harmony with the principles of strict justice and uprightness.

It may fairly be assumed, however, that the motives at the back of this shady wirepulling were not all unworthy. The curious duality of standard shown by Beethoven in morals is apparent also in the inequality of his music. No other composer of his calibre has so often and so completely touched the extremities of good and bad, and that he himself was well aware of the disparity seems evident from remarks in his letters and conversations. And, just as publishers make the frankly popular works in their catalogue pay for their unprofitable masterpieces, so did Beethoven sustain himself during a long flight by disposing of rapidly written works, or by rescusitated early efforts that most composers would have burned.

We have seen how the Mass engrossed him and how it grew in dimensions. He was in earnest when he told Schott it was one of his "greatest works," and it is not difficult to understand that each respite gained by a loan or sum in advance from a prospective publisher enabled him to rewrite and improve the work still further. In fact, as Thayer puts it, the Mass was "several times completed, but never complete so long as it was within reach." But in a big work where proportion and structure count for so much, one alteration almost inevitably leads to another, and so we see the hapless Beethoven becoming more and more involved, and buying an extension of time at the cost of his honour. Some excuse for his conduct in this affair is found, then, in the fact that he needed the money to sustain himself during the writing of two masterpieces (for the Ninth Symphony was also in hand at this time) and to make provision for the future of his nephew. When all is said, however, and the most favourable view taken, the affair is explained rather than condoned.

CHAPTER XVI

Appointment of Johann as business agent—" Landowner " and " Brainowner "—Beethoven and Rossini—The genesis of the last Quartets—The Mass: more negotiations—The real Beethoven tragedy.

ONE result of the financial entanglements into which Beethoven had got himself was the appointment of his brother Johann as a kind of business agent. Beethoven, already in debt to his friend Brentano, Steiner and other publishers, borrowed further from Johann, placing in his hands (as a kind of security) the sale of all manuscripts, finished and unfinished—subject, of course, to the composer's advice. If his prosperity may be taken as a sign, Johann was evidently a shrewd man of business. He was, however, no musician. Is it surprising that in his transactions on Ludwig's behalf his sole concern was to drive as good a bargain as possible? After all, was that not generally Ludwig's own practice? Moreover, despite the ill-repute that has surrounded Johann's name in this matter, there is no evidence of his having been guilty of more than an occasional exceeding of his authority. No doubt he sometimes acted without Beethoven's knowledge, and to this fact is ascribed the publication of some inferior works. But, as we know, the composer himself did not scruple to sell some of his poorer efforts when in need of money.

It has been the custom to condemn wholesale Beethoven's brothers and nephews. True, they were a poor lot, but their defects were largely shared by Beethoven himself, and were due to the unsatisfactory circumstances of their early life. During his researches, Thayer became so convinced of the unjust treatment of Carl and Johann by posterity, that in addition to a defence of them in his life of Beethoven, he followed it up in a pamphlet entitled "Ein kritischer Beitrag zur Beethovenliteratur" (1877); and, later, in a review of Nohl's biography of Beethoven.

The brothers had seen little or nothing of one another since the composer descended on Johann at Linz in 1812, and denounced his association with Therese Obermeyer—a denunciation that was fruitless, as we have seen. Ludwig now invited Johann not only to help in the sale of manuscripts, but also to live with him. As there are no perceptible signs of mellowing in Beethoven's character—very much the reverse, in fact—it is evident that he was not indifferent to Johann's worldly success. There is perhaps more than meets the eye in the familiar story of Johann, in the heyday of his prosperity, sending Ludwig a card, "Johann van Beethoven, Landowner," and the composer's reply, "Ludwig van Beethoven, Brainowner." It is usually quoted as a proof of the composer's scorn for mere worldly prosperity. But may there not have been a touch of envy at the back of it? At all events, we now see Beethoven anxious to make use of the business acumen of the "Land-owner." ("As a merchant you are a good counsellor," Beethoven said in a letter of about this date.) Johann, on his side, was nothing loth. Superficial as he was, and quite devoid of musical ability or taste, he was none the less proud of Ludwig's fame. Acting as the composer's agent appealed alike to his vanity and greed: it gave him both a corner in the limelight and a share of the profits.

The relation of a great composer to his contemporaries is always a matter of interest, so mention should be made of a meeting that took place in this year (1822) between Beethoven and Rossini. That the two met was denied by Schindler and other biographers, but later evidence shows that Rossini was introduced to Beethoven by Carpani the Italian poet. The visit was brief, for conversation was difficult, not only owing to Beethoven's deafness, but also because Beethoven knew little Italian and Rossini even less German. Rossini told Hanslick in 1867 that Beethoven received him "at once, and very politely." That there could be anything more cordial on Beethoven's part was hardly to be expected, for the wild success of Rossini's operas in Vienna had undoubtedly had an adverse effect on Beethoven's popularity. Hence his scornful references to Rossini as "A good scene-painter"; "What have the Italians to show for their famous conservatories? Behold their idol—Rossini! If Dame Fortune had not given him a pretty talent and pretty melodies by the bushel, what he learned at school would have brought him nothing but potatoes for his big belly!" And, "Rossini would have been a great composer if his teacher had frequently applied some blows *ad posteriora*!" On the other hand Rossini, on hearing some of Beethoven's quartets, was enthusiastic; and he said of the "Eroica," "It knocked me over."

The end of this year saw the final touches put to the Mass, and good progress made with the ninth Symphony. Some string quartets also seem to have been sketched. Certainly Beethoven's thoughts were turned towards chamber music at this time, for in November came a letter from Prince Nicolas Boris Galitzin, of St. Petersburg, asking him to compose two or three string quartets at any price he chose to demand—a commission which Beethoven gladly accepted, fixing the fee at fifty ducats per quartet. This is the genesis of the E flat, B flat, and A minor Quartets, Opp. 127, 130, and 132, written at various periods from 1824 to 1826. To these closing months of 1822 belongs also a request from the Handel and Haydn Society, of Boston, U.S.A., for an oratorio—a commission that bore no fruit, though it enabled Beethoven to mention proudly that he had requests "from all parts of Europe, and even from North America."

On March 19th, 1823, exactly a year after the ceremony for which it had been projected, Beethoven handed over to Archduke Rudolph the manuscript of the Mass. The work had occupied him on and off for five years, and an interesting evidence of his constant revision is the fact that the tympani part in the *Agnus Dei* was altered so many times that a hole was made in the paper, although it was "very thick," says Thayer.

As we have seen, there was no definitive shape to the Mass so long as the manuscript remained within Beethoven's reach: he must still be revising. He seemed no less reluctant to let it go beyond his control as a source of revenue: he must still be exploring every possibility of obtaining cash by it. The reader is probably tired of this financial aspect of the work—certainly the writer is. As briefly as may be, therefore, let the fact be stated that, having settled the publication of the Mass in as roundabout and lucrative a manner as possible, Beethoven now conceived the plan of deferring the actual publication for a time in order that manuscript copies might be sold to European crowned heads! The petition to the various Courts was a duplication of the following, sent to Cassel:

> The undersigned cherishes the wish to send his latest work, which he regards as the most successful of his intellectual products, to the Most Exalted Court of Cassel.

It is a grand solemn Mass for 4 solo voices, with choruses and complete grand orchestra in score, which can also be used as a grand oratorio.

He therefore begs the High Embassy of His Royal Highness, the Elector of Hesse-Cassel, to be pleased to procure for him the necessary permission of your Exalted Court.

Inasmuch, however, as the copying of the score will entail a considerable expense the author does not think it excessive if he fixes an honorarium at 50 ducats in gold. The work in question, moreover, will not be published for the present.

LUDWIG VAN BEETHOVEN.

Vienna, 23 January, 1823.

How many of these letters were sent out we do not know, but ten acceptances were received—too few for the composer, however, and in some cases, too tardy. Hence a long letter to the Archduke Rudolph, begging him to use his influence in certain quarters. Subscriptions have come in well, and certain Majesties have risen to the occasion: " In spite of all this, however, [he says] though others also have become subscribers I do not get as much as I would as fee from a publisher, only I have the advantage that the work remains *mine* "—after having sold it over and over again! Thayer calls attention, (" as an unpleasant duty ") to a discrepancy between the letters to the Courts and one to Zelter offering the work to the Singakademie of Berlin. In the former Beethoven says the

Mass will not be published "for the present"; to Zelter he says plainly that it will not be published at all. "Except the copies subscribed for, none will be issued, so that the Mass is practically only a manuscript." Such letters and transactions make one marvel at the canonisation of Beethoven as a ruggedly-independent democrat who abolished the patronage system. Ardent worshippers have too readily taken at their face value such utterances of Beethoven as the following, from a letter asking for the advocacy of Director-General von Könneritz:

> I know that you will scarcely think of me as among those who write simply for vulgar gain, but when do not circumstances sometimes compel a man to act contrary to his habits of thought and principles? My Cardinal is a good-hearted prince, but he lacks means.
>
> Up to now, in spite of all external glory, I have scarcely received for the work what I would have been paid by a publisher, the costs of copying have been so great. My friends conceived the idea of thus circulating the Mass, for I, thank God, am a *layman* in all speculations. Besides, there is no citizen of our country who has not suffered loss, and so have I. Were it not for my sickness of years' standing, I should have received enough from foreign lands to live a care-free life, caring only for art. Judge me kindly and not unfavourably. I live for my art alone and to fulfil my duties as a man, but alas! that this cannot always be done without the help of the *subterrestrial powers.*

It can only be said that if Beethoven was a mere layman in such matters it was not for lack of practice.

The answer to the petition was not confined to money: King Louis XVIII added to his fifty ducats a gold medal weighing twenty-one Louis d'ors, with his bust on one side, and on the other the legend *Donnée par le Roi à Monsieur Beethoven*—" a distinction than which [says Schindler] one more significant never fell to the lot of an artist during his life."

That the subscribers had, after all, considerable difficulty in obtaining the copies for which they had paid was largely due to the slowness of the copyists, but the fact is one for which the composer must take part of the blame. Even so, the whole of the degrading business would have been less conspicuous had Beethoven been merely a Court musician of the ordinary type. But (as Thayer says in discussing this point) he had " preached a new ethic as well as artistic evangel":

> And so, to minds untainted by trade and attuned to a love of a moral as well as æsthetic beauty, the spectacle which Beethoven presents in 1823 must be quite as saddening as that disclosed by his dealings with publishers in the years immediately preceding.

Yet there are signs that he felt some of the humiliation attendant on this touting for subscriptions. He protests too much for one quite at ease. To get the better of publishers was one thing: he regarded them as lawful prey. (In a letter to Holz written in 1825 he describes them as hell-hounds who licked and gnawed his brains.) It was quite another thing to go cap in hand and ask favours from a class for whom one of his mildest terms of abuse was "princely rabble."

Motives of no ordinary kind must have been at work to lead him to stoop so low. Counsel for the defence would find no lack of material for an eloquent plea. His health was failing rapidly; to the deafness that prevented him from appearing in the concert hall was now added impaired sight; his nephew was becoming an increasing charge on his purse and patience; his income tended to diminish, for the increase in the fees he was now able to command was more than set off by his reduced output and slowness in working; and he became more and more entangled in debts and disputes with publishers, patrons and friends. It has generally been held that the tragedy in Beethoven's life was his deafness. But was it? So far as his creative work was concerned, it certainly was not, for most of his finest work was written under the affliction. One cannot but feel that the real tragedy lay in the fact that at this period, when his powers were at their height, he was so beset with hindrances (many of them avoidable) as to be unable to make the most of his gifts. Probably he alone was fully aware of the discrepancy between his powers and the quantity of his output ; and the knowledge must have been an added touch of bitterness to a cup already full. . . . On the whole, it must be a tough-bowelled jury that will convict and pass sentence out of hand.

Chapter XVII

The Philharmonic Society—The Diabelli Variations and last two pianoforte Sonatas published—First performance of ninth Symphony—An enthusiastic reception, but small profits—Beethoven's generosity to the "Queen of Night."

Meanwhile the ninth Symphony was growing. On April 6th, 1822, Beethoven had written to Ries in London, asking, "What would the Philharmonic Society be likely to offer me for a Symphony ?" The answer was "fifty pounds." Not enough, said Beethoven; he might get more elsewhere. He accepted, however, adding a rider not without its touching side :

> I would write gratis for the first artists of Europe, if I were not still poor Beethoven. If I were in London, what would I not write for the Philharmonic Society! For Beethoven can write, God be thanked, though he can do nothing else in this world. If God gives me back my health, which has at least improved somewhat, I shall yet be able to comply with all the requests which have come from all parts of Europe, and even from North America, and I might yet feather my nest.

Other projects in the air at this time were an opera (commissioned by the Karnthnerther Theatre as a result of a successful revival of "Fidelio"); an oratorio, the story of Judith being considered; further settings of the Mass;

and the Diabelli variations. Only the last-named came to fruition. The works actually published in 1822-3 were few—the last two pianoforte sonatas, some Bagatelles, etc.

The beginning of 1824—February—saw Beethoven relieved by the conclusion of the Symphony. Its first performance took place at Vienna on May 7th. The announcement of the concert is shown overleaf.

(The "Grand Overture" was that written in 1822 for the opening of the Josephstadt Theatre, Vienna, and hence called "The Blessing of the House." The "Three Grand Hymns" were the *Kyrie*, *Credo*, and *Agnus Dei* from the Mass.)

There still persists a tradition that so far as his later works were concerned Beethoven was a prophet without honour in his generation, and that the ninth Symphony was too hard a nut for the public of his day. The facts give no support to this. At the concert at which the Symphony was first performed the theatre was crowded, only the Imperial box being empty—not through indifference, but because the Court had left Vienna some days before. As to the reception of the work itself: despite a poor performance, and the great length and strangeness of the Symphony, it made a deep impression and was enthusiastically applauded. Indeed, the audience could scarcely restrain itself during the Scherzo. Beethoven sat gazing at the score,

GRAND
MUSICAL CONCERT
BY
MR. L. VAN BEETHOVEN
WHICH WILL TAKE PLACE
TO-MORROW, MAY 7, 1824
In the R.I. Court Theatre beside the Karnthnerther.

The Musical Pieces to be performed are the latest works of Mr. Ludwig van Beethoven.

First : A Grand Overture.

Second: Three Grand Hymns with Solo and Chorus Voices.

Third: A Grand Symphony with Solo and Chorus Voices entering in the finale on Schiller's Ode to Joy.

The solos will be performed by the Demoiselles Sonntag and Unger and the Messrs. Haizinger and Seipelt. Mr. Schuppanzigh has undertaken the direction of the orchestra, Mr. Kapellmeister Umlauf the direction of the whole, and the Music Society the augmentation of the chorus and orchestra as a favour.

Mr. Ludwig van Beethoven will himself participate in the general direction.

PRICES OF ADMISSION AS USUAL.

Beginning at 7 o'clock in the evening.

oblivious till his attention was drawn to the waving hats and handkerchiefs. Says Schindler:

> Never in my life did I hear such frenetic and yet cordial applause. Once the second movement was completely interrupted by applause, and there was a demand for a repetition. The reception was more than imperial, for the people burst out into a storm four times. When the parterre broke out into applauding cries the fifth time the Police Commissioner yelled "Silence!" The Court only three successive times but Beethoven five times.

(The Police Commissioner yelled because of the hint of sedition in the fact of a mere composer receiving more than the three salvoes traditionally allotted to the Court on its entry to a public hall.)

This memorable concert produced little but honour and glory, however, for the cost of rehearsal and copying were so heavy as to absorb almost all the receipts (2,200 florins, of which Beethoven's profits amounted to about 400 florins). Hence a stormy scene between Beethoven and the little group of friends who had done their best for him. The composer asked Schindler, Umlauf, Schuppanzigh to dine with him at the inn "Zum wilden Mann," where he had ordered "an opulent repast." But the wild man of the sign was tame compared with the wild man of the dinner party. The company had scarce sat down when Beethoven exploded, asserting that the manager and Schindler had cheated him. In vain did his friends bring forward the carefully checked accounts in their defence; Beethoven still stormed, and the party broke up in disorder, the friends adjourning to a neighbouring inn for a meal.

A second concert fared even worse, despite a re-arranged programme that made concessions to popular taste—two of the Mass extracts being dropped in favour of a Rossini aria and other light vocal numbers. Unfortunately, fine warm weather kept folk out of doors (the concert was at 12.30 mid-day on a Sunday in May), and there was a loss of 800 florins. Moreover, there was little enthusiasm—naturally, with an almost empty hall—and Beethoven was bitterly hurt in pride as well as in pocket.

It is pleasant to note at this time an act of magnanimity on Beethoven's part towards his sister-in-law, young Carl's mother. She seems to have fallen on hard times, and in a letter to his friend Bernard, Beethoven shows himself ready to do his best for her—a sign of real generosity, for it was done in spite of the animosity that persisted between the pair. He writes to Bernard:

> I beg of you before the day is over to make inquiries about F.v.B. [Frau van Beethoven] and if it is possible, to have her assured through her physician that from this month on *so long as I shall live* she shall have the enjoyment of the whole of her pension, and I will see to it that if I die first, Carl shall not need the half of

her pension. It was, moreover, always my intention to permit her to keep the whole of her pension as soon as Carl left the Institute, but as her illness and need are so great she must be helped at once. God has never deserted me in this heavy task, and I shall continue to trust in Him. If possible I beg of you to send me information yet to-day and I will see to it that my *tenacious brother also makes a contribution* to her.

As for Carl (who was showing himself to be a lad of parts) his unsatisfactory moral development was due largely to Beethoven's unfitness to act *in loco parentis*. Nothing could be worse for the boy than his uncle's mixture of passionate severity and maudlin tenderness. Carl inherited his father's shrewdness and eye to the main chance, and no doubt found it easy to take advantage of his doting uncle.

It was at this time that the eleven-year-old Liszt made his sensational debut in Vienna. Beethoven, after some persuasion, went to the concert (he disliked infant prodigies), joined in the applause, and ascending the platform, kissed young Franz repeatedly—amid "loud and prolonged applause," of course. More interesting is the story of the boy being taken by his father to see Beethoven. "What can he play?" growled Beethoven. (The meeting is said to have taken place on the morning of the concert.) "Almost anything you like," replied papa Liszt. "Can he play this, for instance?" said Beethoven, hammering out with one finger the subject of the C sharp minor Fugue in Part I of the "Forty-eight." Here the boy (provoked by being referred to in the third person) interposed, "Oh, yes, in what key shall I play it?" Beethoven was non-plussed for the moment. Then, "In what key? Try it in D minor." Whereon the boy promptly transposed the first page from memory. Then Beethoven stopped him, and bade him continue in E minor, which was easily done. "You young streak of lightning!" cried Beethoven, and kissed him on both cheeks.

In 1824 there was much talk of Beethoven composing an oratorio, among the subjects under consideration being "The Victory of the Cross," written by Bernard. Nothing came of it, and the early and unsatisfactory "Mount of Olives" remains his only essay in this form.

The publication of the Mass and ninth Symphony involved the composer, as usual, in a tangle of correspondence and negotiations which lasted over many months. As we know, Schott obtained both, publishing the Symphony in 1826, and the Mass in 1827.

Chapter XVIII

Beethoven and England—A talk with Stumpff—Negotiations with Philharmonic Society—Schindler superseded by Holz—Beginning of the End—Visit from Sir George Smart—An old friendship renewed—Financial dispute with Prince Galitzin.

The project of a trip to England was revived by a visit from Johann Stumpff, a Thuringian resident in London. Stumpff records that Beethoven lauded England and the English, and showed (says Stumpff) " an exaggerated opinion of London and its highly cultivated inhabitants." Said Beethoven, " England stands high in culture. In London everybody knows something and knows it well; but the man of Vienna can only talk of eating and drinking, and pounds and sings away at music of little significance, or of his own making." Something of this attitude was due to the financial failure of the two recent concerts, and to Schindler's emphatic comment on the balance sheet of the first: " In Paris or London the concert would certainly have yielded from twelve to fifteen thousand florins; here it may be as many hundreds. After yesterday you must now too plainly see that you are trampling on your own interests by remaining longer within these walls. In short, I have no words to express my feelings at the wrong you are doing yourself."

Beethoven discussed the possibility of sending Carl to London, and clearly had an idea of going there himself. After he and Stumpff had toasted each other (Beethoven drinking " to a meeting in London ") the conversation ended thus, according to Stumpff's report :

> I beckoned to him to fill the glasses again, and hurriedly wrote in his notebook : " Now for a pledge to the welfare of the greatest living composer, Beethoven."—I arose from my chair, he followed my example, emptied his glass and seizing my hand, said : " To-day I am just what I am and what I ought to be,—all unbuttoned." And now he unbosomed himself on the subject of music, which had been degraded and made a plaything of vulgar and impudent passions. " True music," he said, " found little recognition in this age of Rossini and his consorts." Thereupon I took up the pencil and wrote in very distinct letters :
>
> " Whom do you consider the greatest composer that ever lived ? "
>
> " Handel," was his instantaneous reply ; " to him I bow the knee," and he bent one knee on the floor.
>
> " Mozart," I wrote.
>
> " Mozart," he continued, " is good and admirable."
>
> " Yes," wrote I, " who was able to glorify even Handel with his additional accompaniments to the ' Messiah.' "
>
> " It would have lived without them," was his answer.

I continued writing. "Seb. Bach."

"Why, is he dead?"

I answered immediately, "He will return to life again."

"Yes, if he is studied, and for that there is now no time."

I took the liberty of writing: "As you yourself, a peerless artist in the art of music, exalt the merits of Handel so highly above all, you must certainly own the scores of his principal works."

"I? How should I, a poor devil, have got them? Yes, the scores of 'The Messiah' and 'Alexander's Feast' went through my hands."

If it is possible for a blind man to help a cripple, and the two attain an end which would be impossible to either one unaided, why might not in the present case a similar result be effected by a similar co-operation? At that moment I made a secret vow: Beethoven, you shall have the works for which your heart is longing, if they are anywhere to be found.

Stumpff kept his word, and Handel's works, in the edition of Arnold, forty volumes, folio, reached Beethoven two years later.

So far as actual composition is concerned, only one work of importance was produced during 1824—the Quartet in E flat, Op. 127.

The following year almost brought the oft-projected English tour to fruition. On behalf of the Philharmonic Society Neate wrote (December 20th, 1824), inviting Beethoven to conduct at least one of his works at each concert during the coming season, and to compose a symphony to be produced by the Society (though it was to remain his property). The fee offered was three hundred guineas; and Neate pointed out that Beethoven could easily earn a further £500 by a concert on his own behalf, as well as additional sums through other engagements: for example, performances of the new String Quartet ought to yield at least £100. Neate added that the ninth Symphony had been received, and that the Society had arranged for a rehearsal on January 17th; he hoped Beethoven would come in time to direct the performance. Beethoven replied, asking for a further hundred guineas for travelling expenses, as it would be necessary for him to buy a carriage and bring a companion. The Philharmonic Society declined to make an increase but Neate offered to advance the extra sum.

Beethoven's brother, nephew and friends strongly urged him to go, but in the end his fears for his health and other anxieties prevailed. He wrote to Neate putting off the visit: he hoped to come in the autumn.

A new character entered Beethoven's circle at this time. Schindler had been Beethoven's loyal helper since 1814—even publishing his devotion by inscribing on his visiting-cards "Friend of Beethoven." After the concert-fiasco of May, 1824, however, the composer had turned against him, and poor Schindler was banished from the presence. Probably this step on Beethoven's part was due to the arrival on the scene of an attractive young fellow named Carl Holz, a capable musician, a good hand at business and also something of a rascal. ("A hard drinker, between ourselves," wrote Beethoven of him; and "a terrible fellow for the women.") His business ability seems to have attracted Beethoven, whose knowledge of arithmetic was unequal to negotiations with foreign publishers, especially when complicated rates of exchange had to be mastered. "It seems as if Holz might become a friend," says Beethoven in a letter to his nephew. Holz soon acquired great influence over him, helping him in correspondence, music copying, keeping an eye on Carl, and so forth. He broke down Beethoven's isolation, too, and undoubtedly did him good by taking him into cheerful company—at the cost, perhaps, of some lapses from temperance on Beethoven's part, though the allegations of Schindler on this score seem to have been exaggerations due to jealousy. Holz's devotion cooled towards the end of 1826, and Schindler, letting bygones be bygones, returned in time to be the faithful watchdog during Beethoven's last and fatal illness.

That illness began to cast its shadow during the Spring of 1825, when Beethoven was laid up with an indisposition that threatened to develop into inflammation of the bowels. Strict diet was enjoined, and spirits were taboo—a regimen that Beethoven took ill. There can be little doubt that a consistent adherence to it would have lengthened his life. (" You are very liable to inflammatory attacks . . . I'll wager that if you take a drink of spirits you'll be lying weak and exhausted on your back in an hour. If you want to get entirely well and live a long time you must live according to nature." So wrote his doctor.)

In the summer of this year came a visit from Sir George Smart, then touring Germany with Kemble. His main object in calling on Beethoven was to ascertain direct from the composer the exact *tempi* of the movements of various Symphonies, especially the ninth. A good deal of the conversation at the various meetings was noted in Smart's Journal, and may be read in Thayer (Vol. III, 207-211). In it we find Beethoven still being pressed to visit London. Here, from one of the Conversation Books, is an extract of the talk, Smart's side written down by Carl, Beethoven's part being of course oral:

> He asked why you had not come before now; he said the 300 pounds of the Philhar. Society were not to be looked upon as the principal thing. For that you needed only to appear 2 or 3 times in the orchestra and make money with your own concerts.—He said that in a short time you could make at least a 1,000 pounds and carry it away with you.—10,000 florins, Vienna money.—If you would only go. The 1,000 pounds would be easily earned and more. You can do better business with the publishers there than

here. And you'll find a 1,000 friends, Smarth [*sic*] says, who will do everything to help you.—The sea fish. —In the Thames. . . . We'll wait till the year is over before going to England. . . . You'll not leave London so quickly if we are once there.— Others are living there too, like Cramer, etc.—In two years at least 50,000 florins net. Concerts.—I am convinced that if you were to want to go away from here they would do everything to keep you.

This meeting ended convivially. Here is Smart's account:

We had dinner at two o'clock. . . . I overheard Beethoven say, "We will try how much the Englishman can drink." *He* had the worst of the trial. I gave him my diamond pin as a remembrance . . . and he wrote me a droll canon on "*Ars longa, vita brevis*" as fast as his pen could write in about two minutes of time as I stood at the door ready to depart. "Written on the 16th of September, 1825, in Baden, when my dear talented musical artist and friend Smart (from England) visited me here.—LUDWIG VAN BEETHOVEN."

Within a few weeks of this episode Beethoven's numerous flittings ended with his signing of a lease for rooms in the Schwarzpanierhaus, where he took up his abode early in October: they were destined to be his last lodgings. He occupied four rooms on the second floor, in addition to a kitchen and quarters for his servants. A happy result of this move was a renewal of his friendship with Stephan von Breuning, who lived in the neighbourhood. The two had drifted apart some years before, when von Breuning had offended Beethoven by trying to dissuade him from undertaking the guardianship of Carl. Thrown together again, the two old playmates sank their differences, and Stephan and his family did much to ease the lot of Beethoven till his death.

The compositions of this year were the A minor and B flat Quartets, written in this order, though the respective opus numbers are 132 and 130. These two works make up the set of three quartets commissioned in 1822 by Prince Galitzin. (Unfortunately, for some unexplained reason, the Prince's attitude towards Beethoven changed just as the quartets were finished, and a long squabble over payment for them ensued—lasting in fact till eight years after the composer's death, when, after repeated dunning by Carl, the Prince sent the balance of 75 ducats, not admitting his liability, but describing it as a voluntary tribute "*pour honorer sa memoire, que m'est chére.*")

Chapter XIX

Carl attempts suicide—Beethoven goes to Johann's home—The last Quartet—Projected works—Return to Vienna—Illness develops—Delight in the Handel volumes—Help from the Philharmonic Society—The Bank Shares.

The year 1826 was a black one for Beethoven. Carl had gone from bad to worse, and the climax was reached when he attempted suicide, shooting himself in the head. The effect on Beethoven was to age him by many years. "He soon looked like a man of seventy," says Schindler. To make matters worse, it came to his ears that in some quarters the blame was placed on his shoulders. And Carl himself, during his trial, told the magistrate that he had committed the act because his uncle tormented him too much. "I grew worse because he wanted me to become better"—a remark which is, perhaps, as severe an indictment of Beethoven's methods of control as of Carl's disposition. Those alternations of fond indulgence and excessive rigour were heavily paid for! The harassing business of the trial over, and Carl discharged from hospital, the question arose: where was he to go? Beethoven had with difficulty been persuaded to allow him to go into the army. Holz was urgent on this point: "Why do you want further to restrain him? Once with the military, he will be under the strictest discipline, and if you want to do anything more for him you need only give him a small allowance. Make him a soldier at once!" And von Breuning backed up Holz. But an interval before his entry to the army had to be filled. Beethoven was ready to welcome the prodigal, who, however, was not eager to be welcomed. Nor did von Breuning approve of his return. "If he were here," he said to Beethoven, "you would talk to him too much, and that would cause new irritation; for he testified in the police court that the reason why he had taken the step was because you harassed him constantly." Beethoven, for his part, objected to the youth being sent to his mother. Johann was staying in Vienna at this time, and solved the difficulty by inviting both uncle and nephew to his home at Gneixendorf ("the name sounds like the breaking of an axle-tree," wrote Beethoven soon after his arrival); and thither the three set out on September 28th.

Leaving them there, we return to Beethoven's activities as a composer during the year—the unhappiest of his life. There were many projects—a tenth symphony, an Overture on B.A.C.H., an opera, an oratorio, and a Requiem among them—but more and more Beethoven turned to the string quartet as the most congenial means of expression. The B flat Quartet had its trial trip at the hands of Schuppanzigh and his comrades on March 21st. The Cavatina captured them at once (as well it might) but the terrible Fugue beat them, as it has beaten almost every quartet since. Kolz tells us that Beethoven had shed tears when writing the Cavatina, and even the remembrance of it was sufficient to move him afresh. The publisher, Artaria, who had bought the Quartet, fought shy of the Fugue, and asked Beethoven to write another finale in place of it, offering to publish and pay for the Fugue as a separate work. Beethoven agreed, reluctantly.

When Holz remarked to Beethoven that the B flat work was the greatest of the Quartets, the composer replied, "Each in its way. Art demands of us that we shall not stand still. You will find a new manner of part-writing, and, thank God! there is less lack of fancy than ever before." Probably he had the C sharp minor Quartet in his mind when he spoke; the fugue with which it opens was certainly "a new manner of part-writing" so far as the string quartet was concerned, the polyphony suggesting an endeavour to adapt to the medium the idiom of the organ. If so, the attempt was probably due to Beethoven's interest at this time in various kinds of ecclesiastical music of severe type. He declared this to be the greatest of his quartets.

The Quartet in F. Op. 135, the last of the five works which crown Beethoven's chamber-music achievement was finished at Gneixendorf in October. A few weeks later the finishing touches were put to the finale which Artaria desired for the B flat Quartet in place of the fugue. Several other works were started, among them a Quintet, the completed portion of which was afterwards published in a pianoforte arrangement entitled "Beethoven's letzter musikalische Gedanke."

Apparently some fugues were in the air; for Artaria, writing in the following January says, "I hear of six fugues.—We will empty a bottle of champagne in their honour." There is also some ground for supposing the Rondo, "Rage over a lost penny," to have been written at this time.

The visit to Gneixendorf had been planned to last a week. By that time the bullet wound on Carl's head would be healed, and he would be fit to present himself to the army authorities. In the upshot, however, Beethoven stayed two months. He seems to have had as happy a time as was to be expected, seeing that he was ill, and that he was under the same roof as his old aversion, Johann's disreputable wife. Thayer shows that, concerning this visit, tradition has done some injustice to brother, sister-in-law and nephew. Such evidence as is available indicates that the three did their best for the comfort of one who was as trying a guest as could be imagined. Some well-authenticated stories of his sojourn have come down to us. Most of them show that the neighbours regarded him—not without some grounds—as mentally deficient. How else could they account for such episodes as that, *e.g.*, in which his wild ejaculations and waving of arms scared a yoke of oxen? And his demeanour on the occasion of a visit with Johann to a local official was such that the clerk (who happened to be an enthusiastic amateur and a warm admirer of his music) when asked subsequently by his master, "Whom do you think the man was who stood by the door?" replied, "Seeing that you treated him with such politeness, his may be an exceptional case; otherwise I should take him for an imbecile." He was confounded on being told that the "imbecile" was his favourite composer.

Beethoven returned to Vienna on December 2nd, having, it appears, caught a chill on the journey—whether from exposure owing to Johann's failure to provide him with a closed carriage, or from the wretched accommodation at a village inn where a night was spent *en route*, is uncertain. Apparently he regarded the matter rather lightly, for in a letter to Holz written a day or two after his arrival, he merely says he is "indisposed" (*unpässlich*). The Conversation Books show that Holz called in a physician (Wawruch) on December 5th. This evidence clears Carl of the charge that, bidden to summon the doctor, he forgot the matter for several days and then, remembering it during a game of billiards, entrusted the errand to the billiard-marker, who also failed. Carl's list of misdemeanours is long enough, without this crowning piece of heartlessness.

A complication of diseases developed with terrible rapidity. Wawruch found symptoms of inflammation of the lungs, with spitting of blood and impeded respiration. After a temporary relief on the seventh day, the patient became "jaundiced all over his body," dropsy began to develop, and "the liver showed plain indications of hard nodules."

However, the reader who wishes for the pathological details of the last three months of Beethoven's life is referred to the conscientious Thayer, who spares us little of their unpleasantness.

The Conversation Book gives us glimpses of Beethoven's methods of passing the weary hours. In the early days of his sickness there was correspondence with Schott in reference to the works that publisher had recently bought. Perhaps this set his mind running on financial calculations, and so led to the belated arithmetical studies already mentioned. The Conversation Book used on December 4th contains a series of multiplication tables with simple sums. There is also an explanatory note written by Carl (who had not yet joined his regiment, and was in frequent attendance): "Multiplication is a simplified form of addition, wherefore examples are performed in the same manner. Each product is set under its proper place. If it consists of two digits, the left one is added to the product of the next. Here is a small illustration: 2348, multiplied by 2"—an explanation that probably left the elderly student wondering whether, after all, there was not a great deal to be said for the primitive method of calculation by fingers that had served him all his life. At all events, his efforts to grasp the mysteries of arithmetic seem to have ceased at this point.

A more congenial way of whiling away the hours was at hand a few days later, with the arrival of the forty volumes of Handel's works, promised by Stumpff during his visit in 1824. Gerhard von Breuning (Stephan's son) tells us of Beethoven's joy over this gift. The sick man asked him to bring the books from the top of the pianoforte to the bed. "I have long wanted them," he said to the boy, "for Handel is the greatest, the ablest composer that ever lived. I can still learn from him." There are few pleasant pictures of Beethoven in these last days, so it is good to think of him, leaning the big folios against the wall, and turning the pages with frequent expressions of admiration[1]; and to reflect that of the few pleasures that were now left to him, one of the best came from his mighty predecessor, little of whose music he had ever heard, and with whom he had a good deal in common. A touching proof of the extent to which these scores of Handel were present in Beethoven's mind during the last

[1] Thayer iii, 277.

weeks of his life is seen in a note by Doctor Wawruch, written after the fourth operation for dropsy (February 27th). Beethoven appears to have given up hope—as well he might, in such disgusting sick-room conditions as those described on page 296, Vol. iii of Thayer. Wawruch says:

> No words of comfort could brace him up, and when I promised him alleviation of his sufferings with the coming of the vitalising weather of Spring he answered with a smile, "My day's work is finished. If there were a physician could help me his name should be called Wonderful." This pathetic allusion to Handel's "Messiah" touched me so deeply that I had to confess its correctness to myself with profound emotion.

Carl's departure for the army early in the New Year was no doubt a relief. His attendance in the sick-room was often unwillingly given, and Beethoven's frequent fits of anger with him led to warnings and protests from the doctors. The two never met again. To the end Beethoven was solicitous for Carl's welfare, and did all that was possible in regard to his future.

On February 8th Beethoven wrote to Stumpff, thanking him for the "royal present" of the Handel works, and begging him to approach Smart and Moscheles with a view to a Philharmonic concert for his benefit: "I recall right well that several years ago the Philharmonic Society wanted to give a concert for my benefit.

It would be fortunate for me if they would come to this determination now. It might save me from all the needs that confront me."

Stumpff, it appears, had already heard of Beethoven's illness, and, with Smart and Moscheles, at once brought the matter before the Philharmonic directors. At a meeting on February 28th (the minute-book records):

> It was moved by Mr. Neate, and seconded by Mr. Latour:
>
> That this Society do lend the sum of One Hundred Pounds to its own members to be sent through the hands of Mr. Moscheles to some confidential friend of Beethoven, to be applied to his comforts and necessities during his illness.
>
> Carried unanimously.

Before the decision could reach Beethoven, he wrote two further appeals, first to Smart, then to Moscheles, pleading poverty in such terms that Schindler and von Breuning warned him of the bad impression such an appeal might make. They pointed out to Beethoven that he possessed bankshares of substantial value (about 7,000 florins, say nearly £700); but he insisted on their remaining intact, as they were a part of his intended legacy to Carl.

His mind was soon set at ease by a favourable reply from Moscheles, to whom Beethoven dictated the following letter:

Vienna, March 18th, 1827.

My dear good Moscheles,

I cannot describe to you in words with what feelings I read your letter of March 1st. The generosity with which the Philharmonic Society anticipated my petition has touched me in the innermost depths of my soul. I beg you, therefore, my dear Moscheles, to be the agency through which I transmit my sincerest thanks for the particular sympathy and help, to the Philharmonic Society.

. . . .

Concerning the concert which the Philharmonic Society has resolved to give, I beg the Society not to abandon this noble purpose, and to deduct the 1,000 florins already sent to me from the proceeds of the concert. And if the Society is disposed graciously to send me the balance I pledge myself to return my heartiest thanks to the Society by binding myself to compose for it either a new symphony, which lies already sketched in my desk, a new overture, or whatever else the Society shall wish.

May heaven very soon restore me again to health, and I will prove to the generous Englishmen how greatly I appreciate their interest in my sad fate. Their noble act will never be forgotten by me, and I shall follow this with especial thanks to Sir Smart (*sic*) and Mr. Stumpff.

The letter concluded with a list of metronome marks for the ninth Symphony.

The Philharmonic gift was duly received by Beethoven on March 15th, and was evidently much in his mind until the end, for Schindler says that on the 24th (two days before his death) he whispered, "Write to Smart and Stumpff."

The letter from Rau (the Viennese banker through whom the money was sent) to Moscheles, should be quoted, in fairness to the Viennese public of that time:

> I have with the greatest surprise heard from you, who reside in London, that the universally admired Beethoven is so dangerously ill and in want of pecuniary assistance, while we, here at Vienna, are totally ignorant of it. I went to him immediately after having read your letter to ascertain his state, and to announce to him the approaching relief. This made a deep impression upon him, and called forth true expressions of gratitude. What a satisfactory sight would it have been for those who so generously relieved him to witness such a touching scene! I found poor Beethoven in a sad way, more like a skeleton than a living being. He is suffering from dropsy, and has already been tapped four times; he is under the care of our clever physician Malfatti, who unfortunately gives little hope of his recovery. . . . His friend and ours, Mr. Schindler, dines with him every day and thus proves his sincere attachment to him. S. also manages his correspondence and superintends his expenses. You will find enclosed a receipt from Beethoven for the 1,000 florins (or hundred pounds). When I proposed to him to take half of the sum at present, and to leave the rest with Baron Eskeles, where he might have it safely deposited, he acknowledged to me openly that he considered this money as

> a relief sent him from heaven; and that 500 florins would not suffice for his present want. I therefore gave him, according to his wish, the whole sum at once.

The touch of avarice shown in Beethoven's desire to receive the lump sum was not unnoticed by Schindler. Writing to Moscheles on March 24th, he says:

> I much regret that you did not express more decidedly in your letter the wish that he should draw the 100 pounds by instalments, and I agreed with Rau to recommend this course, but he (Beethoven) preferred acting on the last part of your letter. Care and anxiety seemed at once to vanish when he had received the money, and he said to me quite happily, "Now we can again look forward to some comfortable days." We had only 340 florins remaining and we had been obliged to be very economical for some time in our house-keeping. . . . His delight on receiving this gift from the Philharmonic Society resembled that of a child. A letter from the worthy man Stumpff arrived here two days before yours, and all this affected Beethoven very much. Numberless times during the day he exclaimed: "May God reward them a thousand-fold."

A letter from Rau to Moscheles on the 28th is a further sidelight on the trait, and is quoted here, although it anticipates events somewhat:

> Beethoven is no more: he died on the 26th inst. at five o'clock in the afternoon, in the most dreadful agonies of pain. He was, as I mentioned to you in my

> last letter, according to his own statement, without any relief, without any money, consequently in the most painful circumstances; but on taking an inventory of his property after his death, at which I was present, we found in an old half-mouldy chest, seven Austrian bank bills which amount to about 1,000 pounds. Whether Beethoven concealed these purposely (for he was very mistrusting, and hoped for a speedy recovery) or whether he was himself ignorant of his possession, remains a riddle. We found the whole of the 100 pounds which the Philharmonic Society sent him. . .

As was shown above, the bank shares had been hoarded for Carl. The Philharmonic Society asked for the return of the £100, as the money had not been used to the relief of Beethoven; but they yielded to the plea of Moscheles that they should forego their claim "in honour of the great deceased," and for the benefit of Carl. A portion of the sum was spent by Schindler and von Breuning in payment of the funeral expenses; "otherwise [says Schindler in a letter to Smart] we could not have had him decently buried without selling one of the seven bank shares which constitute his entire estate."

CHAPTER XX

Sick-room Visitors—"*Plaudite, amici, comœdia finita est!*" The Viaticum—Death and Burial.

AMONG the visitors to the sick man were Schuppanzigh and Linke, to whom Beethoven showed his Handel scores. Diabelli also came, bringing a picture of Haydn's birthplace. "Look," said Beethoven to young Gerhard von Breuning; "I got this to-day. See this little house, and in it so great a man was born."

The entries in the Conversation Books for January and February fill 123 pages, and show that Beethoven was by no means forsaken by his circle of friends. The last letter Beethoven wrote by his own hand was to Schindler, about a month before the end. It shows him unable to think connectedly. Schindler had been kept from the sick-room by some mishap, and Beethoven had sent him a gift—evidently of some eatable:

> Concerning your accident, since it has happened, as soon as we see each other I can send to you somebody without inconvenience—accept this—here is something—Moscheles, Cramer—without your having received a letter—There will be a new occasion to write one Wednesday and lay my affairs to his heart,

if you are not well by that time one of my—can take it to the post against a receipt. *Vale et fave*, there is no need of my assuring you of my sympathy in your accident—do take the meal from me, it is given with all my heart—Heaven be with you.

If Schubert ever visited Beethoven (as he is reported to have done) the occurrence was probably about a week before the end. This would account for the absence of any record in the Conversation Books, as their use ceased during the last few days of Beethoven's life. Schindler reports that he had previously (in February) shown Beethoven a parcel of songs by Schubert, and that Beethoven said, "Truly the divine spark lives in Schubert."

On March 24th Beethoven signed his will and various other necessary documents. He was almost in a state of stupor; his brother Johann, Schindler, and von Breuning supported him while he wrote with shaking hand, in one signature omitting an "e," in another the "h." It was apparently on this same day that he delivered himself of an utterance that has become famous among death-bed sayings: "*Plaudite, amici, comœdia finita est*"—probably a half conscious quotation, for a similar remark has been ascribed to a number of dying men long before Beethoven.

On the morning of March 24th, the Viaticum was administered in the presence of Johann's wife, Schindler, von Breuning, and Jenger. The ceremony over, Beethoven said to the priest, "I thank you, reverend sir; you have brought me comfort." Shortly afterwards, he spoke to his friends about a document consigning to Schott's the rights of the C sharp minor Quartet; it was at once drawn up, and his signature—the last he was to make—added.

At mid-day came a present of wine from Schott; Beethoven looked at the bottles which Schindler placed on the table, and murmured, "A pity; too late!" They were his last words. Towards the evening he became delirious, and began a two days' unconscious struggle with death. At about five o'clock on the afternoon of the 26th, there came a flash of lightning and a violent thunderclap—some say there was a snowstorm as well; at all events snow was on the ground. Beethoven had been unconscious for some hours, but, roused by the thunder, he opened his eyes, raised his right hand, clenched (more probably an involuntary muscular action than the defiant gesture of picturesque tradition), and so remained for several seconds. With the dropping of his hand, he died. There were present only his sister-in-law and Anselm Hüttenbrenner; Schindler and von Breuning had gone to the cemetery of Währing to choose a spot for the grave.

Beethoven was buried on the afternoon of March 29th, amid an imposing demonstration of public regard. In the square before his lodging a crowd of 20,000 had gathered, the military being called on to preserve order. All the artistic notables of Vienna were present. The coffin was placed in the court, in view of the people; round it were grouped the dead man's friends, "with draped torches and white roses fastened to bands of crape on their sleeves;" a choir of men sang the *Miserere* and *Amplius lava me* to arrangements made by Seyfried of the Four Equali for trombones. The psalms over, the choir carried the coffin to the Trinity Church in the Alserstrasse. So crowded were the streets that the procession was made with difficulty. Among the pall bearers and torch carriers were Eybler, Hummel, Seyfried, Kreutzer, Schubert, Czerny, Holz, Linke, and Schuppanzigh.

After the service at the church, the coffin was placed in a hearse, and taken to Währing Cemetery, where another dense crowd had assembled. At the cemetery gate the actor Anschütz delivered an oration written by Grillparzer, and after the committal, three laurel wreaths were placed on the coffin by Hummel. Mozart's Requiem was sung at the Augustinians' Church on April 3rd, with Lablache as one of the soloists; and that of Cherubini at the Karlskirche on the 5th. The grave was marked by a pyramid inscribed simply "Beethoven." The Viennese who flocked to the funeral neglected the grave, and, forty-five years later, the Vienna Society of Music-Friends exhumed and reburied the body. But Beethoven's last resting-place was not found until June 21st, 1888, when his remains, with those of Schubert, were removed to the Central Cemetery of Vienna.

PART II

BEETHOVEN'S PERSONALITY

One of the best of recent books on Beethoven—that of Paul Bekker—opens its discussion on the composer's personality thus:

> The general tendency to idealise the figure of a great man has resulted in the creation of a portrait of Beethoven which bears little resemblance to reality. . . . Many interesting particulars of Beethoven's life are now established, free from fictitious embellishments. In view of these facts it is clear that he has hitherto been presented to us in a falsely romantic light, and the need to dispel this is obvious.

The fact that the author, after laying down this sound principle, frequently succumbs to the prevailing tendency, and adds his own quota to the "falsely romantic light," is a further proof of the persistence with which we prefer pictures to portraits where great men are concerned. "Warts and all!" said Cromwell to the artist about to paint his portrait, and that a remark concerned with mere externals should have become historic is significant of the falsity of the attitude of the public in regard to its heroes.

Even biographers who subscribe to the "nothing extenuate" ideal rarely get beyond the theoretical stage. Ries, for example, fell out with Schindler over their proposed collaboration in a life of Beethoven; he courageously maintained that the whole truth should be told, whereas Schindler was for drawing a decent veil. Yet when Ries joined with Wegeler later in a biography, his courage seems to have failed him. There is a good deal to be said for the theory that posterity's concern is with a man's works and not with his private life; but no word can be brought forward in defence of a biographical method that gives us a picture of the man as we think he ought to have been, instead of a portrait of him as he was. The time for biographical haloes is past: we want to know our composers, partly because of our interest in them as fellow-humans, and even more for a fuller understanding of their music. Their work was influenced by their faults as well as their virtues—sometimes an excellence in the music may even have its source in a weakness of the composer, and vice versa. "Warts and all!" should be the motto of the biographer, no less than of the portrait painter—though we must take care that, in our present-day reaction against the whitewashing methods of tradition, the warts do not become boils.

It is true to say that only in very recent years has the personality of Beethoven come to light. During the half century that followed his death there was gradually built up a picturesque figure that subsequent search has proved to be little more than a fanciful sketch of the original. This translation of a very human and fallible being into a kind of demi-god would be easy to understand had Beethoven lived some centuries earlier. Few, if any, authentic records being available, we should be thrown back on legend, and on such deductions concerning his personality as would suggest themselves from a study of his works. The epic grandeur of the best of these, together with their vivid dynamic quality, and their strongly personal and emotional content, would naturally lead us to evolve a Colossus, whose failings (if such there were) would be of the large and picturesque type that are easily condoned in a genius—there would be even a tendency to regard them as a kind of inverted goodness.

But Beethoven lived very near our own time, and there is available an unusually large amount of biographical material. He was a familiar public character all his life. Even in his boyhood he had no mean place in such limelight as was to be had at Bonn, being recognized as something of a prodigy in his eighth year, and becoming more and more prominent in local musical happenings until his departure to Vienna.

The best of his early teachers, Neefe, had recognised his genius, had written about it in the public press and (we may be sure) had not failed to talk about it. In Vienna he quickly made his mark, though as a pianist rather than as a composer; so long as his hearing permitted of successful public appearances as player and conductor (and even after) he was a popular figure on the concert platform; and thereafter, though shut off by his deafness from easy and constant intercourse with his friends, he remained a local lion.

There was never any mystery about his personal traits. Many of his friends, as well as the publishers concerned, were well aware of his dishonesty (there is no justification for using a less frank term than would be applied to similar shufflings by a mere business man); some of his unpleasant personal habits were so publicly exhibited as to become a byword (again it is necessary to be frank concerning demeanour that led folk to avoid his table at the restaurant where he was wont to dine—and those were far from squeamish days); in private he was at least as bad, for Stephan von Breuning's wife, though she bore him nothing but compassionate goodwill, could not bring herself to accept Beethoven's invitations to his house owing to "his domestic arrangements . . . his habit of expectorating in the room, and his neglected clothing." As we have seen, more than one account of his condition in the matter of personal hygiene discreetly draws a veil after a few generalizations. All these faults were of the miserably unheroic type that are far more damning to an artist's fame than violent and lurid breaches of the criminal code.

Perhaps it was the very sordidness of his shortcomings that led to the conspiracy of silence which in its turn brought to birth the Beethoven of tradition.

A frank and conscientious writer on the personality of Beethoven has an ungrateful task. To the laurels earned by the composer, tradition has added a halo for the man. No amount of critical examination can disturb the laurels by more than a stray leaf; but the halo must go. Only the sentimentalist will regret its displacement, for there remains an intensely human figure—a blend of mean failings and great qualities—that presents one of the most engrossing psychological studies in the history of art. To many devout worshippers the unsparing biography of Thayer must have come as a shock. Yet its complete justification is found in the fact that the open-minded reader, a century after Beethoven's death, finds himself at the last page in pretty much the position of the composer's intimates. Like them, he is painfully conscious of Beethoven's lapses; but, also like them (though of course in a lesser degree) he is dominated by the sheer personal power of the man, and won over by sterling qualities that could be fully appreciated only by those who were aware of the terrible handicaps, domestic, mental, and physical, under which the whole of his life's work was done.

It is not difficult to understand how the Beethoven legend was evolved. First, there is the traditional attitude towards the dead—an attitude so inconsistent and illogical that to it may be ascribed most of the obscurities and perversions of history. *De mortuis nil nisi bonum*, we say piously, and proceed to apply the principle to such of the dead as have not shown themselves to be notorious malefactors ; for those that have, there is the Newgate Calendar. Want of frankness in the case of a great man does his reputation nothing but harm in the long run, for sooner or later diaries, correspondence, and similar intimate sources of information begin to point to signs of clay in the idol's feet ; and in the inevitable reaction, fed by rumour and surmise, posterity is apt to see only the clay. In the case of Beethoven, the character of his music naturally suggested a heroic figure, to which his reported utterances on personal and political independence added a few inches ; his physical infirmities (and, above all, his deafness) made a powerful appeal ; his poverty—merely reputed, as we now know—was a virtue in the eyes of a public that likes to think of a genius as being necessarily unappreciated ; and his portraits, the most popular of which exaggerated the rugged and beetling-browed aspects of his physiognomy, added the finishing touches to a figure suggestive of Prometheus, with a dash of Ajax defying the lightning.

Yet the real Beethoven proves to be a far more interesting figure than Prometheus-cum-Ajax. His gifts were his own, and here he moves on a plane shared by few; but his failings were those of the least distinguished and least heroic of the sons of men. Given his parentage and up-bringing, his deafness and all that it involved, and there, but for the grace of God, goes any one of us.

Beethoven was about five feet five inches in height, broad-shouldered and very sturdily built. His head was massive, high and broad of brow, and his hair was abundant. So vigorous was the growth of hair on his face that he shaved up to his eyes; but the operation seems to have been both irregular and calamitous. (Czerny found him with an inch-long beard, and we read of habitual gashes and sticking-plaster). His jaw was big and determined; evidence is conflicting as to the colour of his eyes (they are alternatively described as black, bluish-grey or brown), but all agree as to their brilliance and expressiveness. (The reader will remember the "extremely animated eyes" of grandfather Louis.) He was "very ugly" says Countess Gallenberg (who, as Julia Guicciardi, was one of his conquerors); "ugly and half crazy," says the daughter of another flame—Magdelene Willmann; and this seems to be no more than a crude statement of a fact. But ugliness is little or no handicap to a man. "Since I be so ugly," said du Guesclin, "it behoves that I be bold," and the remark is one that might have come from Beethoven. "What a beautiful brow he has!" exclaimed a doting woman to the company in general. "Well then—kiss it!" said Beethoven, bending the admired brow for the purpose—and not in vain, we may be sure. Certainly he had a way with him, as is shown by Wegeler's remark as to his conquests exceeding those of many an Adonis. As the brow and the brilliant eyes were his only beauties, a good deal must be ascribed to his eager animated manner, concerning which all who came in contact with him are agreed. These attractions must have been considerable in order to outweigh his ugliness, pock-marked face and squat stature, to say nothing of his clumsiness, bad manners (especially at table) and his habit of casually spitting indoors—sometimes even into a mirror, the reflection evidently suggesting an open space suitable for long-range effort.

Much has been made of his radicalism, and no doubt his political bent was in that direction. But the evidence shows that his interest in politics of any kind was, after all, slight, and his fine-sounding democratic principles were promptly thrown overboard when they became between him and his patrons. Nor was it merely an occasional bowing in the house of Rimmon; no composer under the despised patronage system kow-towed more obsequiously than Beethoven, as is shown over and over again in his correspondence. It is amusing to see on what slender bases the legend of his rugged independence has been founded. For example, here is a passage quoted in the introduction to the English translation of Romain Rolland's " Beethoven " :

> Unlike the musicians who went before him, he could brook no dependence upon condescending nobilities. He was not going to be a Court fool. The man who could rush into the courtyard of his really sincere friend and patron, Prince Lobkowitz, and shout " Lobkowitz donkey, Lobkowitz donkey ! " for all the valets and chambermaids to hear . . . must have had something of the devil in him.[1]

Yet what was Lobkowitz's offence ? The third bassoonist being absent from a rehearsal, he had merely tried to placate the enraged Beethoven by pointing out that, as two bassoonists were on the spot, the defection of the third was no great matter. In this episode at least, the " condescending nobility " cuts a better figure than the " independent " composer. The donkey was outside the palace, not inside.

Consider, too, the story of Beethoven and Goethe meeting the Imperial family—Beethoven drawing his hat tightly on his head, forcing his way through the crowd, and ignoring the royal salutes :

> Duke Rudolph raised his hat to me, the Empress bowing to me first. The great ones of the earth know me and recognise me. I amused myself in watching the

[1] *Angels' Wings*, by Edward Carpenter.

procession pass by Goethe. He remained on the roadside bowing low, hat in hand. I took him to task for it pretty severely and did not spare him at all.[1]

Now, had Beethoven consistently maintained this attitude towards royalty, we might have respected the " man's a man for a' that " principle it expressed, though the method of expression might strike us as ill-mannered. But when we set the incident beside such an episode as the touting among all the courts of Europe for subscriptions for the Mass (which, remember, had already been sold) we can hardly be expected to be impressed by Beethoven's radicalism. Yet Rolland describes the Goethe affair with warm approval, saying that " the haughty republican gave the courtly Councillor of the Grand Duke of Weimar a lesson in dignity which he never forgot." To the plain, unbiassed mind, it will seem rather that such dignity as was in evidence was shown by the Duke, the Empress, and Goethe (It is hardly necessary to add that Rolland is silent concerning the " haughty republican's " begging letters " to the great ones of the earth.")

Yet to Beethoven more than any other composer is due the breaking-down of the old system of patronage, and the placing of the creative musician on a footing that, for the first time, enabled him to live by the sale of his works. In regard to the latter point it is hardly too much to

[1] Letter to Bettina von Arnim.

say that the publication of serious and exacting music—especially instrumental—on a large scale, and with lucrative results to all concerned, was made possible by Beethoven. Never before, and perhaps not often since, have publishers "queued up," so to speak, for new works as they did for Beethoven's during the last twenty years of his life. This development alone was of immense significance for the future of the art, for without it a large proportion of the finest music would have remained in manuscript—as indeed was the case with much of Haydn's. The determining factors in any change are necessarily mixed, so it would not be safe to assume hastily (as is usually done) that the end of the patronage system (at all events in its old frank form) was due to Beethoven's independence. For Beethoven himself owed much to patrons all his life, and he never hesitated to make use of them. But he wanted, and obtained, the patronage without undergoing the quasi-servitude that had hitherto been a recognized feature of the system. His attitude on this question was not due solely to his love of independence. Thus, whatever scruples he had were not sufficient to prevent him from accepting from Prince Lichnowsky not only a handsome allowance but quarters in the palace for a considerable time—at least two years, says Wegeler. Why did he leave? Not because he felt there was anything degrading in the position (as indeed there was not) but merely because of his objection to the regular habits and hours it involved. "Every day [he said] I have to be at home at half-past three, change my clothes, shave myself, etc.; I can't stand that." Hence (as we have seen) he preferred to take his meals at an inn, where the time-table was elastic, and where a certain sketchiness in regard to dress, shaving and other amenities would matter little. So he may be said to have "contracted out" in the matter of patronage—which is quite another thing from dispensing with it, as some biographers have credited him with doing. Being able, as he was, to show that a composer could live by composition, he was able to modify the patronage system, once and for all.

Much has been written concerning Beethoven's religion, and it still remains doubtful in quality and quantity, chiefly because his orthodoxy has varied in accordance with that of some of his biographers. Thus, to d'Indy the fervour of the Mass in D is proof that the composer was by way of being a pillar of the Church—a shaky deduction, as is proved by applying it to the unequal and in places flippant Mass of the devout César Franck. Bekker, like d'Indy, takes the Mass in D as the test, saying that Beethoven "has made full avowal of his faith, not in words, but in the music of his great Mass." And he goes on to describe Beethoven's religious beliefs as being "firmly grounded on the root principles of Christian faith, yet free of dogma." He does not explain, however, how "firmly grounded belief" of any kind can be "free of dogma". Perhaps the best clue is found in Beethoven's own remark when pressed by Schindler to define his religion: "Religion and thoroughbass are both things that settle themselves; there is no need to discuss them"—a remark which has a well-known parallel in the replies of an English peer to similar enquiries: "What is your religion?" "That of all sensible men." "And what is that?" "Sensible men don't talk about it." The chances are that both composer and peer hedged thus, not so much from reluctance to define their religion, as from inability. Without attaching much importance to Beethoven's copying out of a few passages from Oriental religious literature, we may describe him as a vague kind of Pantheist with a Roman Catholic label. Towards his end he undoubtedly came nearer to the Church of which his membership hitherto had been little more than nominal. In the course of the legal dispute between Beethoven and Carl's mother for the guardianship, the boy testified that his uncle "prayed with him every morning and evening"; and we learn from Beethoven himself in a Conversation Book of 1820 that he once escorted the lad to the very door of the confessional. ("That will show you what I think of confession," he said.) Nor can the title of the Adagio in the A minor Quartet be overlooked in this connection:—"Sacred Song of

Thanksgiving of a Convalescent to the Divinity ", which was a modification of the title as it appeared in a Conversation Book, " Hymn of Thanksgiving to God," etc. The characteristic comment of d'Indy is worth quoting :

> Et puis, c'est le " Chant de celui qui est revenu à la santé, offrant à Dieu son action de grâces." Nous disons : à Dieu, car, si on considère la nature de la musique, il serait souverainement ridicule de prétendre que cet hymne parfaitement catholique pût s'adresser à un quelconque Esculape !

Certainly there is significance in Beethoven's use of one of the ecclesiastical modes for the Adagio, especially when we note some of his utterances on Church music at this period.

Some people see in his death-bed Communion no more than a passive bowing to convention, and have even regarded his " Comœdia finita est " as a scoffing reference to the ceremony. But on both points the evidence is against them. His grateful words to the officiant have been quoted (p. 174) ; and Schindler says :

> On the day before (the 23rd) there remained with us only one ardent wish—to reconcile him with heaven and to show the world at the same time that he had ended his life a true Christian. The Professor in Ordinary [Wawruch] therefore wrote and begged him in the name of all his friends to receive the Holy Sacrament; to which he replied quietly and firmly (*gefasst*), " I wish it."

With regard to his remark about the Comedy being over, the most reliable evidence points to its having been made on a previous occasion, after the first consultation of the physicians.

Beethoven's violent changes of mood and lack of self-control have been sufficiently manifest in the chronicle of his life. We have seen him coming to blows with his brother, insulting his best friends, throwing a dish of food at a waiter, and generally demonstrating his inability to govern his passions. Without this failing his music would have been wanting in the characteristic that, more perhaps than any other, differentiates it from all the work of his predecessors and that has profoundly affected the art since. From the throwing of a dish of stewed lights at a waiter's head is a far cry to such features as sudden changes of mood, vivid dynamics, the interpolation of detached powerful chords and unisons, and no less arresting silences; but the connection is obvious. No doubt other composers, before and since, have felt like throwing things and have even thrown them; but Beethoven was the first to impose so purely personal (and undesirable) a quality on music, and by its means to enlarge enormously the resources and appeal of the art. It is a commonplace to talk of the defects of a man's qualities, but we are apt to overlook the qualities of his defects—" your pearl in your foul oyster." Hitherto composers had all more or less stood outside their work, and the connection between their music and their personality was merely general. With Beethoven it became particular. To a degree without parallel in music (and perhaps in any art) his work and his character are one. His life has to be written, partly in order that it may be available in chronological form, and expressed in terms comprehensible to those who can hear his music only in part, or at infrequent intervals. But he wrote it himself in his music, and few autobiographies are more vividly convincing—though necessarily diffuse—than that of Beethoven. Chantavoine admirably sums up the autobiographical nature of his work:

> Beethoven est l'homme de toutes les impulsions, même les plus inattendues, des contrastes les plus soudains. Ce caractère, qui rend son portrait si difficile à tracer est celui qui donne à son œuvre tout son accent et toute sa force. Et c'est dans cette œuvre qu'il faut chercher la vraie vie de Beethoven et sa vraie image.

The question naturally rises: if his music is so faithful a reflex of his character, how comes it that the latter has been so misread?

This is a real difficulty with many people, and it is therefore worth while making the attempt to reconcile an apparent inconsistency. The matter is perhaps best dealt with under several heads:

(1) Posterity has inevitably seized on the finest quality of his best work—the heroic passion

which was practically a new element in music—and from it evolved the legendary Beethoven.

(2) The distorted view of all his biographers previous to Thayer has already been alluded to. Inevitably it led people to read into his music some personal characteristics with which he was not liberally endowed.

(3) Certain of his less desirable qualities—for example, lack of self control and coarseness of humour—underwent a sea change during the process of being expressed in music, and, so far as they were read as indications of character, were misleadingly favourable.

(4) As a result of the traditional bias in his favour, many of his inferior works have been far too leniently judged, and his admirers have seen in quite feeble examples the great Beethovenian qualities that they wanted to see. Even distinguished critics seem to be curiously blind to defects where Beethoven is concerned. It would be easy to quote from well-known living critics some extraordinary encomiums on works such as "The Mount of Olives," the Choral Fantasia, the Septet, "Adelaide," and other works which even Beethoven himself decried in his latter years.[1] Obviously, the result of this attitude, persisted in for a generation after Beethoven's death, is an overestimate of the man

[1] It is true that the critical opinions referred to were written about twenty-five years ago; almost certainly the writers would modify them to-day. But this does not affect the point under discussion.

and an undiscriminating judgment of the composer. Moreover, in overlooking this inequality we miss its autobiographical significance.

The third and fourth of these points seem to call for amplification.

First: there is no question as to Beethoven's essential nobility of character. It is as evident as the nobility of his best music. But it is no less certain that this fine character was warped by the squalid circumstances of his early life; the resultant defects and irregularities, accentuated by his temperament, were further developed by his deafness. Some of these irregularities, as we know, so far from adversely affecting his music, actually made for freedom and for an enlargement of its expressive qualities. It is generally agreed, too, that the intensity and absorption of the best of his last works—especially the posthumous quartets—are the result of the isolation brought about by his deafness. Is it fanciful to see in this absorption, this withdrawal into himself, and above all in certain crabbed—even splenetic—passages in the third period works, some reflection of the vein of suspicion and misanthropy that marked his later years? In all music there is nothing analogous to these works in searching quality and personal revelation. Yet, on the whole, with all its beauty and nobility, it keeps us at arm's length: the very inmost door is opened, but rarely more than ajar. The mature Beethoven does not rouse, even in those of us who admire him most, the personal affection that we feel for certain other composers—Bach and Haydn among the great ones, Schubert and Franck among those of the next rank. He can never be "Ludwig" or "old Beethoven" to any of us, as Bach is "John Sebastian" or "old Bach"; and a nickname is as unthinkable in his case as it was natural with Haydn and Franck. In a word, it is a great personality that stands revealed by his best works, but hardly a lovable one.

Beethoven's humour was of the elementary sort that delights in puns and horse-play. His letters are full of the former, and anecdotes abound concerning the latter. Both his conversation and correspondence tended to the Rabelaisian. Of wit he seems to have had none. Here again his music is autobiographical, and reflects this side of his character as truly as it does his violence of temper and his sudden changes of mood. The parallel goes further, for in both cases the characteristics were transmuted in his music.

Just as he was the first to show the possibilities of strong emotional contrast, so he was the first genuine musical humourist. There is geniality in Bach, Handel and Haydn, and (especially in Bach) an abundance of the quality which may be defined as good humour. In Scarlatti, Couperin, and Rameau there are hints of a neat pointedness that are very nearly the equivalent of verbal wit. But it was left for Beethoven to give us in terms of music outbursts of unmistakable humour that make one sit up, and even laugh, and that are irresistible in their blend of gusto, high spirits, and unexpectedness, often touched with the incongruity which is an element of the best fun.

But perhaps the characteristic in his music that more than any other is a reflection of the man is its marked inequality. To quote one of the best Beethoven critics, " compared with many of the great composers, and especially with Bach and Brahms . . . his output is distinctly unequal." In spite of his " supreme feeling for organic structure, he could pen and publish separately, for his own concertos, cadenzas which are mere incoherent meanderings, that no modern pianist with a reverence for the rest of his works would venture to perform."[1]

We do not ask of a creative artist that he shall be always at the peak of his achievement, but we expect him never to fall below a certain level, and even his descents should be manifestly those of genius—working hastily, it may be, or under some other disability, but never meanly. Now, it is incontrovertable that Beethoven, more than any other composer of the first flight, touched the extremes of sublimity and banality. Only occasionally was this the result of haste; more

[1] Ernest Walker, *Beethoven*, p. 184.

frequently it was due to a conscious departure from his own standard. Hence the feeble works bearing high opus numbers—works written in his youth, or abandoned as unsatisfactory and touched up and made saleable later. There is no need to particularize. Every student with any critical sense must have found himself marvelling at some inept movement bearing Beethoven's name—music devoid of the technical skill and mental quality that makes an uninspired work of Bach at least tolerable; or lacking the fluency or high spirits that enable much of the merely casual writing of Handel, Mozart, Haydn, or Schubert to pass muster. Faced with such works as (say) the Fantasia in G minor op. 77, the "Ruins of Athens" music, the "Mount of Olives," or the Triple Concerto, one can only marvel that they should be signed by so august a name. "Did he who wrote the 'Ninth' write *thee*?" we may ask, Blake-wise.

It was said above that these weak works were not as a rule the result of haste. The fact is easily demonstrable, for we have documentary evidence concerning almost the entire output of Beethoven, and we find in it nothing analogous to the well-authenticated instances of rapid production by the four composers named above. And it is significant that his only reference to speedy work (or at all events the only one that readily comes to mind) is his innocent remark when writing one of his worst works (the dreadful *pièce d'occasion,* "Wellington's Victory"), "It is certain that one writes more quickly when writing for the public!" We must look elsewhere, then, for an explanation of Beethoven's extraordinary lapses, and we need not look farther than the motive that led to his shifty dealings with publishers. His nature was an odd blend of generosity and parsimony, and both qualities seem to have led him to publish works that a more consistently stern self-critic would have destroyed. "You see," he said in a letter to Wegeler, in the first flush of his success as a composer, "if I see a friend in need, I have but to sit down and write, and his necessities are relieved." And over and over again he helped himself out of a difficulty by the same easy process. His correspondence with publishers is full of the sheerest huckstering, with lists of wares, duly priced, such an one going cheap "because it is not one of my best works." Clearly, as Ernest Walker says in the book just quoted, "enormously self-critical as he usually was . . . his self-criticism took occasional holidays."[1] His brother and nephew have sometimes been blamed for the publication of certain of the inferior works that were issued in his later years, but Beethoven's attitude throughout in this matter seems to justify the assumption that he was a party to it. He seems to have recognized frankly the distinction between his best works

[1] *Beethoven,* p. 184.

and those written or sold *faire bouillir le pot.* It was perhaps inevitable that the first composer to strike a blow for the independence of the creative artist should also be the first to recognize the pot-boiler's place in the scheme of things. To his credit, let us remember, first, that the pot to be boiled was not always his own, and, second, that his motives often redounded to his honour. His anxiety to make provision for his nephew's future, and the need of ready money while he was engaged on masterpieces over which many months (sometimes years) were spent—these usually explain the "occasional holidays" of his self-criticism. There is thus a clear connection between this bargaining side of his character and the pronounced inequality in his work. It is a reminder, too, that his money-grubbing propensity went hand in hand with (and was in part a result of) his improvidence and his failure to realize the value of money—an apparent contradiction that has its analogy in the common failing known as "penny wise and pound foolish."

Some writers have claimed for Beethoven a wide knowledge of literature and an enthusiasm for intellectual pursuits. The bases for such claims are slender, however. On the other hand, Ernest Newman's description of him as "purely and simply a magnificent musical instrument"[1] is perhaps too sweeping. True, he seems

[1] *Musical Times*, January, 1922.

never to have made up the deficiencies in his early education, if we may judge from badly phrased and sometimes barely coherent letters.[1] In his conversation, however, (and in some of his letters) there is an amount of plain bullion sense and shrewdness indicative of a mind that, better schooled, would have been above the average. And, in the connection, we must not overlook the fact that the production of such works as, for example, the ninth Symphony and the Rasoumovsky and posthumous Quartets calls for an intellect of uncommon energy and quality. Mr. Newman, we know, would be the last to underrate the mental factor in these works—and indeed in all Beethoven's best music. But his epithet is dangerous, because it is apt to confirm the general public in its habitual and flagrant underestimation of composers as compared with other creative artists, especially writers. Justice will never be done until it is realized that the writing of an extended cyclic work calls for a power of invention, a sense of balance, contrast, and proportion, an ability to develop the constituents (or, better still, to give an appearance of allowing them to develop themselves, like the characters in a narrative) and an unerring instinct in the leading to and from a climax, that mark a

[1] It is, however, easy to make too much of this, and even of those death-bed studies in arithmetic. Many a farmhand who is an indifferent performer in the second and third of the three R's does in his daily work a score of tasks requiring a skill of hand and an amount of commonsense beyond a roomful of dapper junior clerks for whom arithmetic has no secrets.

great piece of imaginative literature. There may have been a few inspired idiots among the great composers, though none comes easily to mind. But if ever music was beaten out as much by sheer mentality as by any emotional stimulus, it was the best of that produced by Beethoven in the last fifteen years of his life. Not in Bach himself is there a finer fusion of brain and heart. The mind at work here must have been of such calibre and quality that beside it the mental equipment of many a brilliantly successful politician or business magnate is little more than a well-developed low cunning.

One other side of Beethoven's character (and on the whole the finest) is revealed in the great works of his third period. We have seen him spending several years on the Mass—improving and re-writing till the function for which it had been projected was long past. There is hardly one of his masterpieces that was not the fruit of a similar passionate quest of perfection. This is not a mere matter of experimenting with themes, as in the Sketchbooks.[1] Rather, it is a

[1] Perhaps too much stress has been laid on this side of his methods in composition. After all, every composer worth his salt evolves rather than creates his themes, but much of the process is mental, and if it is done on paper the sketches are rarely kept. Had every composer carried in his pocket a sketchbook, used it at all sorts of odd moments, and (owing to a habit of working at several compositions side by side, and so spreading their completion over a long period) kept the volumes, we should probably find that many an apparently spontaneous theme was almost as painfully brought to birth as the most typical Beethoven examples—*e.g.*, the air "Die Hoffnung" in "Fidelio," of which the sketchbooks give no fewer than eighteen variants.

proof of Beethoven's innate strength and nobility of character. At what a sacrifice were these later masterpieces achieved! There is no reason to regard as overdrawn any of the pictures Schindler and others give of his plight at such times. How his friends found him one day during the composition of the Mass has been told on page 122; and the records contain enough anecdotes of a similar sort to indicate that with scarce an exception his best works were the result of a long struggle, beset with all the discomforts that come from want of proper food, rest, and the ordinary domestic amenities.

The traditional garret and crust are in comparison a trifling inconvenience—indeed, much might be said for them as a healthy regimen and incentive to work. There is irony in the fact that the creative artist who more than any other wrought in a kind of desperation, with physical and mental suffering that affected his health and hastened his end, was so far above the poverty line as to be able to rent a set of rooms (sometimes two), keep at least one servant, and even a horse, and regularly spend his summers in the country. Life could have been easy for Beethoven had he followed up his brilliant success as a pianist with a little aristocratic teaching, and an occasional " best-seller " in the shape of a showy pianoforte piece or set of dances. His crooked financial dealings have to be mentioned as a matter of fact, but before looking round for a stone, let us remember that the very considerable sums he received for the whole of his compositions would probably have been exceeded had he taken the easy line and reaped his harvest as a performer and teacher before deafness shut him off from the concert room. But he not only answered his vocation; he threw himself into the task of giving the utmost that was in him. And of the heavy price he paid perhaps the most bitter part was the sense of ignominy that must have oppressed him at the thought of the questionable means by which he bought the liberty to work at his masterpieces till even he was satisfied. A less perfect result would have been more popular and lucrative. The gain is ours, the loss Beethoven's—loss of health, of length of days, and not least (let it be repeated), loss of honour in a hundred petty transactions easily avoidable by one less faithful in the pursuit of his ideal. The Beethoven of romance may be left to those who prefer the picturesque dummy to the human being. The rest of us will continue to see in the real man, who both in his life and music touched the extremes of greatness and pettiness, one of the most affecting and absorbing figures in history. It was no "comedy" on which the curtain came down on that stormy March day in 1827, but a tragedy—and a tragedy the more poignant because of the squalor of many of its episodes.

PART III

BEETHOVEN THE COMPOSER

A DETAILED discussion of Beethoven's output, or even of any one of its more important sections, is not within the scope of this volume, in which the chief object is the presentation of the composer's life in accordance with the researches of Thayer and other recent writers. Moreover, the series to which it belongs is designed for the general reader rather than the specialist. It would, however, be doing the general reader an injustice to suppose that his interest in Beethoven is confined to the biographical. The ensuing pages will, therefore, aim at a consideration of Beethoven's music. Such a treatment must necessarily be brief, and will be limited as a rule to works that are familiar, or to which reference is easy; and to a few that are at present hardly known to the general reader. By this means it is hoped to show some of the directions in which Beethoven's influence has been, and still is, most marked; and also to indicate directions in which the reader should increase his acquaintance with the composer. At the same time, something in the nature of an appraisement of Beethoven's output as a whole will be attempted. Certain aspects of his work, *e.g.*, his vocal writing, humour, use of fugue, etc.—will also be discussed briefly.

If, as was implied above, the average man is to be credited with an interest in the discussion of purely musical questions, he must of course be prepared for the use of technical terms. This is generally regarded as an obstacle to the popular discussion of the art, but it will be removed when the average man realizes that the amount of labour necessary for the grasp of the fundamentals of music is less than he spends on many of his recreations. As all sorts of helps are now available—talks on the wireless, annotated player-piano rolls, simply-expressed booklets, etc.—the old-time excuses for ignorance no longer exist. Musical discussion that is not merely puerile is impossible without the aid of at least a few technical terms, so no apology is made for their use in the following pages. They will, however, be confined as far as possible to the less abstruse type, and to such as are familiar to the intelligent amateur who regards music as being worth at least as much trouble as bridge or cross-word puzzles.

It is generally agreed that Beethoven's most important contributions to music were on the constructional side. The terms "form" and "construction," when used in connection with music, are looked on with suspicion by many amateurs, who regard them as connoting the mechanical and calculated as against the free and inspired. Yet these same amateurs must often be conscious of the fact that many an otherwise excellent novel is spoilt by faulty construction—a defect that comprises want of balance, clumsy management of climax, lack of variety, and so forth. There have been, and always will be, composers whose fertility of invention has been largely negatived by their weakness in the management of form. Schubert, for example, was one of the most gifted of composers so far as melodic invention was concerned, but he had little sense of design; hence the neglect of his pianoforte works to-day. In song writing there was less responsibility thrown on him, because the poem generally determined the structure. It is said that Schubert, looking at a manuscript of Beethoven, and noting the numerous corrections and re-writings that the composer had found necessary in order to get his climaxes, changes of key and rhythm, etc., in just the right places, shook his head doubtfully, as if to say, "Is all that worth while?" How Time has answered his question we all know. The points that need emphasis here are: (1) There is a world of difference between formalism and a mastery of form; (2) Form, or design, has a beauty of its own in music no less than in the graphic arts, and is as real a source of pleasure as melody, harmony, and rhythm; (3) Beethoven, was, above all, a master of this type of beauty—indeed, few are likely to quarrel with Hadow's claim that "he had the greatest constructive genius of any musician who ever lived—perhaps of any artist except Shakespeare."[1] Consequently, the student who neglects this side of Beethoven misses a constant source of delight and instruction.

It falls out happily for the amateur with a limited library that the best known and most easily accessible of Beethoven's works—the pianoforte sonatas—are a kind of epitome of his contribution to music. Including, as they do, typical examples of his work spread over the period covered by opus numbers 2 to 110—that is, from his twenty-fifth to his fifty-second year—they give us a more comprehensive view of his creative activities than any other branch of his output; and in them are represented practically all his expansions and developments on the structural side of music and almost everything he did in the direction of extending its emotional appeal through dynamic contrast and variety.

It is significant that we need go no farther than the opening page of the first sonata for a striking instance—one first pointed out by Parry, and discussed with masterly insight on pages 263-6 of his "Art of Music." The theme with which the sonata begins is almost identical with that of the Finale of Mozart's G minor Symphony. Let us look at them together: (The Mozart subject is transposed into F minor for greater ease of comparison).

[1] *Beethoven's Op.* 18 *Quartets*, p. 8.

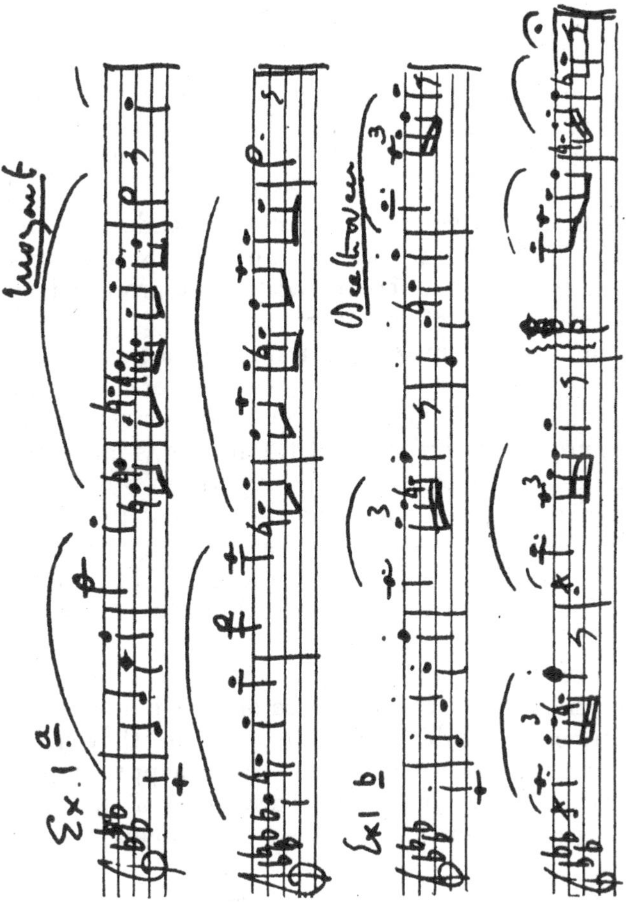
Ex. 1 a.
Mozart
Ex 1 b
Beethoven

Mozart is content to round off the phrase with a conventional cadence (technically known as a half-close in the dominant). His next step is to repeat the opening phrase, this time in the dominant, followed by full close, now in the tonic. The four sections are nicely contrasted and balanced in movement, harmony, texture, and scoring (the wind instruments are added for the two cadential passages). Yet how square and precise the effect compared to that produced by Beethoven's treatment of this simple series of notes! Here, instead of the impetus of the opening figure being checked by a piece of harmonic padding, it is increased by a repetition of the figure a note higher, and the feeling is made yet more urgent by a two-fold repetition of its final bar leading up to a *ff* chord—the first to appear in the right hand, and therefore all the more effective. The climax reached, the music quietens down to a *p*, followed by a silent pause. The harmony in both examples consists of nothing more than tonic and dominant; but note how, whereas Mozart at the close of his eight bars has arrived at a full close in the tonic, Beethoven has left us in a state of suspense. What happens next? Mozart leaves this theme and switches off into four bars of matter that do little more than mark time:

Ex. 2

after which he takes up his opening theme at its fifth bar, and repeats it note for note.[1] Beethoven's plan is very different. His silent pause is followed, not by something fresh, nor, as we might expect, by a kind of answer to the urgent question of his opening eight bars, but by a repetition of the theme, now in C minor, and in the bass:

He asks the question again, so to speak, and increases its appeal by means of the darker tone of the lower pitch. Mere repetition would weaken the emotional effect, so instead of going over the same ground again, he takes the tail-end of the theme and uses it four times while he modulates to E flat, as the dominant of A flat. Even when this latter key is established he does not give us a fresh theme (a "second subject," as it would be called technically). Instead we have a free inversion of the opening theme:

[1] What is said here is not in disparagement of the movement as a whole. Its interest develops later, chiefly through Mozart's treatment of the little conventional figure in bar 5 of the theme quoted above.

so he is still asking the question, with a difference. In fact, the movement has no real second subject. Practically the whole of it is evolved from the opening theme.

The remainder of this sonata foreshadows some of the later methods of Beethoven. Thus, the Adagio, though Mozartean in melody and mood, is more richly laid out than most of the slow movements in Haydn and Mozart's pianoforte sonatas.

The Minuet and Trio shows even more advance, its abrupt contrasts in power, and the emotion of the second half of the Minuet already giving a hint of what Beethoven was to do later when he had found the Minuet form too small for his purpose, and had replaced it by the Scherzo.

The Finale, though its interest droops midway, is nevertheless a powerful movement, with a foretaste of the finale of a later sonata in the same key—the "Appassionata."[1] The melody

[1] This similarity of mood and key is of frequent occurrence in Beethoven's works, and has probably done much to induce and confirm the general association of certain keys and moods, *e.g.*, C minor and F minor with passion and pathos, C major and D major with triumph, G major with felicity, etc.

of the middle section of the Finale under discussion, by the way, is sometimes regarded as a modification of the opening theme of the first movement, quoted above (see Ex. 1):

This may be a mere accident, but such likenesses happen so frequently throughout the sonatas that they may usually be regarded as a deliberate means of ensuring unity.[1] This Finale contains what may well be a further instance: the ascending theme in crotchets in bars 7-8 and the descending one in bar 12 seem to be anticipations of the second subject which begins in bar 34. Thus we see Beethoven, even in the very first of his sonatas, beginning (perhaps unconsciously) to tighten up the form by introducing little touches of relevance between the various sections. Hitherto, even in some of the best examples of Haydn and Mozart, the constituents—first and second subjects, episodes, bridge passages, etc.—had been very sharply defined. The result was contrast, but it was obtained at the cost of

[1] See, as an outstanding example, the Hammerklavier Sonata, in which each movement begins with a rising major third.

unity. As Parry says, "Prior to Beethoven, the development of a long work was based upon antitheses of distinct tunes and concrete lumps of subject representing separate organisms, either merely in juxtaposition, or loosely connected by more or less empty passages."[1] "More or less empty" is, in fact, a kindly term to apply to the typical bridge passage of that period. So vapid was it, and so irrelevant, that it separated rather than connected the main constituents of a movement.

Even in the most mature works of Haydn and Mozart these connecting passages usher in a fresh subject by a repercussion of the dominant chord ("presenting arms," as somebody aptly calls it) that is both amusing and irritating.[2] Beethoven relapsed occasionally into this mechanical procedure throughout most of his life, but he usually saved the result from threadbareness by means of something fresh in the disposition of these parts. In many of his ripest works, however, the material is so continuous and unified that we are barely conscious of the passage from one theme to another. Sometimes the structure is so closely knit that even the searching eye of the analyst is defied. For example, one writer, discussing the structure of the first movement of the Sonata

[1] Grove's Dictionary: Art. *Sonata*.

[2] Wagner described the conventional bridge passages as "the clatter of plates and dishes between the courses of a meal."

in A, Op. 101, describes it as being in sonata-form, and tabulates its component parts. He then adds: "This plan does not conform with all authorities. For example, one starts the second subject with the fourth beat of bar 16; [the analyst quoted is satisfied that it begins on bar 11], another on the last beat of bar 7 (a very difficult view to accept); still another well-known professor told the writer he did not consider there was a second subject at all!"[1] And on the whole, the "well-known professor" is nearest the mark, for if even the close inspection of experts cannot discover an unmistakable juncture between a first and second subject, it seems obvious that there is only one theme. In fact, Beethoven often puts a considerable strain on the terminology of form. Thus, the first movement of the Sonata in E flat, Op. 81a ("Les Adieux"), is clearly based throughout on the opening three notes, G, F, E flat, set to the word "Lebewohl." They are never absent from many bars, and turn up in all sorts of shapes—lengthened, shortened, upside-down, rhythmically changed, etc. The most important of these modifications has to be described as a second subject, though it is only a modification of the first. This movement (one of the most poetic Beethoven ever wrote) is so wonderful an example of unity in variety that the chief forms in which

[1] G. Egerton Lowe, *Beethoven's Pianoforte Sonatas: Hints on their Rendering, Form*, etc., p. 128.

the little thematic germ appears are given below:

Ex. 6. Adagio

This does not exhaust the list, but it will serve to show the reader how far Beethoven had travelled from the sonata-form as he found it. From the start he seems to have been impatient with its restrictions. His method of thematic development called for a scheme of greater amplitude (hence the fact that even among the early sonatas are some longer than many of the Symphonies of Haydn and Mozart), and the structural limitations were ill-suited to music of an intensely emotional character, in which freedom of expression and the element of unexpectedness are factors.

In this connection it is important to realize a fundamental difference between Beethoven's instrumental music and that of his predecessors. Haydn and Mozart wrote mainly for social and recreative purposes. Their music had beauty in balance and design; its mood was usually cheerful, often even frivolous; at other times it merely touched the fringe of melancholy, and then chiefly for purposes of contrast. It was, in fact, music that in its polish and charm, and in its general freedom from violence and the unexpected could at once be listened to and talked through—in other words, *salon* music, though of a beauty and quality hitherto unknown, and perhaps never attained since. But Beethoven, even in his earliest works, introduced disturbing elements. Here was no polite—almost apologetic—background for conversation. Instead there was a monologue, with the composer as speaker. It must be remembered, too, that whereas the bulk of Haydn's and Mozart's music was designed for private performance by Court musicians, that of Beethoven, almost from the first, had the public in view. Music was just emerging from the *salon* to the concert hall, from the patron to the public, and—note again the happy coincidence of the hour and the man—Beethoven, with his forcible idiom and wide human appeal, was the composer most fitly endowed to speak in these larger surroundings and to the new audience.

When Beethoven produced the group of three sonatas, Op. 31, he said to Krumpholz, " In future I mean to compose in a new way." But the remark was late—and not even true, except in regard to the second of these three sonatas, the splendidly dramatic work in D minor. Beethoven had started composing " in a new way " with his Op. 2 ; even his Op. 1 is not without its surprises and novel touches. And this was inevitable. Beethoven's northern origin gave him a tenacity of purpose and depth of feeling that had not found expression in music since Bach. The former quality naturally led him to adopt, from the first, the longest of instrumental forms—the sonata ; and to the latter is due his prompt and continuous development of it both in size and content. He must have found at once that in some respects the sonata form of Mozart and Haydn was unsuitable as a medium for intense or dramatic expression. The problem to be solved is the reconciliation between the exigencies of form, and the freedom demanded by emotion. Thus, a certain amount of recapitulation—even literal restatement—is necessary in a lengthy movement, in order to obtain cohesion and balance. But, generally speaking, repetition—especially of a long theme or a complete section—tends to reduce the emotional level.[1] The reappearance of a theme usually needs to be made significant in some way. If a restatement is exact, the context should be so designed as to throw it into relief, or to reveal some hitherto latent quality; its reappearance may raise—or even lower—the emotional tension; it may provide variety by contrast of key, tone, power or pitch. The one thing it should not appear to be is mere repetition for its own sake.[2] The surest way of avoiding this is to expand or intensify the free portions of the movement (known as the "free fantasia"), and it is here above all that Beethoven shows his supreme mastery. To give examples would involve too much detailed reference and numbering of bars, or the use of music type; an

[1] For example, in Bach's cantata, *Weinen, Klagen*, the opening chorus consists of an intensely poignant movement (later used by Bach for the *Crucifixus* in the B minor Mass) followed by a contrasted section, which in its turn gives way to a complete repetition of the opening. It is impossible to hear this without feeling that the *da Capo* is a bad error of judgment. Neither performers nor hearers can be expected to reproduce, and retain through a lengthy slow section, the emotional state that was easily evoked at the beginning.

[2] An apparent exception is the Rondo, in which regular recurrence of the main theme is an essential feature, and indeed gives the form its name. But even here Beethoven did wonders, expanding the structure and modifying some of its details, so that from being a slight and somewhat rigid form the Rondo became a fit medium for some of his finest inspirations. The reader should compare some early specimens—*e.g.*, the Rondeau in Bach's C minor Partita, or any Rondo from Mozart's Pianoforte Sonatas, with the beautiful example in Beethoven's Op. 90.

examination of any of the best of the sonatas will readily yield instances.

The conventional scheme was: first subject in tonic; bridge passage ("rattling of dishes"); second subject in dominant; short codetta, generally followed by a complete repetition *ab initio*; brief passage consisting of free treatment of material taken from the opening section; return to first subject, now in dominant; bridge passage (dishes rattled again—perhaps a different rattle, but the same dishes); second subject, now in tonic; brief winding-up section, called the coda. The hearer always knew what was coming next.

When music was gradually being developed from the small forms of dance and song, in which one theme and one mood sufficed, this inevitability was no bad thing. Listeners had to be helped through the ordeal of a long movement by regular landmarks and boundaries. Beethoven was fortunate in arriving at a juncture when folk were so thoroughly at home in the sonata form that they were ready (some bold spirits even anxious, perhaps) for a less obvious type of construction. Beethoven achieved this in a variety of ways, *e.g.*, by a great extension of the section in which the themes were discussed (the "free fantasia"), by replacing the cut-and-dried bridge passage with matter derived from the preceding theme or anticipatory of the new one, and by greatly extending the coda in size and significance. Even the recognized number of movements—three—was frequently dropped, and in the character and order of the movements themselves similar freedom was shown. Thus, thirteen of the thirty-two sonatas have four movements, thirteen have three, and six have two. In ten there is no minuet or scherzo, and in two the place of the slow movement is taken by an Allegretto. The choice of keys for the various movements of a sonata is as unconventional as that for the themes in the movements themselves. In a word, there is not one principle of sonata form that was not thrown overboard by Beethoven when it suited the needs of the moment. The matter has been admirably summed up by Dr. Dyson in his book, "The New Music:

> He left thirty-two piano sonatas and nine symphonies, yet the more intimately they are known the less can one hazard even a guess as to what the thirty-third sonata or the tenth symphony would be like. They would be Beethoven, and that is but the statement of a formal enigma. How many movements they would have, and which would be which; what would be the psychological mood of any or all of them either in detail or as a whole; whether the themes would be slight and the handling sublime; whether there would be an orgy of rhythm or a feast of melody, or both; whether they would follow an old form or invent a new one; all these are matters on which nothing intelligible can be said. He would state, in some new and surprising way, ideas which so soon

as they were grasped would seem to be as inevitable as they were unaccountable. We talk somewhat glibly of sonata-form and attach it to the name of Beethoven. There never was a greater deception. It is no doubt possible to extract from his movements two themes and a coda, and to say that here is, or might be, or should be, a double bar, and so forth. But it is often equally possible to extract three or four or five themes, though what will be their order or importance is beyond anyone to lay down. . . . The late sonatas and quartets are admitted to be beyond formal classification. He was descended in a measure from Haydn and Mozart, but it is none the less true that the moment we recognize his models we lose him. The things he himself said were just those that had no place in his inherited architecture. Beethoven is the creative iconoclast.

But the mere enlargement of scope was insufficient—indeed, by lengthening the movements Beethoven increased his responsibility to the hearer. The interest in a long movement must be cumulative, or at least sustained. A wider range of keys, a reduction of mechanical repetition, an increase in the proportions of such sections as the "free fantasia" and coda—these features could do much. Beethoven, however, called on a further constituent—variety and contrast of power. Nuance there had always been, of course, but its range was limited owing to the lack of power in all solo instruments save the organ, and to the smallness of the forces employed for concerted music.[1]

Here again circumstances favoured Beethoven. The delicately tinkling clavichord was just giving way to the new instrument whose very name was derived from its ability to produce both soft and loud tones. The orchestra of Bach—practically a chamber combination—had grown in size and variety, and its dynamic possibilities had been developed considerably by Haydn and Mozart, especially the former. A new factor in musical expression was thus available at the moment when it was needed by Beethoven for the double purpose of expressing his violent and impulsive personality, and helping him to keep the interest alive in the greatly extended forms he was adopting. The reader who has at hand sonatas of Haydn, Mozart and Beethoven, will see that Beethoven is not only far more liberal with expression marks; he is also unusual. Frequently we find a *crescendo* leading unexpectedly to a *p* or *pp*; *diminuendo* and *piano* passages are often interrupted by *sforzandi* on a weak part of the bar; occasionally he surprises us by a demand for a dead level of

[1] Even in the organ the possibilities of contrast were few owing to the clumsy mechanism of the instrument. Until long after Beethoven's day an organist could make no gradual increase from *pp* to *ff*; the power came on in chunks, as the player pushed out sections of stops by means of a lever worked by a strong thrust of the foot. The organist was the only soloist who could rapidly alternate between *ff* and *pp*, by means of two keyboards widely contrasted in power. But this quasi-echo effect (used a few times by Bach, and much more frequently by the early French organ writers) soon palled.

tone—for example, the final eight bars of the Sonata in D, Op. 10, No. 3. It is a pity some editors see fit to add expression marks in such passages as this; Beethoven was so lavish with his indications that we may be sure his abstention for a few bars was deliberate. A similar and even more striking example is to be found in the Finale of the C sharp minor Sonata, —the "Moonlight"—where the rising arpeggio leading to a couple of quaver chords has no expression mark. It is a convention that such passages should be played with a *crescendo*, but Beethoven's desire for an exceptional treatment is clear. The passage occurs in various forms over and over again, but always with the same indication—the arpeggio *p*, and a *sf* on the first of the two chords to which it leads. There can be no question as to the effectiveness of this unusual dynamic scheme, yet so commonly is the composer's intention disregarded that one editor—Casella—feels it necessary to add a footnote: "Each ascending arpeggio *without crescendo*." And he is careful to point out, too, that the *sf* applies only to the *first* of the two chords. This passage is discussed in some detail because it is only one of many instances in which the casual player misses the explosive effect that the composer clearly had in view.

"Explosive": perhaps that word more than any other sums up the dynamic side of Beethoven's music. There had been nothing like it before, and that there has been an overdose of it since is due to the fact that it is easily imitated by composers who can follow Beethoven in nothing else.

Not so easily imitated, however, is another element of surprise and contrast introduced by Beethoven. We saw how in the eighth bar of his first pianoforte sonata he induced a feeling of suspense by means of a silent pause after a questioning chord (page 210). This is an early hint at one of various devices of the kind that he developed and used with tremendous effect. An early and typical example is found at the close of the first and last movements of the Sonata in C minor, Op. 10, No. 1. In the former there is a mere subsidence of power and movement (but no change of pace) on which the two final chords burst with shattering effect. The close of the Finale carries the idea a great deal farther, a climax in the tonic being followed by a quiet modulation to D flat, on the dominant of which is a pause. Then, *calando* and *ritardando*, follows a reference to the second subject in D flat, which ends with a pause on the dominant seventh of that key; a widespread chord of the diminished seventh (ambiguous here, because to the ear the A natural is B double-flat, and so belongs to the key of D flat) is built up deliberately and very softly from the very bottom of the keyboard, and paused on; and from this leaps a six-four chord in the tonic, arpeggio, *ff*, at the original speed—

prestissimo. There is no further change of pace, but the power drops gradually, and the end come eight bars later with an effect of exhaustion. The sonatas contain many examples of this dramatic subsidence followed by a final outburst; and there seems to be no limit to Beethoven's fertility in varying the scheme. It is, of course, only another aspect of the faculty that enabled him to substitute for the conventional close of a movement (a mere "amen," so to speak) a coda sometimes almost as long as the rest of the movement, and frequently the most significant part of the work. Without this gift Beethoven's extension of the existing forms would have led to mere length and tedium. He has no superior—and perhaps no equal—in this respect. Bach could manage the long flight (none better) but his course is generally even, and such growth of interest as is almost invariably achieved at the end is the result of the closer weaving of a polyphonic texture; Wagner could stay the course too, thanks largely to the lessons he learned from Beethoven himself, and even more to the aid given him by the drama; but Beethoven is alone in that his reserve of power and invention at the close of a long and purely instrumental movement is such as to enable him not merely to maintain his level, but to overtop it.

The pianoforte sonatas having been used to illustrate some of Beethoven's developments, this is perhaps a convenient moment to discuss in some detail a point that has been already mentioned—his frequently unsatisfactory writing for the keyboard. Even the casual student of the sonatas must feel aware that the finer they become the less pianistic is the idiom. Great gaps occur between the hands, a muddy clump of notes at the bottom of the keyboard being poorly balanced by a chord at the top.[1] Frequently notes that require sustaining are written in that part of the keyboard where the tone is most brittle. And so on. Various reasons are put forward for this, among others the composer's deafness. This is to suggest that a composer of Beethoven's genius and experience was not equal to realizing mentally the effect of what he wrote! The defect is partly explained by the inherent disabilities of the keyboard itself—some of which were removed by the perfecting of the damper, or so-called "loud" pedal. In regard to Beethoven, however, there is a personal reason which at once presents itself if we compare the latest sonatas with certain of the earliest.

[1] Dr. Dyson's remarks on keyboard writing are too happy to remain unquoted. After pointing out that "the piano thrives on chords, not on counterpoint," he goes on, "The playing of true polyphony is very difficult, and the result often ambiguous at best. Chords are only too easy, within the compass of the hands. And it is a commonplace of criticism that the piano classics are full of crude splashes of hand-music as raw and ugly as anything in the whole history of technique. A thick splash in the bass combined with a thin splash at a remote distance in the treble—this was an accepted formula."—*The New Music*, p. 75.

The C major Sonata, Op. 2, No. 3, for example, contains much writing that is clearly designed for technical display. The B flat Sonata, Op. 22, is another reminder that Beethoven's first success was as a pianoforte virtuoso; and other instances might be given—*e.g.*, the "Waldstein." As his deafness increased and prevented him from playing in public, he naturally became less and less interested in pianistic effect as such. His concern was rather with ideas, and that he found the keyboard less and less satisfactory as a medium is shown by his gradual turning from it to the string quartet—a combination that was particularly suited to the intimate moods of one cut off from orchestral conducting and pianoforte soloising. The idiom of the string quartet is polyphonic, and polyphony plays an increasingly important part in the sonatas. Now, despite the fact that Bach wrote the "Forty-eight" for the precursor of the pianoforte, that instrument is, as we have seen, ill-fitted for the presentation of music in which distinct strands of sustained melody are combined. In the first place, unless the various parts, or "voices," form a compact texture, one pair of hands cannot cover them without the aid of the pedal; the use of the pedal in such music is fatal to clearness, and without clearness polyphony loses most of its beauty. That Beethoven had at an early date acquired the knack of writing good keyboard counterpoint is shown over and over again in the sonatas.[1] He could be compact, too. See the breezy little fugal Presto that ends the early Sonata in F and the passages in double counterpoint in the Scherzo of the A flat Sonata, Op. 26 and in the first movement of the so-called "Pastoral" Sonata. But with Beethoven's growing fondness for the string quartet his keyboard writing, and especially his keyboard polyphony, began to sprawl. The four stringed instruments constitute the most perfect of all media for a contrapuntal texture, and Beethoven's use of it remains one of the marvels of music. No wonder he felt hampered by the necessity for moderating his transports to the limitations of a pair of hands on a keyboard. Hence, as an outstanding example, the tortuous fugue of the "Hammerklavier" Sonata, barely practicable on the pianoforte, and in an idiom suggestive of no particular medium. Indeed, Paul Bekker says that this Sonata and the Diabelli Variations "ought not to be played":

> They are written for an instrument which never existed and never will exist. In these works Beethoven moves in an abstract world of music; he plays not with

[1] It is commonly said that he was a poor contrapuntist, at all events until his later years. But this view seems to be based merely on the familiar stories of his early struggles with the subject under Albrechtsberger. That he had to struggle is true, but it is no less certain that he struggled with complete success, as is seen by the excellence of the polyphony even in his early chamber music. The fact that it rarely "ran on velvet" at any time of his life is not due to lack of technical mastery, but to the character of the thought behind it. The vigour of his counterpoint—above all its frequent touch of asperity—is as characteristic, and therefore inevitable, as is the ease and grace of Haydn's.

> sounds, but with conceptions of sounds, using the language of the pianoforte symbolically. Actual physical tone is but a coarse materialization of the artistic idea, given here to the mind's ear alone. These two works are the most immaterial creations of human art hitherto. We see instrumental art carried to the point of absolute perfection, and carried beyond it by the urge to the immaterial; physical sound is rejected, and an experiment is made with tone abstractions which can only be grasped intellectually.[1]

This is surely going too far. Music is for the ear, as food is for the palate, and we don't want Barmecide feasts of either. The explanation of the impracticability of this sonata as a whole and of detached passages in other works of Beethoven's last years is simple. Even Mr. Bekker himself goes on to admit that "with increasing age Beethoven 'instrumentated' worse and worse both for the orchestra and for the pianoforte." This was partly for the reasons set forth above, and also because of Beethoven's lifelong impatience with technical limitations. Instances of this were mentioned on page 124. Nevertheless, when all is said as to Beethoven's clumsiness and lack of consideration for the player, the fact remains that the splendour of his conceptions is such that his maladroitness is forgotten. The matter is everything, the manner a mere detail.

Perhaps the most astonishing fact concerning the sonatas is that despite their great scope and

[1] *Beethoven*, p. 143.

elaborate structure they remain among the most intimate things in music. And so rich are they in every kind of beauty, and so wide in their appeal, that had Beethoven written nothing else they would be sufficient to ensure his immortality. Musicians sometimes amuse themselves with conjectures as to what work they would choose if cast away on a desert island with one only. Invariably the selection is narrowed down to the "Forty-eight" and the "Thirty-two," and the problem then becomes so acute that most of us would be forced to decide the matter by the spin of a coin.

Apart from the sonatas, Beethoven's pianoforte music contains little of importance. There are many sets of variations, but only a few written in his maturity, such as the wonderful "Diabelli" group,[1] are of interest to-day. A few of the later Bagatelles are worthy of their composer; the remainder, like the numerous detached pieces—dances, rondos, etc.—merely remind us that Beethoven was rarely able to work successfully in miniature. His great strength lay in construction and thematic development—features which call for ample space—and only in some modification of the sonata-form could he give of his best.

[1] This masterpiece had a curious origin. About the year 1823, Diabelli composed a waltz, and asked a number of composers to write each a variation on it. Beethoven was among those invited to contribute. Instead of sending one variation, however, he produced thirty-three, which were published by Diabelli as a separate set.

§

A symphony being merely a sonata for orchestra, there is no need to say much concerning Beethoven's developments on the structural side of that form. Practically all of what was said on this aspect of the sonatas applies to the symphonies, though, of course, as the scope was larger, the developments are on a scale of architectural grandeur rarely possible (or perhaps even desirable) in a work for solo instruments.[1] Beethoven's symphonies are so familiar that they need not be discussed separately. It must suffice to treat of them in bulk, with special reference to their character and instrumentation.

Beethoven's output for the orchestra contains at least half-a-dozen of the most popular works ever composed for that medium. Volumes have been written on the symphonies alone, and the details concerning their origin, instrumentation, construction, and interpretation, have been set forth with a care and elaboration given to no group of compositions by any other composer. There must be some unique quality in works that have thus provoked the closest thought and discussion in so many and diverse types of critic. In this matter of universal commentary, the only obvious analogy is that of Shakespeare, and the fact at once indicates the quality by virtue of

[1] If the "Hammerklavier" Sonata, for example, is a magnificent failure (as is sometimes said), the fact is due chiefly to its being too big for its medium.

which the symphonies have made and retained their extraordinary hold over generations of musicians of practically every degree of learning and standard of taste. For in the symphonies, as in the plays of Shakespeare, there is something for everybody, and apparently for every period. Argument as to which is the greater, Bach or Beethoven, is fruitless, because both are so indisputably great in different ways. It is sufficient to recognize that both possess above all composers, and to a degree rarely equalled by any other creative artists beside Shakespeare, this quality of inexhaustibility.

The symphonies are sometimes described as nine mountain peaks, standing out above all other works of the kind. This is typical of the uncritical attitude that does a composer's reputation nothing but harm. No composer—least of all Beethoven—is always at his best. If he were, as Sir Henry Hadow points out in discussing a bad lapse of Beethoven,[1] he would have no best. Can it be denied that the interest of No. 1 is almost solely historical? Is No. 2 much better, judged strictly on its merits? It is easy to see in both works portents of the splendours that were to come, but only because the splendours *did* come. Had Beethoven stopped at No. 2, we should feel bound to confess that for a composer of over thirty years of age, with a good list of fine works already to his credit, they were of no great merit. For

[1] "*Beethoven's Op.* 18 *Quartets*," p. 55.

every one of the novel touches in them we could find two in the best symphonies of Haydn and Mozart, plus (in Haydn especially) a surety in handling the orchestra that Beethoven never acquired.

There are not nine peaks, then, but four (Nos. 3, 5, 7, and 9) with a delightful eminence (No. 8) and pleasant foothills in the remainder. Of these No. 1 is scarcely discernible from the plain, and No. 6, the "Pastoral"—a dreadful decline and fall from No. 5—would be a depression but for the idyllic atmosphere of its opening and the genuine humour of the Scherzo.

It is natural that the first symphony should show some signs of the unpractised hand. At the time of its first performance (1800) Beethoven had written about a third of the pianoforte sonatas, and a fair number of chamber works, including the set of string quartets Op. 18. Despite its characteristic touches, the first symphony is not on a level with the bulk of these other works, especially in regard to originality of idea. Beethoven had to acquire the mastery of the symphony, and even to some extent of the orchestra itself. His instrumentation shows, on the whole, no advance on that of Haydn and Mozart, both of whom had carried this branch of the art much farther than any of their contemporaries. The increased significance Beethoven gave to various members of the orchestral family was to a large extent the inevitable result of the great emotional intensity of the music itself. It was inevitable, too, that from the first he made the most of the dynamic possibilities of the brass and tympani. In fact, it may be said that his developments in orchestration were not the outcome of experiments in instrumental tone colour for its own sake, but the natural correlative of the idea he happened to be expressing. This is the reverse of the process of some later composers—Berlioz, for example—who seem rather to devise an orchestral effect, and then concoct a passage for its exploitation. The present-day hearer who, finding much of Beethoven's orchestration primitive and bleak, subscribes to the suggestion sometimes made as to the symphonies being re-scored, fails to realize that much of their strength and hard-wearing quality is due to this unity of conception. Both idea and scoring have a common origin, and the frequent starkness and occasional gleams of tenderness are a true reflection of the composer's personality. A re-scored No. 9, for example: what a gorgeous edifice of sound an Elgar would make of it! But it would not be Beethoven. Less austerely garbed, that tremendous opening movement would lose both in stature and strength.

In another category are the occasional bad balance and some of the ugly effects due to the limitations of the brass instruments for which Beethoven wrote. In regard to the former, two possible explanations are given: (a) the constitution of the orchestra in Beethoven's time, in which the proportion of strings and wind was different from that of to-day; and (b) the composer's deafness. There is not much in either reason, especially the latter. The likeliest cause is that alluded to on a previous page—Beethoven's preoccupation with the idea rather than with the medium.

The uncomfortable—sometimes even hideous—effect of the undue stressing of tonic and dominant by the brass (*e.g.*, in the Finale of the seventh Symphony) makes one wonder why Beethoven, usually so intolerant of technical restrictions, did not at times boldly disregard the limitations of the old "natural" trumpet and horn, and trust the manufacturer and player to rise to the occasion in due time. He would not have had to wait long, for inventors were busy with valve trumpets and horns long before his death, and the instruments began to appear in full scores soon after. We might thus have been spared the comparative ineffectiveness of passages where Beethoven, modulating to a distant key, has to drop the brass till his return home. The result is a lack of power when a climax occurs in a remote key, and too sudden a burst when the brass is resumed. Yet these limitations, like the occasional ineptitudes, in the long run bear witness to the greatness of the music. There could be no severer test than the frequent performance the symphonies receive to-day, when we are accustomed to orchestral effects that in richness and variety of colour, and magnificence of sound, exceed anything Beethoven could have imagined. Beside this opulence his most lavish pages look meagre, and, in a sense, sound so. Yet the best of the symphonies and overtures remain standing dishes. We cut, and cut, and come again as we do to little else in music. Once more a parallel with Bach suggests itself: in the instrumental works of these two men there is enough plain living and high thinking to cure all our present discontents, with a good margin left for those round the corner.

Although we talk of "The Nine," there are really ten, and there might have been a round dozen. In 1809 there was discovered at Jena a symphony in C, undoubtedly by Beethoven. It was published two years later by Breitkopf and Härtel. Clearly it was a very early work, owing much to Mozart, and even less mature than No. 1. It received a few performances at the time of its discovery, but has since gone to its own place—the shelf.

About the year 1815 Beethoven made sketches for a symphony in B minor; and at the time of his death he had definitely started on a No. 10, in C minor. The sketch promises an opening far less arresting than that of No. 9. Beethoven's peculiar gift for producing a masterpiece from an unpromising sketch makes one cautious in surmises of this sort, but it seems very probable that the alternation of peaks and foothills (1, 2, 3, 4, 5, 6, 7, 8, 9) would have been continued. Moreover, the Choral Symphony, like the B minor Mass, clearly marks the culminating point in its particular direction.

Fine symphonies have been written since the Ninth, but all have stopped well on this side of it. Not only has there been no Tenth: it is extremely unlikely that there ever will be. For Beethoven's last Symphony was the product of a combination of factors that can never occur again. It would not be sufficient for the future to throw up another composer of equal genius; certain circumstances, personal and social—especially personal—must be reproduced as well. The first movement and Scherzo of the ninth Symphony and the posthumous quartets bear on every page the marks of a terrible concentration hardly possible save in one shut off from the world of sound. Beyond a doubt, this splendid fruit of Beethoven's genius owes much to his affliction; one is tempted to suggest that composers should not only be kept reasonably poor: they should be made deaf as well.

The best of the overtures—"Coriolan," "Egmont," and the "Leonora" group—are worthy companions of the symphonies. They may be enjoyed without reference to the operatic or other bases. Yet, satisfying as they are as pure music, there is drama on every page. They exemplify one of the most remarkable of Beethoven's inconsistencies. "Fidelio," "The Mount of Olives," and the songs as a whole, show that his dramatic sense was hampered by a text. On the other hand, he has no equal in conveying by means of purely instrumental music a sense of drama. Nor is the drama that of mere emotional crises: often there is an impression of actual incident as well.

The "song without words" has long been a popular form of small instrumental solo. Beethoven gave us the thing itself, long before the name was invented. There are no more eloquent songs without words than the dozens merely labelled "Adagio" and "Andante," scattered about among the sonatas and chamber music. He went farther, however, and in the overtures and symphonies he wrote dramas without words, and sometimes without plots. In many movements—*e.g.*, the first and the Scherzo of the C minor (and above all in the passage from the Scherzo to the Finale), the Allegro and the Funeral March of the "Eroica," the Allegretto of No. 7, and in all the Choral Symphony except the Adagio—this sense of the momentous is constantly present. Real beings seem to walk some shadowy stage in the background, and real things to happen, though beings and things vary with the hearer. No doubt this quality has led to the saddling of his music with so many programmes—

mostly ridiculous. (This point is discussed later.)

It is important, however, to note that the dramatic quality is almost certainly a by-product of his unique constructive skill. Many composers before and after his time have given us wealth of detail, and some—though fewer—have done miracles in the opposite direction.[1]

In all his finest works Beethoven combines these extremes as few others have done before or since his day. As was said above, the secret lay in his genius for construction. It is the first of his two essential qualities, the second being intensity and vigour of expression.

As a result of "his supreme mastery over the whole architectonic scheme of musical design, not only is the balance perfect—it is often perfect in Haydn and Mozart—but it attains its perfection through a fullness and wealth of detail which in their best work they never commanded . . . every bar, every phrase is relevant to the main issue, and the canvas is crowded with figures and incidents all significant and all indispensable. To let the mind flag for a moment is to risk losing some point of vital importance: the actor who crosses the stage may be carrying

[1] See, for example, the completeness of the harmonic implications in works so widely dissimilar as the countless movements in two-part harmony by Bach, and Morley's Canzonets for two voices. To the eye, such things are the bare bones of music, yet the indispensability and exact rightness of every note make the effect more full and satisfying than the fattest chords of the unskilful.

the key of the plot, the modulation thrown out with studied carelessness may be the explanation of the whole organic scheme."[1]

Clearly the writer of this passage was influenced, though perhaps unconsciously, by the dramatic quality discussed above. And his reference to the crowd of figures and incidents reminds us that perhaps we have to look to literature for the best analogy of certain of the finest movements of the mature Beethoven. Over and over again they suggest the lavish profusion of a Shakespeare or a Dickens, controlled by the compactness and concentration of a Bacon.

And the more we realize this intense relevance, the more we see that the Beethoven orchestra —grey and incomplete as it seems to us to-day —is the right medium for the music. An increase of colour would no doubt please the ear, but it would also lure that all-too-easily-distracted member from essentials. With Beethoven, as we have seen, the thing said matters more than the manner of speech, and half his message is missed unless we join him in putting the idea first and the medium a long way after.

§

Beethoven wrote five pianoforte concertos,[2] one for violin, the Triple-Concerto, Op. 56, for violin, violoncello and pianoforte (one of his

[1] Hadow, *Oxford History of Music*, v. 276.

[2] There are also two youthful efforts now rarely or never heard.

worst works, and therefore very bad indeed), besides several pieces for violin and orchestra. The level is lower in this part of his output than in the symphonies or the pianoforte sonatas, chiefly because a good many of the movements date from an early period, and none from his ripest years. The form itself is also responsible to some extent, because it attempts what is practically impossible in the combination of two factors—soloist and orchestra—whose interests are essentially opposed. Indeed, we might now say three factors, for the orchestral conductor of to-day is as much a virtuoso as the pianist. These personal and communal elements never really blend, and the average audience is perhaps not altogether wrong in refusing to regard a concerto as anything more than an unusually opulent solo with an expensive and frequently distracting accompaniment. Moreover, as Hadow says, there is the problem of disposing the unequal forces of soloist and orchestra "in such a manner as to secure for each its due measure of interest and beauty, to prevent the larger from being artificially subordinated, or the smaller absorbed through sheer weakness of tone."[1]

The E flat pianoforte Concerto (known as "The Emperor," but not so named by Beethoven) retains its popularity, owing chiefly to its opportunities for keyboard display, and also to an undeniable spaciousness. Its unauthorized

[1] *Oxford History of Music*, v. 243.

but not inappropriate label is also an aid to popularity. So far as actual musical value is concerned, however, most musicians would probably place above it the delightful No. 4 in G major. The relative value of the two works is shown by the fact that there is unanimity concerning No. 4, whereas musicians are divided concerning the "Emperor." Pianoforte enthusiasts revel in the latter, but to many of the rest of us the work smacks too much of a scale and arpeggio primer *in excelsis*.

About six years after the composition of the "Emperor," Beethoven made considerable progress with a pianoforte Concerto in D. It promised so well that it would probably have eclipsed its predecessors, and we can only account for its non-completion by the fact that owing to his enforced retirement from the rôle of concert pianist Beethoven lost interest in a form which existed chiefly for the exploitation of virtuosity.

The violin Concerto in D is as great a standby to the violinist as the "Emperor" is to the pianist, with the further claim of being better music.

Beethoven's sonatas for violin and pianoforte, and violoncello and pianoforte, are as a whole below those for pianoforte in quality and level of interest. There are two principal reasons for this. First, only two of the sonatas (the pair for violoncello and pianoforte, Op. 102) were written in his last period; second,

Beethoven was as a rule less happy in this type of work than in the sonatas for pianoforte alone. The problem of catering for two virtuosi, and at the same time of producing a good ensemble and a balance of interest throughout, is not always solved. Moreover, the needs of the sonata form involve the delivery of a good deal of the material by both soloists, and inevitably many themes that suit the keyboard are less satisfactory on the stringed instrument, and vice versa. This, of course, is an inherent disability of the type, and it is only overcome when the musical worth of the material throughout is so high that an occasional lack of suitability to the medium is scarcely observed. This is not often the case in Beethoven's duo-sonatas, because most of those for violin were written rather hastily for the use of eminent players, and so the element of display had to be considered, even at some cost in musical value. The five works for violoncello are on the whole more successful, partly because of the expressive character of the instrument, and also because its tenor compass would enrich the middle of the texture, and so allow of the increased variety obtainable by a liberal use of the extremes of the keyboard instrument.

Fine movements there are throughout these fifteen sonatas, and one or two are successful wholes, but it cannot be said that they show us the best of Beethoven save in glimpses.

His other duo-sonatas for various pairs of

instruments, mainly for pianoforte and flute, are almost negligible. As a curiosity may be mentioned a sonatina for mandoline and pianoforte—surely as unpromising a combination as could be devised.

There is also a considerable mass of works—duos, trios, etc.—for various combinations of wind instruments, mostly dating from his early period, and containing little of interest.

With the trios for pianoforte, violin, and violoncello, however, we step on to another plane. Here was a medium that from the first proved congenial. The addition of an extra instrument removed much of the virtuoso element that was almost inevitably prominent in the duo-sonatas; and the possibilities in the direction of richness of tone and texture were very largely increased. High, low and middle registers were present on both stringed and keyboard sides; the form was definitely one of ensemble rather than of a solo shared between two performers; and as a result the interest could be more easily maintained at a high level. In spite of all that may be said against the use of pianoforte with strings on the ground of the unblending effect of the keyboard instrument, the pianoforte trio has proved itself to be a highly effective medium. It is significant that even in the three Trios of his Op. 1, Beethoven at once reached a high level; Op. 97, (the "Archduke") is one of Beethoven's finest works; and almost, if not quite, in the same class are the two trios (D and E flat) that make up Op. 70.

Beethoven's natural genius for string writing was shown very early in the Trios for violin, viola, and violoncello, Opp. 3, 8 and 9. The medium is a difficult one, owing to the risk of the texture lacking "body." But Beethoven surmounted the obstacle with ease, and with results that are still delightful. Curiously, he returned no more to this type of work, perhaps because he found the string quartet a far more satisfying medium for the ideas of his maturity.

But with a few outstanding exceptions, such as the "Archduke," all these chamber works,[1] good as many of them are, seem to be comparatively unimportant when placed beside the string quartets. In every respect—thematic invention and development, richness of polyphony and harmony, depth of thought, mastery of construction, intensity and intimacy of expression—the quartets show the sum of Beethoven's power as they are shown in no other part of his work—not even in the symphonies. It happens that they were composed in three groups which represent more fully than any other department of his output the "three periods" concerning which a good deal has been written. Indeed, so much has been made of this triple division of his creative life that one would

[1] This term, of course, includes all the sonatas for two instruments of any kind, of which Beethoven wrote about forty.

imagine it to be a phenomenon peculiar to Beethoven, whereas it represents the normal stages through which every creator, be it in literature, music, or any other art, must needs pass, given anything like the allotted span of life. First comes the period when even the most gifted composer imitates the models of his predecessors; then the stage when, the models assimilated, the lessons learned, his originality can work freely (this second period is also of course the heyday of his physical life when emotional and other stimuli are most powerful); finally comes the age of reflection, wisdom, and experience. These three periods are sometimes only vaguely indicated; there must be occasional overlapping, and the transition is sometimes so gradual as to set up something more nearly corresponding to Jacques's "Seven Ages of Man." Moreover, in the case of Beethoven's work as a whole the boundaries are apt to be obscured by his habits of working at several compositions simultaneously over a long period, and of taking up and finishing a work sketched many years before. But the three groups of string quartets exemplify the "three-period" idea with a clearness that has probably no equal in the work of any other composer.

Beethoven wrote sixteen string quartets. The first six (Op. 18) date from 1798 to 1801. They contain many delightful pages, with originality shown in occasional touches rather than in thematic invention generally; and there is admirable finish in workmanship. Incidentally a study of these Op. 18 quartets makes one wonder how musicians could have regarded Beethoven as a poor contrapuntist. There is no more severe test of a composer's mastery of polyphony than the string quartet, and in these, his first essays, Beethoven passes with ease. The faults of the Op. 18 are decidedly not those of any department of workmanship. As was implied above, there is no remarkable power of invention, nor is there much depth of thought or feeling. In a word, the Op. 18 group is best appraised by remembering that its composition belongs to the period that gave us the first Symphony, the early pianoforte Concertos in B flat and C (now rarely heard), the "Mount of Olives" (also deservedly neglected to-day), and the "Pathétique" Sonata. All these diverse works show the blend of discipleship, promise, and immaturity, that belong to first period work.

The assured composer, with a message of his own, and fully equipped for its delivery, is revealed in the next group, the three great works known as the Rasoumovsky Quartets (Op. 59). These, with the E flat Quartet (Op. 74), called the "Harp" on account of the frequent pizzicato arpeggio passages, and the F minor Quartet (Op. 95), cover roughly the period from 1807 to 1810, and are among the cream of the "second period" works. In mood and style, however, the F minor Quartet foreshadows the group of five masterpieces which belong to Beethoven's last years—the Quartets in E flat (Op. 127), B flat (Op. 130), C sharp minor (Op. 131), A minor (Op. 132), and F major (Op. 135).[1] Of these five only the E flat work was published during Beethoven's life.

Round the last five quartets (especially the C sharp minor) there has grown up a tradition of obscurity. No doubt the public of Beethoven's day found some difficulty in them, partly because of their departure from the usual three- or four-movement sonata form,[2] their intensity of thought, their introspective and swiftly changing emotion, and above all, perhaps, by reason of a harmonic freedom—even roughness—that resulted from the vigour and unconventionality of the polyphony.[3] Yet the present-day hearer who is accustomed to modern music will wonder at the persistence of this reputation for obscurity. Indeed, it is more than likely that such a hearer will at once feel that

[1] The *Grosse Fuge*, which originally formed the Finale of the B flat quartet and was afterwards published separately as Op. 133, will be discussed later.

[2] The C sharp minor Quartet contains seven movements; the B flat six; the A minor, though nominally in four movements, contains several sub-sections as important as sonata movements of normal length. In fact, it is difficult to define the number of movements in some of Beethoven's greater quartets.

[3] It is worth noting, however, that the first of the set, the E flat major Quartet, was received with enthusiasm, and given six performances in a few months—a tribute to the discernment of the public of that time, even when it is admitted that this quartet is comparatively straightforward.

here, if anywhere, is the Beethoven with a message not only for to-day, but for a long series of to-morrows.

The last quartets have always been among the least familiar of Beethoven's works, for obvious reasons. Their technical and interpretative difficulties have restricted their performance; and the type of concert at which these scattered performances were heard has always been that attended by a small proportion of the general musical public. Happily, the gramophone, the broadcast concert, and the player-piano[1] have now brought them within everybody's reach. It is to be hoped that the hosts of people who are making a first acquaintance with these masterpieces will not allow themselves to be bothered by the alleged " obscurity " mentioned above. Of course, no music worth the hearing yields all its secrets at once. This truism is so harped on, however, that there is some danger of our thinking that such music has nothing to say to us at a first hearing. The very reverse is the case—indeed, we might almost go so far as to deny merit to a work that begins by holding us completely at arm's length. The essential difference between good and bad music is not in immediate appeal. So far as this quality is concerned, there is a wealth of classical music so rich in melodic and rhythmic attractiveness that it is able to capture the lay ear as readily as the most alluring

[1] In reproductions of four-handed pianoforte arrangements.

vulgarity. The hall-mark here, as in everything else, lies in durability. The better the music, the longer we can live with it; and in all music there are few works to which the word "perennial" may be so truly applied as to these last works of Beethoven.

Adequate discussion of the sixteen string quartets would call for nothing less than a volume—indeed such a work has recently appeared.[1] But, as was said above, guidance of the sort is not indispensable. The music tells its own tale—not all at once, and not always in the same way. Indeed, the tale itself may vary with the mood of the hearer. No doubt this elusiveness and variability has been partly responsible for the reputed obscurity of the last quartets. So sudden are the changes of mood, so unusual the structure at times, that we feel there must be a "programme," lacking which we miss the significance of the music.

Some critics are so much concerned with the strangeness of certain of the late quartets—the C sharp minor especially—that they regard them as signs of a transition stage. Beethoven, they think, was about to enter on a fourth period, and they hold that the quartets show the composer feeling his way towards new means of expression.

[1] *Les Quatuors de Beethoven*; Joseph de Marliave. (Paris: Felix Alcan) pp. 406; 322 music-type examples.

The early quartets are very fully discussed by Sir Henry Hadow in *Beethoven's Op.* 18 *Quartets*. The Oxford Press.

But are not the " new means " already there? Beethoven had evidently found the customary quartet cycle of movements insufficient for his purpose. We may imagine him casting round for something to put in its place. Would not the old suite form seem to present possibilities? Its sequence of half a dozen or so short contrasted movements gave rise to the sonata, contrast being effected partly between the three movements—quick, slow, quick—and partly in the contents of the movements themselves. But the sonata had proved too small a medium. Its three—or at most four—movements had to be lengthened unduly in order to contain all that Beethoven wished to put in it, *e.g.*, the great B flat pianoforte Sonata. The framework of the suite would give him all the scope he wanted. The various movements could be lengthened, some of them connected, and for the contrasted dances that had formerly filled the original framework could be substituted movements in which far more vivid contrast could be provided—a contrast of mood as well as of mere pace and rhythm. This is only conjecture, but it is at least as probable as the theory that Beethoven was groping his way towards something new. The composer of the ninth Symphony and the Rasoumovsky Quartets was hardly likely to " grope "! Curiously hesitating passages abound, it is true. For example, at one point in the first movement of the B flat Quartet are six changes of time-signature and speed in the short space of nine bars. But need we regard such things as signs that Beethoven was in any way at a loss? Are they not further developments of a device he employed in some of his earliest pianoforte sonatas?[1]

Beethoven, we know, regarded the C sharp minor Quartet as the best of the group. He said, "You will find a new manner of part-writing; and thank God there is less lack of fancy than ever before." This was undoubtedly a reference to the polyphony of the opening fugue, which was that of the organ rather than of strings. But probably the term "fancy" has to do with the structure. For its seven movements, all vividly contrasted and intended to be played without break, represent a striking fusion of suite, sonata, and single-movement forms. But we must meet the composer half-way. To the hearer who listens with a "sonata ear," so to speak, the Quartet is apt to sound scrappy—though such a word is curiously out of place when the "scraps" comprise such things as the profound and heartsearching fugue ("the most melancholy movement in all music" Wagner called it), and the passionate and powerful final Allegro.

In considering this development of the suite form, two points have to be noted. First, it is foreshadowed in the Op. 59 Quartets: and,

[1] See page 225.

second, a scheme somewhat similar to that of the last quartets is found in the Divertimenti of Mozart, wherein the number of movements varies from four to ten. But the music in the Mozart works is very slight in texture and emotional significance, and contrast of any kind (sometimes even that of key) is lacking. Beethoven was probably more familiar with the Divertimenti than with the ancient suite from which it descended, and may well have seen in it possibilities ignored by Mozart.

BEETHOVEN AND THE FUGUE

In these last quartets, in the C major of Op. 59, and indeed in many other works of his maturity, we see Beethoven making liberal use of the fugue form. It is true that his complete fugues are few in number, but among these few are some tremendous examples, and his use of the form altogether is so individual as to call for a brief discussion.

It will be remembered that in his prime as a pianist he excelled as a player of the "Forty-eight," and to the influence of Bach thus assimilated may be ascribed the habit of introducing brief fugato sections into his works. Thus the Finale of his pianoforte Sonata in F, Op. 10, No. 2, is an excellent fughetta, or free fugue; and the slow movement of his first Symphony opens fugally. One of the most impressive moments in the "Eroica" Funeral March is a fugal section; and so on. Various explanations have been put forward to account for Beethoven's increasing use of fugue during the last years. The fact of the Finales of the A major, B flat, and A flat pianoforte Sonatas suggests to some writers that Beethoven adopted the form because he saw in it an ideal means of expressing the triumph of will. For example, Paul Bekker carries this theory to its extreme limits when, discussing the "Grosse Fuge," he says:

> "The ideas of Freedom and Necessity are blended by Beethoven in his Fugue, upon which he wrote 'Tantôt libre, tantôt recherché.' The inscription is more than a note on form; it is the poetic 'programme' of the movement, indicating the reconciliation of the two great opposites of Freedom and Necessity which here find symbolic expression."[1]

We may ask, as was asked concerning Burleigh's shaking of his head in *The Critic*, "The devil! did he mean all that?" Surely the simplest explanation is the likeliest. Is not the inscription analogous to that over the Fugue in the B flat pianoforte Sonata—"Fuga . . . con alcune licenze"? And the "recherché" labels it as a *ricercare*—a "sought out" fugue, and the biggest ever written.

It is more likely (as d'Indy suggests) that Beethoven's preoccupation with the fugue form

[1] *Beethoven*, p. 332.

was merely one manifestation of his third period tendency to return to such traditional forms as the fugue, the suite (as in the structure of the last quartets) and even the figured-choral (see the slow movement of the A minor quartet, the second subject of the third movement of the F Minor quartet Op. 95, etc.). The clue to the immense and unusual fugues of Beethoven lies in the second half of a remark made late in life to Holz: "To make a fugue requires no particular skill; in my student days I made dozens of them. But the fancy wishes also to exert its privileges, and to-day a new and really poetical element must be introduced into the old traditional form." If Beethoven's are "splendid failures," (as they have been so frequently called) it is probably because of a lack of unity. The "poetical element" is usually there, but it is too often overwhelmed by the "old traditional form." Beethoven might talk of his "licence" as a fugue writer, but in fact he is rather more academic than Bach—or, rather, he allows the academic element to become more obtrusive. Sometimes, indeed, there is little else, *e.g.*, the fugue that closes the Violoncello Sonata, Op. 102, and the Fugue in D for String Quintet. In gnarled, dry roughness it would be hard to find the equal of these. There is not a touch of feeling or relief of any kind. Here we see perhaps Beethoven's chief weakness as a fugue writer. He seems to undervalue the true fugal episode (relief and relevance in one) to which we owe some of the most delightful moments in the "Forty-eight." Evidently, like the post-Bach generation as a whole, he was blind to the poetry in Bach. For him, the introduction of the "poetical element" meant something that in mood and style was analogous to the second subject of the sonata form. But the essence of the fugue lies in its unity and continuity, and the genuine poetry that marks a fine example results from the presentation of a theme under varying aspects. Most of the modern romantic school of pianoforte music (from Schumann to the crowd of Russian composers with their unending stream of preludes) has this in common with the fugue—that its effect is obtained, not by the contrasting of material, but by making the utmost of the emotional possibilities of a single theme. The dramatic element in the ground bass was probably recognized very early, in spite of the fact that it owed its origin to the ease with which it enabled a composer to obtain variety in unity.[1] Hence Purcell's use of it for some of his most expressive songs—*The Evening Hymn*, *Dido's Lament*, *The Elegy on Mr. John Playford*, etc. And present day audiences of every sort subscribe to the dramatic power of the "ostinato" or "ground

[1] As the early composers were usually organists, the popularity of the various members of the ground bass family was probably due in part to the facility with which the "ostinato" could be played on the pedals.

bass" every time they hear Rachmaninov's well-known prelude, in which the principle of insistence is carried out in harmony as well as in theme.

Beethoven's interruption of his fugues by the interpolation of some entirely fresh matter (*e.g.*—the *una corda* passages of the "Hammerklavier" Fugue) or a recapitulation of material from a previous movement (as in the Arioso quotations in the A flat pianoforte Sonata fugue) may have meant much to him, but most hearers are conscious of little more than an interruption of the main stream. In the "Grosse Fugue" Beethoven gets nearer the ideal method of imposing "the poetical element" when, in the *meno mosso pp* section in G flat, he makes one of the two fugue subjects the basis of some fresh and exquisitely delicate music.

Concerning the "Grosse Fuge," the verdict of the past is likely to be reversed, or at least considerably modified. Until very recent times it was held to be beyond the endurance not only of hearers, but also of players. Even so enthusiastic a Beethovenian as Dr. Ernest Walker calls it "outlandish," adding that not even Joachim (to whom public knowledge of the late quartets was at that time almost entirely due) had ventured to include it in a programme.

To-day performances of it may be heard, though infrequently. A single hearing is likely to leave one convinced that the work is little more than a monstrous freak. Increased study of the score, and of the pianoforte duet arrangement (an invaluable means of getting at the inside of things) soon brings us round to the view that we have here one of Beethoven's greatest works—imperfect, and not well carried out in some of its details, but a truly magnificent creation as a whole. Its weaknesses are: over-insistence in the opening section, by all the parts, of the dotted rhythm ; the fact that the second subject, when used in augmentation, is not easily identifiable, and so loses relevance ; overmuch repetition (always a risky expedient in a form whose essential quality is continuous growth) ; too many full closes and pauses towards the end (which induce a feeling of finality too soon) ; and, above all, undue length. No wonder the publisher of the B flat quartet for which it was designed as Finale protested ! Even heard alone, it makes so great a strain on the attention that the hearer can hardly appreciate fully the splendours of the second half. Moreover, it is often too big for its medium. Such music demands not four soloists, but an orchestra. It should be scored, and played in place of a symphony (which indeed it is, of a new kind).

The mention of excessive length reminds us that in his fugal writing Beethoven failed sometimes to realise the value of terseness both in subject and working. His fugue subjects generally are not good. They lack the epigrammatic significance of many dozens of Bach's best subjects. The subject of the "Hammerklavier" fugue, for example, is suggestive of a kind of vigorous meandering (only so contradictory a term seems to meet the case) and when later on Beethoven reverses it, and energetically meanders backwards, the effect is little more than odd. Yet here again we have a fugue that has been underrated merely because it had so few chances of justifying itself. It is rarely heard in the concert room, and the domestic pianist can do no more than helplessly look at it, and turn with relief to such old friends as the opening movement of the "Moonlight." Happily, the player-piano has come to the rescue. The reader who turns on a roll of this fugue, setting a good pace, and playing no tricks with it, will have a thrilling experience.

The Finale of the Op. 59 Quartet in C is perhaps Beethoven's most popular fugue. Its subject is overlong, and not unlike that of the B flat fugue in the vigour with which it says nothing of importance. It is worked at too great length also, but its brilliance is undoubted; and structurally it is more successful than some of the later examples in that it combines fugue and sonata forms with no loss of continuity or flagging of interest.

The double fugue in the finale of the ninth Symphony must not be forgotten. Perhaps the best proof of its towering success is the fact that very few hearers realize that the *Allegro energico* section is a fugue at all—and a very skilful double one at that.

On the whole, perhaps, the chief drawback in the biggest of these fugues is their diffuseness, apparently due to Beethoven's over-concern with the scientific side of the form—an odd complaint to make of so emotional a composer. But this is merely one of the contradictions of his character. His habit of jotting down canons on all sorts of occasions and sending them to his friends as personal greetings is quite in keeping with his liberal use of such fugal ingenuities as inversion, augmentation, and the like. He seemed loth to leave anything to be taken for granted—the reverse of Bach, who is usually content to end his fugue without exhausting either his subject or his hearer. Perhaps Bach's unique perception of the possibilities that lay in a few notes made him aware of the special risks of the fugue in the matter of length. In no other form does one thing bring up another with such dangerous facility. Indeed, it is literally true to say that a composer might begin his career by starting a fugue, and, issuing it in monthly parts, might go on with it all his life—or at least as long as he had a subscriber left. Having finished with a subject in the ordinary way, he has only to invert, augment, or diminish it in order to open up for it a new career of usefulness, and when these are exhausted, the subject in any of its forms may be made the countertheme of a new one, and so on to infinity.

In the "Grosse Fuge" Beethoven fell into this snare—partly as a result of combining the fugue and variation forms (a kind of tautology, for the fugue form itself is one of the most subtle and comprehensive types of variation); and, by not knowing when to stop, placed beyond our reach some of his most magnificent music.

BEETHOVEN AND PROGRAMME MUSIC

It was in an unfortunate moment that Beethoven said, "I never compose without a picture in my mind." The remark (which was probably made half in jest) applies little more to him than of any other composer. A very large proportion of works, especially of the smaller instrumental type, owe their origin to some chance incident, to the reading of a poem, or what not, but such origin is rarely avowed. Unfortunately, Beethoven's words have been taken as warrant for all manner of ridiculous interpretations of his music. Some of these have been alluded to in a former chapter, and a complete collection would form not only one of the most diverting and irritating of volumes connected with music; it would be a standing monument to the fatuity of the great mass of folk for whom art of any kind cannot exist without a "story." It is almost incredible, for example, that a German critic of repute could write, and publish in one of the oldest established of German musical journals, in 1924, such a note on the fifth Symphony as that from which the following extracts are taken :

> Fate does not knock; it strikes a man to the ground. Whenever the panting victim struggles to arise (bars 33-34) he is ruthlessly thrown down again (bars 44-56). The second subject, with its downward fifths

Ex. 7.

> outdoes the first. Thus does Fate grind its heel on man's neck and press it hard on the ground (the long-held low B flat) while man begs for mercy :

Ex. 8.

As a result of Beethoven's remark, " So does Fate knock at the door ! " uttered casually long after the Symphony was finished, the work has had more nonsense of this sort written round it than any other with the exception perhaps, of Rachmaninoff's Prelude in C sharp minor.[1]

[1] The most popular programme devised for this piece has also to do with knocking—that of a prematurely-buried man on his coffin lid !

The real source of the so-called "fate motive" may or may not have been the call of a yellow-hammer heard by Beethoven in the public park at Vienna, as Czerny relates. What does it matter, except as a further proof of music's unique power of developing much from little? To-day, when the Fifth Symphony comes to us crowned with the applause of two generations, we are apt to overlook the insignificance of the germ from which it was developed. On the contrary, the glamour of the whole makes us even see power and significance in the part. Yet to over-rate the theme is to under-rate Beethoven's achievement. Find a man who has never heard the Symphony: play these notes:

Ex. 9

and ask him if he doesn't think they make a fine subject. He will answer contemptuously, "*That* a subject? It makes me think of a cuckoo with a stutter! Two cuckoos, in fact, and two stutters!" And is he wrong? But let him hear what Beethoven does with it, and he will take off his hat and say that the notes will never again remind him of a cuckoo. He will be at a loss to say what they suggest, until you mention Fate knocking at the door, after which the postman has only to double a rat-tat in order to send his mind back to Beethoven. And suppose Beethoven to have said, "So does the postman knock at the door!"—a remark quite characteristic of him in his frequent half-cynical jesting moods. Would the Symphony be a bit less esteemed to-day? All but a handful of the least important of listeners (those to whom music without a "story" is nothing) would have seen it for what it is—a work full of vitality and significance, and no more definite in meaning (or dependent on it) than some stern and violent aspect of nature.

Both "Fate" and yellow-hammer origins are almost certainly apocryphal, however. For the little theme that has made such a noise in the world for over a century had already made a good deal before Beethoven worked a miracle with it. Its possibilities lie mainly in its rhythm, and Beethoven had used it finely before writing the Fifth Symphony. It occurs in the finale of the early pianoforte sonata in C minor; the little four-note figure of the Finale of the D minor Sonata is rhythmically the same;[1] and the first movement of the "Appassionata" has it. Beethoven comes back to it once more in the Scherzo of the "Harp" Quartet (significantly in C minor again) and makes it one of the chief constituents of a long movement; and he appears to

[1] It is said to have been suggested by the sound of a galloping horse.

have been obsessed with the figure during the period that produced the Symphony, for the opening subject of the G major Concerto, written during these years, contains the same rhythm. And, after all, it may have been a reminiscence, for the rhythmic figure that was to become the best-known in all music had been made much of by Haydn in his E flat pianoforte Sonata, No. 3.

The more one looks into this aspect of Beethoven's music, the more one is convinced that the popular view of him as an arch-composer of programme music is mistaken. Here and there—as, for example, in the pianoforte Sonata in E flat—the "Adieu"—we have a fine result from the adoption of such bases; and it was natural that so consummate a master of expression as Beethoven should have excelled as he certainly did in the operatic overtures. But amongst his acknowledged programme music the failures perhaps exceed the successes, if we take (as we must) musical quality as the criterion. As Niecks says, the works written on a definite programme form only a small part of his output, and "this small portion has to be sifted before we get the really noble and notable examples."[1]

Schindler tells us, on what seems to be good authority, that towards the end of his life, Beethoven planned a new and complete edition of the pianoforte sonatas, in which the poetic idea at the back of each would be set forth verbally.

[1] *Programme Music*, p. 114.

Had this plan been carried out Beethoven would probably have been bound to do as Schumann did with his descriptive pieces—that is, he would have found superscriptions to fit the music. The plan is one commonly adopted to-day. A composer hits on a musical idea, develops it, and then finds a title to fit the result. If Beethoven had worked out a similar method in regard to the Symphonies, it would be interesting to see what he would have done with the "Eroica." Nobody has yet succeeded in showing how the Finale can be related satisfactorily to the rest of the work if the dedication to Napoleon is to be regarded as implying a programme. We have seen[1] that Czerny looked on the first movement of the "Eroica" as descriptive of a sea fight! About the Funeral March there can be no mistake: the Hero is being buried. But a composer who buries his hero halfway through a symphony leaves himself with nothing but elegiacs for the remaining two movements. What is the Scherzo doing here? And the not very interesting variations on a dance tune already well-worked by Beethoven years before? "The Scherzo," says Niecks, "represents 'Scenes in the Camp'"; Berlioz calls it "The Funeral Game," and, speaking of the Symphony as a whole, he says, "There is no question of battles or triumphal marches such as many people, deceived by

[1] Page 77.

mutilations of the title, naturally expect; but much in the way of grave and profound thought, of melancholy souvenirs and of ceremonies imposing by their grandeur and sadness—in a word, it is the hero's funeral rites."[1]

The Finale, according to Niecks, represents the "apotheosis of the Hero"; Grove sees in one portion of it "the dance of a band of Scythian warriors round the tomb of the 'hero' of their tribe," and in the *poco Andante* the flight of the hero's soul skywards.

These are only a few of the attempts to discover a connection between the Finale and the title of the Symphony. The complete failure of music to depict (unaided by detailed subtitles and explanations) events and persons could not be more completely demonstrated. Let nobody regret this inability of music to compete with the written word and the graphic arts: musicians can range freely in a field where the writer and painter can do no more than grope insecurely. Beethoven has no equal in the use of this "kind of unfathomable speech," a speech that, as has been well said, begins where ordinary language ends; and no composer's music is more self-sufficing. So far from being the "greatest composer of programme music," his greatness lies in his power to create pure music. With few exceptions his avowedly descriptive works show him below his best;

[1] *A Critical Study of Beethoven's Nine Symphonies.*

and the misguided invention of programmes to fit the remainder results from a failure to comprehend his real strength. No music worth the hearing can be "explained" as you can explain a picture or a poem; it gives us the essence of both, sublimated beyond analysis. To impatient Fontenelles, who ask "Sonata, what do you mean? What do you want of me?" the sonata might reply, "Nothing more than an attentive ear, and a freedom from anxiety as to my meaning. For I have not one meaning, but a hundred, and perhaps even a different hundred for every ear. Why attempt to pin me down to one, and so defraud yourself and belittle me?"

It must be confessed that Beethoven's own attitude in this matter was inconsistent. "All painting in instrumental music is a failure if pushed too far"; so runs a note among his sketchbooks. Again: "People will not require titles to recognize that the general intention is a matter of feeling rather than of painting in sounds." He ridiculed the imitative passages in the "Creation" and "Seasons" of Haydn, and was furious when someone added the title "La Chasse" to the un-named Overture, Op. 115. Yet (putting aside the "Wellington" Symphony as a mere *pièce d'occasion*) he could bring himself to write a Pastoral Symphony in which bird-songs and the murmur of the brook were imitated; and, asked to explain the poetic basis of the F minor pianoforte Sonata (some authorities say the D minor; others mention both in this connection) he replied "read Shakespeare's 'Tempest'"—from which we may infer that his own reading of the play had stopped at the title.

True, he wrote at the head of the Pastoral Symphony "More an expression of feeling than of actual painting." But the thing that matters is not what he said, but what he did. And the bird-calls, the brook, and above all the thunder-storm, simply belie his words. The inconsistency is accentuated by the almost certain fact of Beethoven's having been "inspired" (the expression is Niecks's) by a similar work by Knecht, entitled "Portrait musical de la Nature"—"but [says Niecks], inspired only by the programme, not by the music, or at least not otherwise by the music than the desire of doing well what has been done badly." Nobody to-day knows anything of Knecht's work, but the general criticism of Beethoven's effort would probably be, not that he had done well, but merely less badly than his mediocre model.

Attempts to read autobiography into Beethoven's music are almost as mistaken as the search for programmes. His habit of working by fits and starts at a number of works at the same time makes it very unlikely that a given work can safely be identified with a particular episode.

The romantic glamour that hung for so long

round the "Moonlight" Sonata is a case in point: a plain and simple biographical fact was enough to dispel it. Even more absurd is the tendency to associate certain works (and even movements, especially of the pathetic type) with his vicissitudes. Yet the mere fact of a violent contrast of mood between two movements of a work is sufficient to set players conjecturing as to Beethoven's "soul state" at the time. The following reads like a parody, but is a quotation from the programme-book of a concert given in London in 1924. "In the first movement of the second [violoncello] sonata the drama has begun. An ardent passion consumes him. . . . But in the second movement he so far recovers himself as to be able to joke with us."

Isn't it just possible that Beethoven was by this time (*ætat* 25) a sufficiently practical composer to see the advisability of contrast between the two movements? The first showed passion: very well; there could be no better reason for the second being bright. Even the "passion" of the first movement was probably due to the fact that, the two sonatas being produced as one *opus*, and the first being light throughout, Beethoven deliberately began the second in a different vein. (We see a similar contrasting of sonatas, as well as of movements, in the sets for pianoforte published at this time.)

Again, concerning the third sonata, we read:

"It was written in 1808 . . the same year in which he finished the tragic fifth Symphony. Yet there is no hint of tragedy in this Sonata. Only serenity, and great and infinite tenderness. The lion caresses . . . Beethoven is happy.

Despite the fact that he had just written the "tragic fifth"! And as the Symphony is anything but "tragic" in its Finale, are we to assume that Beethoven was hagridden when writing the first movement and jolly when working at the Finale?

The present day tendency to see in a composer's output a psychical record of his life is dead against the facts of history, and contrary to our own experience of life and of work. The amount of care-free music that we know was written during illness or mental distress is so large as to make us incredulous when a commentator tells us (say) that "in such a year Beethoven was in great agony of mind, as is seen by the Adagio of Opus so-and-so." Beethoven was too great a composer to be content with expressing his own joys and sorrows from day to day. He expressed those of everybody, and just because he was a practical composer we may be sure that he often addressed himself cheerfully to the composition of a sombre Adagio, and no less frequently sat down with the hump to write a graceful Andante or a jolly Rondo for which one of his publishers was impatiently waiting.

As has been said in an earlier chapter,

Beethoven's music is an extraordinarily complete and faithful expression of his character. There are, in fact, few more human documents among literary autobiographies. But it is a portrait, not a life—a character sketch, not a record. And if we attempt to see in it anything more than the merest general connection with his life, or try to discover a "programme" for the more vivid and striking of its movements, we bring between the music and ourselves an element that narrows its appeal and hampers our perception.

BEETHOVEN'S HUMOUR

No discussion of Beethoven's music, however brief and sketchy, can ignore the humour that is so prominent a feature, and that (perhaps as much as any other single quality) gives it the unmistakable Beethovenian character. True, he was far from being the first to jest in terms of music. Readers will recall the capital joke of Handel's in "O ruddier than the cherry." "Bring me a hundred reeds of decent growth, To make a pipe for my capacious mouth" says the giant Polyphemus in the opening recitative, whereupon a flute frisks an obbligato to his aria.[1] Still, the joke depends almost entirely on the text for its point: had Polyphemus not called for a hundred monster pipes the flute would have been unamusing.

Until recent times musical humour was usually fortuitous: the natural result of the contrast

[1] The humour is often underlined to-day by the use of a piccolo instead of a flute.

provided as light relief to the slow serious movements. It was geniality with, perhaps, an occasional rhythmic quip—good humour rather than humour, an atmosphere rather than a definite joke. Apparently music had to wait till Haydn came on the scene for its first purely instrumental jest. Haydn has two to his credit—the elaborate and elementary "Farewell" Symphony (which still "comes off" astonishingly) and the bang in the slow movement of the "Surprise" Symphony—an explosion so mild that it makes nobody jump to-day. Beethoven has killed that joke by a thousand bombinations. In this sense, all his symphonies are "surprise" symphonies and practically all his sonatas are "shock" sonatas. The Sonatina for mandoline is unprocurable, but we may hazard a guess that at some point that ludicrous instrument is called on to concentrate and release its puny resources in a would-be tremendous tinkle.

Beethoven's humour so often consists of dynamic surprise of this kind that we may say it is the chief ingredient. It seems a slender foundation on which to build a reputation as a humorist.[1] At first sight one regards it as little more than the musical equivalent of a slap on the back. But a slap on the back is always and detestably the same, whereas Beethoven works his

[1] Often, of course, the device is employed with serious intent. Here we are concerned only with the numerous cases where the spirit of rough fun is clearly present.

surprise in a hundred different ways. It is something more than a mere contrasting of *ff* with *pp*. Haydn's symphonies contain plenty of examples of this natural and easy help towards vitalizing a long movement. Beethoven usually goes one better by the addition of some other factor. Thus, a dynamic effect of the kind has its significance greatly increased if it occurs in a weak part of the bar, or on a powerful discord, or on a concord in a remote key. Similarly, the famous drum solos in the Scherzo of the ninth Symphony gain their comic character from a variety of causes. One of these that seems not to have been realized generally is perhaps its *apparent* disturbance of the rhythmical scheme. It is commonly said that the drums change the three-bar rhythm into that of four bars.[1] But this is not so. Its first four entries *emphasise* the three-bar rhythm. If a listener feels there is a change of rhythm, it is probably because he is so concerned with the

Ex. 10

[1] Thus, Grove in ***Beethoven and his Nine Symphonies*:** "It will not escape notice how the drum, with characteristic audacity puts the composer's direction at defiance by coming in four times at intervals of three bars, and the fifth time making the interval four."

of the drums that he fails to notice that the two bars that follow, played by the rest of the orchestra :

Ex. 11

complete the three-bar phrase with which this part of the movement is concerned.[1] It is quite possible that this deception was an unusually subtle joke of Beethoven's. If so, it has been one of his most successful. There is, however, another reason why the passage has always been eagerly awaited and unfailing in effect—the choice of instrument.[2] Any composer but Beethoven would almost certainly have given the entry to the bassoons, or to the string basses *pizzicato*. The result would then have been merely a touch of piquancy. The drums, hollow of tone and slightly lacking in definition of pitch, change the humour from the polite to the broad. It is as if, impatient of their traditional rôle of mere rhythm-makers, and jealous of the busy bandying of the theme between other parts, the drums said, " Let us take a hand," promptly take it, and find themselves after all unable to

[1] Apparently Professor Donald Tovey was the first to expose this popular fallacy. See his masterly analysis of the Ninth Symphony. (Patersons, 1922.)

[2] It "seems to have been one of the points which specially enraptured the audience at the first performance." Nohl, " Leben ", quoted by Grove in ***Beethoven and his Nine Symphonies***.

improve on the feat with which they startled us at the opening of the movement—*i.e.*, the delivery of the first three notes of the theme.

This passage has been discussed in some detail because it is one of the few examples of Beethoven's humour that can definitely be regarded as a joke, and in which we can lay our finger on the constituents that make it one. It can still bowl over the hearer whom it takes unawares, as was proved to the writer one day at Queen's Hall when a neighbour laughed aloud at it and immediately apologized, saying that the drums were the cause, though he couldn't explain how. He had never heard the Symphony before, and was relieved and interested on being told that he had laughed in the right place. Another comic effect (less subtle and therefore perhaps even more characteristic) is the uncouth gambolling and the false starts of the double basses in the Trio of the Fifth Symphony Scherzo. (Even funnier, though, is the fact that at one period the passages used to be played by Dragonetti as a solo in order that the notes might be quite clear!) Perhaps the best of all the amusing movements in Beethoven is the Scherzo of the Pastoral Symphony, where the

Ex. 12.

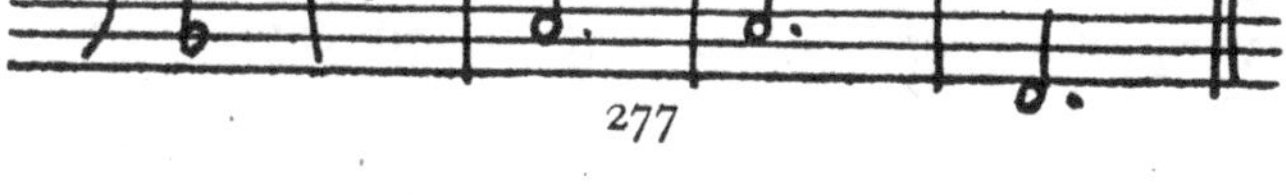

of the second bassoon so funnily hits off the rustic musician of the type we all know well—the player who in the difficult passages is busy adjusting his copy or his glasses, or tuning his instrument, but is ready to pom-pom with gusto on a bit of tonic and dominant if the pace be not too hot. This may surely claim to be one of the few really humorous passages in pure music. It is comedy, which is higher than comicality because it gives us a touch of real life. Even without the title of the movement to help us, the emphatic futility of the passage would amuse us almost as much. And is it too fanciful to suppose that the violas and 'cellos mock the bassoonist four bars after the last appearance of the figure quoted above?

The pianoforte Rondo, "The rage over a lost penny" is a failure because it is labelled, too long, and poor music. The necessary element of surprise is lacking; moreover, the choice of a form so repetitive and mechanical as the rondo is fatal.

It will be found that the direct musical jokes in Beethoven are unexpectedly few. Generally his humorous effects are simply exhibitions of high animal spirits. There is, however, a musical device that he employs frequently in such a way as to remind us of his fondness for puns and such elementary verbal quips. The only way in which music may approximate to verbal wit is in some of its uses of enharmonic change. The taking of a chord in one relation and leaving it in another is a kind of pun, and in so far as it is a sudden revelation of an unsuspected connection between two unrelated keys it has much in common with real wit. Such enharmonic surprises are not necessarily funny, of course—in fact, they are usually serious or dramatic. The pianoforte sonatas contain numerous examples of this playing with the dual aspects of a chord. The effect belongs to the common stock of composition material, and indeed is often over-used as a means of modulation. But we may well suppose that the humorous aspects of its ambiguity appealed to Beethoven. In support of this may be mentioned its striking use in the Finale of the eighth Symphony, where a C sharp, *ff*, in unison, suddenly interrupts the *ppp* cadence in the dominant of F. The ear naturally expects a modulation to D minor, instead of which the opening theme is resumed in the tonic F. Actually, therefore, the note was not C sharp, but D flat, the dominant minor ninth of the key of the movement. The explosive note is twice used thus. In the recapitulation, however, it is repeated in exactly the same circumstances, and the ear expects the result to be as before. But this time it is noted as D flat, and is treated by Beethoven as the tonic of that key. After two bars, *pp*, in D flat, the note is again hurled at us, this time noted as C sharp, and used as the tonic of C sharp minor. A further two bars, *pp*, and it crashes out yet once more. Then, calling on the hearer for special attention by means of a twofold repetition of the note, Beethoven springs his final surprise by using it as the dominant of F sharp minor, and proceeds to present the main theme in that key.

Berlioz devotes a page to this C sharp, and sums up a grave analysis by saying, "All this is very curious."[1]

Not nearly so curious, however, as his own failure to see the joke, humorist though he was. On the other hand, Grove (who is always readier to be thrilled and harrowed than amused by his idol) unexpectedly sees the fun—or half of it, for he regards only the first two entrances of the C sharp as a "huge joke." Huge it is, but we may be sure Beethoven wrote down every one of these five immense ambiguities with a full relish of the way they would make hosts of folk sit up, even if it were but to find them all "very curious."

This Finale is altogether one of Beethoven's best humoreskes. Both its principal themes are distinctly jocular, and in addition to the rousing jest discussed above there is at the end a capital example of Beethoven's fondness for "leg-pulling." A decided cadence and a long series of tonic chords announce the close unmistakably; but Beethoven suddenly launches a further coda, and keeps things going for another thirty

[1] *A Critical Study of Beethoven's Nine Symphonies.*

bars. In fact, the movement is a genuine Scherzo (though not so labelled) and is properly appreciated only when played and heard as such ; and the reason for so unusual a Finale is found in the fact that the place of the Scherzo in this Symphony is taken by a very short slight delicate movement, Allegretto Scherzando—the movement associated with Maelzel.[1] It is a mere bud of a Scherzo, and probably, Beethoven, realizing this, added the full bloom by way of Finale.

Inevitably the finest examples of Beethoven's humour are found in the scherzo form—the development and perfecting of which was his great achievement on the constructional side.

The two assertions so commonly made (1) that he invented the scherzo, and (2) that he evolved it from the minuet, are not correct. Movements called "Scherzo" were written long before his day, by Bach, among others ; and that Beethoven recognized the scherzo and the minuet as distinct forms is shown frequently. In both the A major and C major pianoforte sonatas in Op. 2, there is a Scherzo ; both are characteristic, yet very different in style, and without a trace of the minuet feeling. The F minor sonata in the same opus, on the other hand, contains a no less definite Minuet. In the E flat sonata, Op. 31, No. 3, we find both Scherzo and Minuet, and Beethoven makes the distinction more than usually clear by putting the Scherzo in 2-4 time

[1] See page 105.

(instead of the customary 3-4) and marking the Minuet at a slower pace than usual. And in the Symphony in F, discussed above, we have an Allegretto Scherzando, a genuine Minuet and Trio, and a Finale that is a Scherzo in all but name. If the scherzo is to be regarded as a development of the minuet and trio, the credit belongs less to Beethoven than to Haydn, many of whose Minuets are first-rate short Scherzos, though still wearing the old label. In fact, Haydn was too modest when he expressed a wish that "somebody would write a new minuet": he did it himself over and over again.

The humour in the Beethoven scherzo ranges as widely as the form itself varies in size and shape. The airy-fairy little movement in the A major pianoforte sonata, Op. 2, and the gigantic Scherzo of the Ninth Symphony mark the limits; between this Alpha and Omega are to be found practically every degree both in scale and mood. The humour has a kind of universality that lifts it clean out of the sphere of the mild and decorous good spirits that had hitherto served amply for light relief. The instrumental music of Haydn and Mozart so rarely touched a deep emotional note that the gusto and high spirits of Beethoven would have been out of proportion. On the other hand, the unrestrained emotion in Beethoven's works needed a humour to correspond, and nobody but Beethoven could supply it. Thus, although we might (with an effort) imagine another composer—say Brahms at his very best and a good bit over—writing the first movement of the Ninth Symphony, we can conceive of nobody but Beethoven being able to produce the Scherzo.

It is unfortunate that the word humour, applied to Beethoven's music, is so limited as to be misleading. The more comprehensive meaning (freakishness, eccentricity, variableness of mood) common in Elizabethan times is nearer the mark. But no single term can cover the ground. Dr. Walker calls it "a kind of world humour," and rightly says that it has practically no parallel in all music, and hardly anywhere outside music except in Carlyle.

The reader who approaches the typical Beethoven Scherzo expecting to find in it no more than drollery will miss the very quality that makes it unique. "Scherzo," we know, means a jest, but in many of these examples of Beethoven the jest is almost confined to the title. Despite the drum passages discussed above, the Scherzo of the Ninth Symphony, for example, is about as funny as the opening movement is pretty. Indeed, this Scherzo, and a few others—*e.g.*, those of the Quartets in E flat ("Harp"), and F minor, the violoncello Sonata in A (Op. 69), the Fifth Symphony, and the "Archduke" Trio (in the sinister middle section)—as often as not have a deep underlying seriousness. It is "very tragical mirth."

Time has dealt hardly with many of the slow movements of the classical composers, and not least hardly with Beethoven's. Their leisurely expression of feeling is often too calculated to touch us to-day, and some of the harmonic material that wrung the hearts of a past generation is now discredited by over-use. The pang of a century ago is to-day a mere diminished seventh or minor ninth, worn threadbare by the Spohrs of various nationalities—especially German and English. So it has come about that to many of us the Beethoven movements most charged with emotional significance are those labelled Scherzo. This view of the Beethoven Scherzo is not new, of course, though it appears to have been only partially realized in the past. Too many musicians were misled by the title, and by the restricted use of the word "humour." But Grove saw there was much more than mere release of high spirits—that the thing was, in fact, beyond a joke. Speaking of the Scherzo of the "Eroica," he says: "This is the earliest of those great movements which Beethoven was the first to give to the world, which are perhaps the most Beethovenish of all his compositions, and in which the tragedy and comedy of life are so startlingly combined."[1] It is difficult to avoid literary analogies in this connection, and if Beethoven's humour reminds us at times of the grimness of Carlyle, it no less frequently

[1] *Beethoven and his Nine Symphonies.*

recalls the savage irony of Swift. Reading autobiography into Beethoven's music is to be deprecated, but to many a page of these headlong and revealing Scherzos we feel tempted to adapt the title of a joke that failed: "Rage over a lost penny." For the finest Scherzos in all music were written by one who had lost his most precious faculty, his hearing.

BEETHOVEN AND THE VOICE

Of Beethoven's choral works very few survive, and not one is familiar in the sense that a huge store of Bach's and Handel's choral writings are familiar. The only two that are even passably well-known are the two Masses. The "Mount of Olives" has been performed occasionally during recent years, but no amount of acquaintance can discover in it more than hints of the real Beethoven. The remainder of the cantatas, canons and other choral works have disappeared completely from the repertory—if, indeed, they were ever in it.

Beethoven's comparative failure as a vocal writer is not to be explained by the off-hand and stereotyped statement that he didn't know how to write for the voice. Indeed, we may even say that the statement is untrue. We must remember that he served a long apprenticeship in the Opera House at Bonn, accompanying and conducting rehearsals of works in which the vocal writing was of the most grateful type; and that he realized the importance of this part of a composer's equipment is shown by the fact that on his arrival in Vienna he backed up his former valuable experience by going to Salieri for lessons in vocal writing—apparently with the setting of recitative specially in view. He was so well acquainted with good models that his shortcomings are evidently due rather to lack of sympathy with the voice than want of knowledge. Perhaps if he had been a chorister in his boyhood his attitude would have been different. But he seems to have shown no aptitude for singing, and his vocal efforts when trying over his own works at the pianoforte consisted of the desolating sounds we usually hear from creative musicians in the throes. (In fact, "composer's voice" is now almost a generally recognized classification.) The clue to his ungrateful vocal writing lies in a casual remark: "When I think of a theme, it is always for some instrument." Add to this his constant impatience with any kind of technical limitations, and we can account for those terrible strings of high notes, the ungrateful arpeggios and other florid passages, and the long breathless stretches that make his choral writing so formidable. On the score of excessive range, however, Professor Tovey defends him, saying that the extravagant vocal compass "looks like some enormous violence of Beethoven's genius; whereas it is but little worse than the habits of contemporaries of his who were under no excitement whatever."[1] It was unfortunate for this department of Beethoven's work that he lived in a bad choral period, when the idiom was secular and operatic, and the beauty of unaccompanied singing seems to have been unrealized. Thus in the whole of the Missa Solemnis there are only about a dozen bars in which the orchestra is silent. Moreover, the vocal lines are often obscured by being doubled in an aggressively florid way by the orchestra.

Another reason for Beethoven's shortcomings in writing for the voice was his poor literary sense. He was always unhandy in dealing with words, and a text often hampered rather than inspired him. In this respect he is the very reverse of Bach, who was almost over-ready to respond to the appeal of a graphic phrase. Indeed, a single word sometimes sufficed to set his invention running in a direction contrary to that of the sentence as a whole.

Beethoven, as we have seen, spent four years over the Missa Solemnis, and there is hardly a page that does not bear witness to the intensity with which he wrought. So far as the choral writing is concerned it is a considerable advance on the vocal portion of the Ninth Symphony. Cruel difficulties and desperate moments abound, it is true ; but there is nothing like the grotesque

[1] *Beethoven's Ninth Symphony*.

impracticabilities with which the Finale of the Symphony bristles—*e.g.*—

Ex. 13

The difference between the two works in this respect is summed up by Professor Tovey, who says that, " enormously difficult as is the Mass, the finale of the Choral Symphony is more exhausting in twenty minutes than the whole Mass in an hour and a quarter." And he goes on to conjecture, with good reason, that had the composer lived a few years longer there would have been a fourth period which should have been distinguished by a body of choral work fully equal in power and perfection to the Symphonies and String Quartets.[1]

Although the Mass contains some intensely dramatic moments—*e.g.*, the famous passage in the *Agnus Dei* where the prayer for peace, ushered in by the sound of distant drums and trumpets, begins with halting phrases (*Timidamente*) and rises to anguished appeal against the descriptive war music of the orchestra—there are many signs of Beethoven's interest at this period in the older and more austere forms of music. There is much fugal writing (the *Credo* ends with a

[1] *Beethoven's Ninth Symphony.*

tremendous example, packed with skilful device—a kind of scholastic frenzy hard to parallel) an abundance of good plain diatonic harmony, and several highly effective modal touches. On the whole, one feels that d'Indy is justified in challenging the critics who, presumably on the score of its dramatic nature as a whole, deny its right to the title of religious music. In the course of a lengthy discussion of the Mass, he says:

> Doit-on regarder la *Messe solennelle* comme de la musique liturgique? Répondons hardiment: non. Cet art admirable ne serait sûrement pas *à sa place* à l'église. Hors de proportions avec les cérémonies de l'office divin, la *Missa solemnis* exige l'emploi d'un orchestre considérable, peu propre à sonner de façon convenable dans un lieu de prière.
>
> Musique liturgique, non . . . mais musique religieuse au premier chef, et, de plus, musique essentiellement catholique.—Nous sommes bien éloignés de suspecter la bonne foi de ceux des historiens de Beethoven qui ont prétendu attacher à ce monument unique de l'art religieux un sens simplement philosophique, faire de cette Messe une oeuvre en dehors de la foi chrétienne, une manifestation de *libre examen* . . . (on a été jusque-là!); mais ne pas reconnaître l'esprit même du catholicisme dans la tendresse dont sont entourés les personnages divins, dans l'émotion qui accompagne l'énoncé des mystères, c'est faire preuve d'aveuglement . . . ou d'ignorance.

It was of this work that Beethoven said, "From the heart it came; to the heart it will go."

[1] *Beethoven*, p. 137.

There is no doubt about the first half of the remark, for there can be few things in music with a more authentic stamp of conviction. But it can reach the heart only through the ear, and its difficulties have so far stood in the way by making its performance rare. Now that so many choral societies have conquered the difficulties of its great fellow, the B minor Mass of Bach, the Missa Solemnis may yet be made familiar to thousands to whom it has so far been no more than a title.

It is a terrible decline from the Mass to the songs. Beethoven wrote about seventy, and only a handful are ever heard to-day. The reasons for this neglect are but too obvious. The vocal part is usually uninteresting, consisting often of strings of repeated notes, or of figures based on the common chord. "Neue Liebe, neue Leben," for example, opens with five bars in which the voice is concerned with notes of the chord of C, while the piano has repeated chords of C, twenty of them, all in exactly the same position! Yet this was no boyish effort: it is No. 2 of Op. 75. The accompaniments are frequently casual and unenterprising; no scrap of passage-work seems to have been too feeble for Beethoven's use here. No doubt many of the songs were turned out hastily for commercial purposes, but the weakness of this part of Beethoven's output is to be explained on other grounds. First, he wrote at a time when the form itself was in a transition stage. The bulk of his songs were of a type just then becoming popular in Germany—a kind of half-way house between the folksong and the *lied*. Hiller and other small men turned out such things by the score. The voice-part was straightforward, with some of the stock phrases of folk-song, but minus its rhythmical and modal peculiarities; the accompaniment was modest and conventional; and one setting usually did duty for any number of verses. Beethoven too readily fell into this easygoing method, either wholly or in part. One point about the songs deserves to be noted: they disprove the theory that Beethoven could not write music grateful for the voice. Their failure is due to their weakness as music, not to any lack of suitability to the medium.

It is, however, doubtful if he could ever have been other than a mediocre song composer. His genius was dramatic and epic rather than lyrical. Moreover, his peculiar excellence—skill in development—is one that needs more elbow-room than is found in the smaller vocal forms. Many of the insignificant phrases in his songs would have been made much of had they occurred in an instrumental work. In a form where the confines are narrow, and the exigencies of a text have to be considered, he could not spread himself.

There was an obscure young man in Vienna at the time of Beethoven's death who had little skill in development, but who was blessed with what Beethoven lacked—an inexhaustible fund of lyrical invention. It was left to him to do more than any other composer in founding the modern song. Beethoven lived just long enough to see some of Schubert's songs, and to hail him a possessor of the divine spark.

Although Beethoven composed a good deal of incidental music for the stage, he wrote only one opera. This, though invariably described as a masterpiece, is never performed—presumably for that reason, the opera house (perhaps inevitably) having a curious musical standard of its own. Stanford's eulogy of " Fidelio " may seem excessive, but it claims respect, being evidently based on familiarity with actual stage performances in Germany:

> It remains to this day the noblest, most ideal, most human, and most touching opera in existence. No later work has surpassed or equalled it in the dramatic qualities of the great quartet in the Prison scene, the tenderness of the duet between Florestan and his heroic wife, the delicate handling of the prisoners' chorus, or the sombre colouring of the digging of the grave. Rocco stands out with Don Juan and Hans Sachs as one of the typical figures of the operatic stage, to be ranked with those of Shakespeare, Goethe, and Dumas *père* on the dramatic boards. If less deft than Mozart in his handling of stage effects, Beethoven draws more tears from the eyes than did his great predecessor, and proves more deeply the root-qualities of human nature. The story of *Fidelio* has often been belittled on the score

of the slightness and melodramatic moments of its theme. But Beethoven knew better, and saw that with all its drawbacks (and what opera book is devoid of them?) it contained the germ of the finest quality in human nature, self-sacrifice, and provided him with the means of preaching a great sermon upon a small but piquant text. A crust of bread has become in his hands the means of stirring the world's emotions for a century. *Fidelio* is seldom given, which is as well, for excessive repetition of a very sacred thing is apt to dull its continuous appeal; but it never disappears or lies by for long, and when it is heard the impression is as great as, or greater than, it was a hundred years ago. When Beethoven the composer is compared (not untruly) with Shakespeare the poet, the parallel is not a little owing to the opera of *Fidelio*.[1]

The concensus of critical opinion, however, is that the operatic form, with its restrictions and conventions, was on the whole too much for Beethoven—"This business of the opera is the most tedious in the world," he wrote to Treitschke during the revision of "Fidelio." "I am dissatisfied with most of it and almost every piece in it is patched. It is a very different matter when one can give oneself up to one's own reflection or inspiration." "Fidelio" contains splendid music, but splendid music, minus a sense of stage, makes a poor opera, whereas a sense of the stage plus superficial music may (indeed generally does) ensure brilliant success. For

[1] *Interludes, Records, and Reflections* (1922).

opera you may have music, but you must have a theatrical instinct. Beethoven had only the music ; the drama that eluded his grasp when writing for the stage he put into his overtures, symphonies, and chamber works, where it is of infinitely greater and more permanent value.

BEETHOVEN AFTER A HUNDRED YEARS

The posthumous fame of a composer is an affair of enthusiasms and reactions, becoming less and less violent with the passage of years. Roughly the swing of the pendulum takes about a generation—a natural process, because, dating from the death of a composer, each generation of necessity makes a kind of rough and ready appraisement of his work. We have either to take a composer at his face value, so to speak, or we have to exercise our critical faculties in an endeavour to decide whether he means less or more to us than to his contemporaries and immediate successors. At first sight it would seem that the inevitable changes of taste and fashion during a century would turn the scale heavily against a composer. But experience shows that in the long run only the smaller men suffer. On the other hand, the big ones, profiting by the greater dispersion of musical knowledge and the increased frequency of performance, come out of the ordeal with added laurels.

The centenary of Beethoven's death occurs just after an undoubted reaction.[1] If that reaction has been in some quarters hasty and ill-founded, it is the natural result of the uncritical adulation with which his music was regarded during the

[1] This book was written in 1926.

half century following his death. Curiously, that worship was largely due to one of the very causes that brought about some of the recent depreciation of his music. His great enlargement of the scope and appeal of music on its expressive and romantic sides, and his immense increase of variety in dynamics, were developments of a type calculated to make a strong appeal to the public of his own day and for some years after. As time went on, however, this factor counted for less and less, and in recent times it has even been something of a handicap. The orchestra has grown to double the size of that in Beethoven's day, and in practically every medium there has been an increase in the range of power and colour. A generation to whom the richness and sonority of Wagner is a commonplace is apt to regard as tame many a climax that to the ears of Beethoven's contemporaries must have sounded as the crack of doom. Take one simple and easily verifiable example of the change in this respect. Beethoven's use of *fff* is sufficiently rare to indicate that a passage so marked is intended to be really shattering. An example occurs in the Seventh Symphony, and there is another in the Eighth. Yet many a composer of to-day produces a more stunning effect with a mere *f*. Noise, of course, is only one ingredient in a climax. Ideas count and rhythm helps; and there is the further consideration that degrees of power are relative. But, stoutly as Beethoven may hold his own in regard to energy of thought and rhythm, he inevitably suffers in the matter of power-gradation. His ability to build up a climax depended on the extent to which the limitations of the brass instruments allowed of their being used. If the building-up was chromatic, or in a remote key, the most powerful instruments could be used little or not at all. To-day, the entire orchestra can effect a crescendo from *ppp* to *fff*.

As with novelty in dynamics, so with novelty in harmony. Where to-day is the harmonic daring that caused headshaking among his contemporaries? To our ears his harmony is less striking than Bach's—in fact, owing to his never having quite survived the tonic and dominant obsession that beset the early Viennese school (partly because a large proportion of the thematic material in orchestral music had to be restricted both in compass and key in order to be playable on the brass) much of the harmony in his symphonies even sounds trite. (In his best chamber music, owing to the absence of such instrumental limitations, and also to the polyphonic texture, there is no lack of harmonic variety and interest.)

There are, of course, other reasons for the recent anti-Beethoven phase. At present there is a reaction against the didactic and emotional in music. No doubt it is only temporary, but it inevitably hits Beethoven hard. It spares Bach, probably because of the comparative (often even entire) unfamiliarity of a large proportion of such highly emotional works as the Church Cantatas. Also, many who are indifferent to the ethical and emotional significance of his work are attracted by his astounding workmanship, and the harmonic interest that results from his polyphony.

One of the most pronounced changes in taste during the past century is in regard to the classical slow movement. To Beethoven's public his Adagios must have been poignant experiences; to-day, all but a few of the finest do no more than remind us that although the musical exposition of joy, peace, grace, pastoral pleasure, the dance, and other things that involve pace and animation, remains pretty much what it was a century ago, the expression of intense sorrow has changed. The minor ninths, diminished sevenths and bits of the chromatic scale that formerly meant so much have become obvious.

We see the same thing in literature. Generally speaking, only the simpler forms of expression have retained their power. Hamlet's "Now could I drink hot blood" may have stirred Bankside; to-day it is mere fustian beside Ophelia's "I was the more deceived." And few of the violent takings-off and alarums and excursions in Shakespeare give us the tingling thrill of the knocking at the gate in Macbeth. So far as the composers of the past are concerned, we find it easy enough to rejoice with them that do rejoice, but only on comparatively rare occasions can we weep with them that weep. We wear our rue with a difference.

Further, Beethoven suffers from the modern tendency to belittle the methods of development in which his chief strength lay. Here again Bach, who could develop at immense length, is saved by one or both of two factors—the splendidly energising effect of his basses, and the fugal treatment that was almost the staple idiom of his time. In regard to the latter point, he reaps the benefit of the present survival—we might almost say revival—of the fugue form. Against the handful of splendid, but only partially successful, and excessively difficult examples of Beethoven, Bach comes forward with dozens that are perfect in form and finish, and easily playable by any pianist of good average ability.

Ease of accessibility and performance, so great a help to the Bach cult, has unfortunately been lacking in regard to much of Beethoven's finest music. Performances of such masterpieces as the Mass in D and the ninth Symphony in its complete form have always been rare; the chamber music has necessarily been music for the few; and the later quartets have been familiar to no more than a comparative handful, even among well-informed musicians. Happily science has come to the rescue. Already the gramophone has brought the chamber music into the homes of the million; several of the last quartets have been recorded in full, and at the time of writing the remainder are promised; and the ninth Symphony, complete, is also available for the gramophonist. The player-piano has banished the bogey of difficulty that made some of the greatest of the pianoforte sonatas a sealed book to all but the virtuoso; and it even provides admirable and highly effective arrangements of the orchestral and chamber works. For the listener who owns neither gramophone nor player-piano, there are wireless recitals and concerts, in which the instrumental works are not only played, but expounded as well.

Beethoven's chance of thus reaching everybody, not, as in the past, by a few hackneyed works, but by the very cream of his output, comes late in the day. No other great composer has so large a proportion of masterpieces that are as yet unfamiliar to the great bulk of the musical public; and the overcoming of this handicap could not fall out at a more suitable time than the present, when the centenary will undoubtedly show that Beethoven's recent decline in favour was as temporary as it was inevitable. That such a decline will occur again is unlikely, because our acquaintance with his music will no longer depend on the public concert—a method of music-making which, largely for economic reasons, tended to concentrate on a comparatively small number of his works, and those by no means the best. Indeed, some admittedly feeble works have been allowed to figure in programmes so frequently as to give the uninitiated a totally wrong impression of his genius. His reputation is damaged by every public performance of such works as the Turkish march from the "Ruins of Athens," the Rondino for wind instruments, the Septet, "Adelaide," the pianoforte Fantasia Op. 77, the violin Romance in G, the Thirty-two Variations, most of the Bagatelles, the Choral Fantasia, some half-dozen of the weaker pianoforte sonatas, and other uninspired items, many of which he himself scorned in his later years. Beethoven's worst enemies are not those who frankly object to his frequent and obvious lapses, but the performers to whom the name on the title page matters more than the music it covers. Nor is the damage confined to the perpetuation of inferior works. Almost as much harm is done by the pianoforte recitalists who give the "Moonlight," "Appassionata," and "Waldstein" sonatas fifty performances to one of the E minor or the F sharp,—in fact there are at least a dozen of the sonatas unjustly neglected. Some of the fairly early ones—*e.g.*, the E flat, Op. 7, and the D major, Op. 10, No. 3—are among the most vital and attractive of pianoforte works of any period, and deserve a better fate than to be almost relegated to the examination syllabus and the teaching list. In the orchestral department there is a similar over-insistence on the third and fifth Symphonies, at the expense of the fourth and eighth. And how are we to account for the entire neglect of the Overture "Consecration of the House"? During a good many years of concert-going in London, the writer has never once heard it. Yet, judging from the score, it is far more worthy of performance than half a dozen weak works that are frequently heard.

The reader who settles down to an exhaustive study of Beethoven's output as a whole will have many surprises. He will find an inequality of standard that cannot be matched in the work of any other composer in the first rank. That is his first surprise. His second—the one that really matters—will come from his discovery of two things: first, that, almost without exception, the masterpieces he has known for years prove to be even finer than he had thought them to be; and, second, that there are many more of them than concert-givers had allowed him to suppose. As to inequality of standard: when the heights reached are those of Beethoven at his best, we (and he) can afford to ignore the depths. Posterity's estimate of a master must be based on his masterpieces, and to a critic who says that Beethoven's day is past (because he wrote the "Wellington" Symphony, or was shifty in money matters, or any other reason why) the best and only answer is a performance of one of his finest works.

Even such single movements as the Scherzo of the ninth Symphony, or the Fugue from the C sharp minor Quartet, suffice to show the utter futility of the prophecy; and a survey of his best music in bulk leads to the conviction that no composer's future is more secure. The deciding factor is not quality alone, but something more difficult to appraise, though it is unmistakable in its effect. To his contemporaries a genius is often little more than one of a crowd of mere talents. Time does the sorting-out; the talents drop away, and the genius is seen to be what he is by virtue of having given to art something that is not only fine, but unique and irreplaceable. To many musicians a hundred years ago the chief difference between (say) Beethoven's Op. 111 and the sonatas of a dozen lesser men was in the degree of difficulty. There was no doubt much good stuff in the lesser men's sonatas, but, life being short, art can avoid being too long only by a constant process of selection. The rival sonatas have been shed and forgotten, and if we gave them a re-trial to-morrow we should almost certainly decide that they can still be spared. But imagine the pianoforte repertory bereft of the Op. 111!

And what is true of the C minor Sonata is true of a noble tale of works for other media.

There can be no "greatest" composer. It is not caution but a realization of differences that makes us give the supreme place to a small group rather than to an individual. What dictates our selection? Not a general level of excellence, else some second rank men would qualify; not bulk, or a good claim might be put in for the Boccherinis. The choice depends on the extent to which a composer wrought into his work some quality without which music would be immeasurably the poorer. In this respect no one—not even Bach—did more than Beethoven. No other composer has achieved a like fusion of the personal and universal. His influence on the art during the century that followed his death was so general as to be beyond estimate : as well try to measure the air. " O ye millions I embrace you " ; among creative artists none but Beethoven and a few of the greatest in literature could use the words, not as a rhetorical flourish, but as a plain truth. " It is the peculiarity of Beethoven's imagination," says Ernest Newman, " that again and again he lifts us to a height from which we revaluate not only all music but all life, all emotion, and all thought." He goes on to indicate some of the works of Beethoven in which many people find their supreme musical experiences, and adds, " But whatever the chosen movement may be, the feeling that prompts its choice is the feeling that in it the human spirit has attained to its maximum of wisdom, of purified understanding, of the will set free, and soared to that mystical sense of 'the love' (or whatever it may be) 'that moves the world and the other stars' of which Dante speaks. And we find ourselves then working backwards and testing the 'greatness' of other music by the degree to which it approximates to the sublimated quality of Beethoven's finest work."

It is by virtue of this unique and unexplainable quality that Beethoven takes his place among the elect. If that classification be too vague, and we fine it down to a group of three, there will be general agreement save as to the third name. It may be Handel, Wagner—a half dozen august choices present themselves. But as surely as one of the two undisputed names is Bach the other is Beethoven.

LIST OF WORKS

(This list is complete save for a number of canons and other small vocal works.)

Abbreviations: PF = Pianoforte. V. = Violin. Va. = Viola. Vo. = Violoncello. C. bass = Contrabass. Clar. = Clarinet. Ob. = Oboe. Fl. = Flute. Orch. = Orchestra.

I. WORKS WITH OPUS NUMBERS.

Op.	*Description.*	*Dedicated to*
1	Three Trios, PF. V. Vo. (in E♭, G, C minor).	Prince Carl von Lichnowsky.
2	Three Sonatas, PF. (F minor, A, and C).	Joseph Haydn.
3	Trio, V. Va. Vo. (E♭).	
4	Quintet, V. V. Va. Va. Vo. (E♭).	Count von Fries.
5	Two Sonatas, PF. Vo. (F, G minor).	Frederick William II. of Prussia.
6	Sonata, 4 hands, PF. (D).	
7	Sonata, PF. (E♭).	Countess Babette von Keglevics.
8	Serenade, V. Va. Vo. (D).	
9	Three Trios, V. Va. Vo. (G, D, C minor).	Count v. Browne.
10	Three Sonatas, PF. (C minor, F, D).	Countess v. Browne.
11	Trio, PF. Clar. (or V.) Vo. (B♭).	Countess v. Thun.
12	Three Sonatas, PF. V. (D, A, E♭)	A. Salieri.
13	Sonata Pathétique, PF. (C minor)	Prince Carl von Lichnowsky.
14	Two Sonatas, PF. (E, G).	Baroness v. Braun.
15	Concerto, PF. and Orch. (C.). (Really the second.)	Princess Odescalchi, *née* Keglevics.

Op.	*Description.*	*Dedicated to*
16	Quintet, PF. Ob. Clar. Bassoon, Horn or V. Va. Vo. (E♭). Arrd. by Beethoven as a quartet for PF. V. Va. Vo. Also arrd. as string quartet and marked Op. 75.	Prince von Schwarzenberg.
17	Sonata, PF. Horn or Vo. (F).	Baroness v. Braun.
18	Six Quartets, V. V. Va. Vo. (F, G, D, C minor, A, B♭).	Prince von Lobkowitz.
19	Concerto PF. and Orch. (B♭). (Really the first.) See No. 151.	Charles Nikl Edler von Niklsberg.
20	Septet, V. Va. Horn, Clar. Bassoon, Vo. C bass (E♭).	Empress Maria Theresa.
21	Symphony No. 1 (C).	Baron v. Swieten.
22	Sonata, PF. (B♭)	Count v. Browne.
23	Two Sonatas, PF. V. (A minor, F).	Count M. von Fries.
24	Sonata in F. PF. V. (Op. 23), Op. 24 was originally PF. score of Prometheus, now Op. 43.	*idem.*
25	Serenade, Fl. V. Va. (D.) (see Op. 41).	
26	Sonata, PF. (A♭).	Prince C. v. Lichnowsky.
27	No. 1 Sonata quasi una Fantasia, PF. (E♭).	Princess J. Liechtenstein.
	No. 2 Sonata quasi una Fantasia, PF. (C♯ minor), ("Moonlight").	Countess Giulietta Guicciardi.
28	Sonata, PF. (D), ("Pastoral").	Joseph Edler von Sonnenfels.
29	Quintet, V. V. Va. Va. Vo. (C).	Count M. v. Fries.
30	Three Sonatas, PF. V. (A, C minor, G).	Alexander I. Emperor of Russia.

Op.	Description.	Dedicated to
31	Three Sonatas, PF. (G, D minor, E♭).	
32	Song, " An die Hoffnung."	
33	Seven Bagatelles, PF. (E♭, C, F, A, C, D, A♭).	
34	Six variations on an original theme, PF. (F).	Princess Odescalchi, *née* Keglevich.
35	[15] Variations with a fugue, on theme from Prometheus, PF. (E♭)	Count M. Lichnowsky.
36	Symphony No. 2 (D).	Prince Carl v. Lichnowsky.
37	Concerto, PF. and Orch. (C minor).	Prince Louis Ferdinand.
38	Trio, PF. Clar. V. or Vo (E♭), arranged by author from Septet, Op. 20.	Prof. J. A. Schmidt.
39	Two Preludes, through all 12 major keys, PF. or Organ.	
40	Romance, V. and Orch. (G).	
41	Serenade, PF. Fl. or V. (D), from the Serenade, Op. 25; revised by composer.	
42	Notturno, PF. Va. (D), arranged from the Serenade, Op. 8.	
43	" The Men of Prometheus," Ballet, Nos. 1—16.	
44	Fourteen Variations, PF. V. Vo. (E♭).	
45	Three Grand Marches, PF. 4 hands (C, E♭, D).	Princess Esterhazy, *née* Liechtenstein.
46	Song, " Adelaide."	Matthisson.
47	Sonata [" Kreutzer "], PF. V. (A).	R. Kreutzer.
48	Six Songs :—" Bitten " ; " Die Liebe des Nächsten " ; " Vom	Count v. Browne.

Op.	Description.	Dedicated to
	Tode"; "Die Ehre Gottes"; "Gottes Macht"; "Busslied."	
49	Two Easy Sonatas, PF. (G minor, G major).	
50	Romance, V. and Orch. (F).	
51	Two Rondos, PF. (C, G)	Countess Henrietta v. Lichnowsky.
52	Eight songs:—"Urian's Reise"; "Feuerfarb"; "Das Liedchen v. d. Ruhe"; "Mailied"; "Molly's Abschied"; "Die Liebe"; "Marmotte"; "Das Blümchen Wunderhold."	
53	Sonata, ["Waldstein"] PF. (C).	Count von Waldstein.
54	Sonata, PF. (F).	
55	Symphony No. 3 ("Eroica") (E♭).	Prince von Lobkowitz.
56	Triple Concerto, PF. V. Vo. and Orch. (C).	Prince von Lobkowitz.
57	Sonata, PF. (F minor), "Appassionata."	Count F. von Brunswick.
58	Fourth Concerto, PF. and Orch. (G).	Archduke Rudolph.
59	Three Quartets ["Rasoumoffsky"], V. V. Va. Vo. (F, E minor, C). (7th, 8th, and 9th)	Count von Rasoumoffsky.
60	Symphony No. 4 (B♭).	Count Oppersdorf.
61	Concerto, V. and Orch. (D).	Stephan v. Breuning.
	Concerto, PF. and Orch. (An arrt. by B. of Op. 61.)	Madame v. Breuning.
62	Overture to Coriolan.	M. [H. J.] de Collin.
64	Twelve Variations on "Ein Mädchen" (Zauberflöte), PF. Vo. (F).	

Op.	Description.	Dedicated to
65	Scena ed Aria, "Ah, perfido!" Sopr. and Orch.	Countess v. Clary.
67	Symphony, No. 5 (C minor)	Prince Lobkowitz and Count Rasoumoffsky.
68	Symphony, No. 6 ("Pastoral") (F).	Prince Lobkowitz and Count Rasoumoffsky.
69	Sonata, PF. Vo. (A).	"My friend Baron von Gleichenstein."
70	Two Trios, PF. V. Vo. (D, E♭).	Countess Marie v. Erdödy.
71	Sextet, Clar. Clar. Cor. Cor. Fag. Fag. (E♭).	
72	"Fidelio," or "Wedded Love" Opera.	Archduke Rudolph.
73	Concerto, PF. and Orch. (E♭), the Fifth.	Archduke Rudolph.
74	Quartet ["Harp"], V. V. Va. Vo. (E♭). (The 10th.)	Prince Lobkowitz.
75	Six Songs, "Kennst du das Land," "Herz mein Herz." and "Es war einmal"; "Mit Liebesblick,"; "Einst wohnten" and "Zwar schuf das Glück."	Princess von Kinsky.
	Op. 75 is also marked to an arr. of Op. 16 as a string quartet.	
76	[6] Variations, PF. (D). See Op. 113.	"To his friend Oliva."
77	Fantaisie, PF. (G minor).	Count F. von Brunswick.
78	Sonata, PF. (F♯).	Countess Therèse von Brunswick.
79	Sonatina, PF. (G).	

Op.	*Description.*	*Dedicated to*
80	Fantasia, PF. Orch. Chorus. The theme of the variations is Beethoven's song "Gegenliebe."	Maximilian Joseph, King of Bavaria.
81*a*	Sonata, PF. (E♭), "Les Adieux, l'Absence, et le Retour."	Archduke Rudolph.
81*b*	Sextet, V. V. Va. Vo. 2 Cors. (E♭).	
82	Four Ariettas and a duet. 1. "Dimmi, den mio." 2. "T'intendo, si." 3. "Che fa, il mio bene" (*buffa*). 4. "Che fa, il mio bene" (*seria*). 5. "Odi l'aura."	
83	Three Songs: 1. "Trocknet nicht." 2. "Was zieht mir." 3. "Kleine Blumen."	Princess von Kinsky.
84	Music to Goethe's "Egmont." Overture. 1. Song, "Die Trommel." 2. Entracte I. 3. Entracte II. 4. Song, "Freudvoll und leidvoll." 5. Entracte III. 6. Entracte IV. 7. Clara's death. 8. Melodrama. 9. Sieges-symphonie.	
85	Christus am Oelberge. ("Mount of Olives,") S. T. B. Chorus, Orch.	
86	Mass, S. A. T. B. Chorus, Orch. (C).	Pr. Nicholas Esterhazy de Galantha.
87	Grand Trio for V. V. Va. (C) arranged (not by Beethoven) from a MS. Trio for 2 Oboes and Cor Anglais.	

Op.	Description.	Dedicated to
88	Song, "Das Glück der Freundschaft," (A).	
89	Polonaise, PF. (C).	Empress of Russia.
90	Sonata, PF. (E minor).	Count Moritz von Lichnowsky.
91	"Wellington's Victory, or the Battle of Vittoria," Orch.	Prince Regent of England.
92	Symphony No. 7 (A).	Count von Fries.
93	Symphony No. 8, Orch. (F).	
94	Song, "An die Hoffnung."	Princess Kinsky.
95	Quartet, V. V. Va. Vo. (F minor) (The 11th.)	N. Zmeskall von Domanovetz.
96	Sonata, PF. V. (G).	Archduke Rudolph.
97	Trio, PF. V. Vo. (B♭).	Archduke Rudolph.
98	Six Songs, "An die ferne Geliebte, Liederkreis."	Prince Lobkowitz.
99	Song, "Der Mann von Wort."	
100	Duet, "Merkenstein."	
101	Sonata, PF. (A).	Baroness Dorothea Ertmann.
102	Two Sonatas, PF. Vo. (C, D).	
103	Octet, 2 Ob. 2 Clars. 2 Cors. 2 Fag. (E♭). The original of Op. 4.	
104	Quintet, V. V. Va. Va. Vo. (C minor), arranged by Beethoven from Op. 1, No. 3.	
105	Six very easy themes varied, PF. Fl. or V.	
106	Sonata, PF. (B♭).	Archduke Rudolph.
107	Ten [national] themes with variations, PF. Fl. or V.	
108	Twenty-five Scotch Songs, and 2 Voices and small chorus, PF. V. Vo.	Pr. Radzivil.

Op.	*Description.*	*Dedicated to*
109	Sonata, PF. (E).	Frl. Maximiliana Brentano.
110	Sonata, PF. (A♭).	
111	Sonata, PF. (C minor).	Archduke Rudolph (ded. by publishers).
112	"Calm sea and prosperous voyage." S. A. T. B. and Orch.	Goethe.
113	"The Ruins of Athens." Chorus and Orch.	King of Prussia.
114	March and Chorus (E♭) from "Ruins of Athens."	
115	Overture in C, sometimes called "Namensfeier."	Prince Radzivil.
116	Terzetto, "Tremate," S. T. B. (B♭).	
117	"King Stephen" Overture (E♭) and 9 numbers.	
118	Elegiac Song, S. A. T. B. and Strings (E).	Baron Pasqualati.
119	Bagatelles, PF. (G minor, C, D, A, C minor, G, G, C, C, A minor, A, B♭, G).	
120	33 Variations on a Waltz by Diabelli (C).	Frau Antonie von Brentano.
121*a*	Adagio, Variations and Rondo, PF. V. Vo. (G).	
121*b*	Opferlied, Sopr. with Chorus and Orch.	
122	Bundeslied (B♭), S. A. Chorus and Wind.	
123	Mass in D, "Missa Solennis."	Archduke Rudolph.
124	Overture in C, "Blessing of the House").	Prince N. Galitzin.

Op.	Description.	Dedicated to
125	Symphony No. 9 (D minor), Orch., S.A.T.B. soli, and Chorus.	King of Prussia.
126	Six Bagatelles, PF (G, G minor, E♭, B minor, G, E♭, E♭).	
127	Quartet, V. V. Va. Vo. (The 12th) (E♭).	Prince N. Galitzin.
128	Arietta, "The Kiss."	
129	Rondo a capriccio, PF. (G), "Rage over a lost penny."	
130	Quartet, V. V. Va. Vo. (B♭). (The 13th.)	Prince N. Galitzin.
131	Quartet, V.V. Va. Vo. (C sharp minor). (The 14th.)	Baron von Stutterheim.
132	Quartet, V. V. Va. Vo. (A minor). (The 15th.)	Prince N. Galitzin.
133	Grand Fugue, V. V. Va. Vo. (B flat). Originally the Finale to Op. 130.	Archduke Rudolph.
134	Grand Fugue (Op. 133), arrd. by the Author for PF. 4 hands.	Archduke Rudolph.
135	Quartet, V. V. Va. Vo. (F)—(the last).	Johann Wolfmayer.
136	"Der glorreiche Augenblick" ("The glorious moment"), Cantata, S. A. T. B. Chorus and Orch; 6 numbers. Also as "Preis der Tonkunst" ("Praise of Music").	The Sovereigns of Austria, Russia, and Prussia, etc.
137	Fugue, V. V. Va. Vo. (D).	
138	Overture, Orch. (C), known as "Leonora, No. 1," but really Leonora, No. 3. See Op. 72.	

II. WORKS WITHOUT OPUS NUMBERS.

1. FOR ORCHESTRA, AND ORCHESTRAL INSTRUMENTS.

Description.	*Dedicated to*
12 Minuets.	
12 Deutsche Tänze.	
12 Contretänze. (No. 7 is the dance used in the Finale of Prometheus, the Eroica, etc. No. 11 also used in Finale of Prometheus.)	
Minuet of congratulation (E♭).	
Triumphal March, for Kuffner's "Tarpeia" or "Hersilia" (C).	
Military March (D).	
Military March (F).	
Rondino (E♭), 2 Ob. 2 Clar. 2 Cors. 2 Fags.	
3 Duos, Clar. and Fag. (C. F. B♭).	
Allegro con Brio, V. Orch. (C). Fragment of 1st movement of a V. Concerto. Completed by Jos. Hellmesberger.	Dr. G. von Breuning.
Musik zu einem Ritterballet.	

2. FOR PIANOFORTE AND VARIOUS CHAMBER MUSIC COMBINATIONS.

Sonatina for the Mandoline and Cembalo (C minor).	
Rondo, PF and Orch. (B♭). Probably finished by Czerny. Perhaps intended for Op. 19.	
3 Quartets, PF. V. Va. Vo. (E♭, D, C) (very early). N.B.	

Description.	*Dedicated to*
Adagio of No. 3 is employed in Op. 2, No. 1.	
Trio, PF. V. Vo. (E♭).	
Trio in one movement, PF. V. Vo. (B♭).	
Rondo, Allegro, PF. and V. (G).	
12 Variations on "Sevuol ballare," PF. and V. (F).	Eleonore von Breuning.
12 Variations on "See the conquering hero," PF. and Vo. (G).	Princess Lichnowsky.
7 Variations on "Bei Männern," PF. and Vo. (E♭).	Count von Browne.
Variations on a theme by Count Waldstein, PF. 4 hands (C).	
Air with [6] Variations on "Ich denke dein," PF. 4 hands (D.)	Countess Josephine Deym and Countess Theresa Brunswick.
3 Sonatas, PF. (E♭, F minor, D). (Very early works, see page 4.)	Elector Maximilian Frederic of Cologne.
Sonata [called Easy], PF. (C), two movements only, the second completed by F. Ries.	Eleonore von Breuning.
2 Sonatinas, PF. (G, F). Of doubtful authenticity.	
Rondo, Allegretto, PF. (A).	
Minuet, PF. (E♭).	
Prelude, PF. (F minor).	
6 Minuets, PF. Perhaps first written for Orch.	
7 Ländler dances.	
6 Ländler dances, also for VV. and Vo.	
Andante [favori], PF. (F), originally intended for Op. 53.	

Description.	Dedicated to
6 Allemandes, PF. and V.	
Ziemlich lebhaft, PF.	
Bagatelle, PF. (A minor),	
Andante maestoso (C), arranged from the sketch for a Quintet and called "Beethovens letzter musikalische Gedanke."	
10 Cadenzas to Beethoven's PF. Concertos in C, B♭, C minor, G and D (arrt. of Violin Concerto, see Op. 61). Also 2 to Mozart's PF. Concerto in D minor.	
[9] Variations on a March by Dressler, PF. (C minor).	Countess Wolf-Metternich.
24 Variations on Righini's air "Vieni (*sic* i.e. 'Venni') amore," P.F. (D).	
[13] Variations on Dittersdorf's air "Es war einmal," PF. (A).	
[9] Variations on Paisiello's air "Quant' è più bello," PF. (A).	Prince C. von Lichnowsky
[6] Variations on Paisiello's duet "Nel cor più." PF. (G).	
12 Variations on minuet [à la Viganò] from Haibel's ballet "Le nozze disturbate," PF. (C.)	
12 Variations on the Russian danec from Paul Wranizky's "Waldmädchen," PF.	Countess von Browne.
6 easy Variations on a Swiss air, PF. or Harp (F).	
8 Variations on Grétry's air "Une fièvre brûlante," PF.	

Description.	*Dedicated to*
10 Variations on Salieri's air "La Stessa, la Stessissima," PF. (B♭).	Countess Babette de Keglevich.
7 Variations on Winter's quartet "Kind willst du," PF. (F.)	
8 Variations on Süssmayer's trio "Tändeln und scherzen," PF. (F).	Countess von Browne.
6 very easy Variations on an original theme, PF. (G.)	
[7] Variations on "God save the King," PF. (C.)	
[5] Variations on "Rule Britannia," PF. (D).	
32 Variations, PF. (C minor)	
[8] Variations on "Ich hab' ein kleines Hüttchen nur," PF. (B♭).	

3. WORKS FOR VOICES.

Bass Solo, Chorus, Orch. "Germania!" Finale for Treitschke's Singspiel "Gute Nachricht."	
Bass Solo, Chorus, Orch. "Es ist vollbracht." Finale to Treitschke's Singspiel "Die Ehrenpforten."	
"Miserere" and "Amplius." Dirge at Beethoven's funeral. Chorus of 4 eq. voices and 4 trombones. Adapted by Seyfried from two of 3 MS. Equali for trombones.	
Cantata on the death of the Emperor Joseph II. (Feb. 20,	

Description.	*Dedicated to*
1790), for Soli, Chorus and Orchestra (C minor). (Very early work.)	
Another Cantata (Sept. 30, 1790), "Er schlummert," on the accession of Leopold II.	
Song of the monks from Schiller's "William Tell"—"Rasch tritt der Tod." "In memory of the sudden and unexpected death of our Krumpholz, May 3, 1817." T. T. B. (C minor).	
Cantata, S. A. B. and PF. (E♭).	
Cantata, "Graf, Graf, lieber Graf." Voices and PF. (E♭).	
Incidental music, "Du dem sie gewunden," written for Duncker's "Leonora Prohaska" (D).	
Many Canons and small incidental pieces.	
25 Irish Songs, for Voices with PF. V. Vo.	
20 Irish Songs.	
12 Irish Songs.	
26 Welsh Songs.	
12 Scottish Songs.	
12 Songs of various nationality, for Voice, PF. V. Vo.	
Song, "Schilderung eines Mädchens."	
Song, "An einen Säugling."	
Song, "Farewell to Vienna's citizens."	Obristwachtneister von Kövesdy.

BEETHOVEN

Description.	*Dedicated to*
War Song of the Austrians, Solo and Chorus, with PF.	
Song, " Der freie Mann."	
Opferlied, " Die Flamme lodert."	
Song, " Zärtliche Liebe."	
Song, " La Partenza."	
Song, " Der Wachtelschlag."	
Song, " Als die Geliebte sich trennen wollte."	
Arietta, "In questa tomba oscura."	
Song, " Andenken."	
Four settings of Goethe's " Sohnsucht."	
Song, " Als mir noch."	
Song, " Welch ein wunderbares Leben."	
Song, " Der Frühling entblühet."	
Song, " Des Krieger's Abschied."	
Song, " Die stille Nacht."	
Song, " O dass ich dir."	
Song, " Dort auf dem hohen Felsen."	
Song, "Wenn ich ein Vöglein wär."	
Song, " Wo blüht das Blümchen."	
Song, " Nord oder Sud ? "	
Song, " Lisch aus, mein Licht ! "	
Song, " Wenn die Sonne neider sinket."	
Two songs, "Seufzer eines Ungeliebten," and "Gegenliebe." (For theme of the latter see Op. 80.)	
Song, " Turteltaube."	
Song, " Gedenke mein ! ich denke dein."	

INDEX OF NAMES

INDEX OF NAMES

INDEX OF NAMES

INDEX OF WORKS

INDEX OF WORKS

INDEX OF WORKS